GETTING LISTED ON WALL STREET

The Irwin Guide to
Financial Reporting Standards
in the U.S.

GETTING LISTED ON WALL STREET

The Irwin Guide to
Financial Reporting Standards
in the U.S.

Carolyn Kay Brancato

Professional Publishing

IRWIN Concerned about Our Environment

In recognition of the fact that our company is a large end-user of fragile yet replenishable resources, we at IRWIN can assure you that every effort is made to meet or exceed Environmental Protection Agency (EPA) recommendations and require- ments for a "greener" workplace.

To preserve these natural assets, a number of environmental policies, both companywide and department-specific, have been implemented. From the use of 50% recycled paper in our textbooks to the printing of promotional materials with recycled stock and soy inks to our office paper recycling program, we are committed to reducing waste and replacing envi- ronmentally unsafe products with safer alternatives.

© Richard D. Irwin, a Times Mirror Higher Education Group, Inc. company, 1996

All rights reserved. No part of this publication may be reproduced, stored in a retrieval system, or transmitted, in any form or by any means, electronic, mechanical, photocopying, recording, or otherwise, without the prior written permission of the publisher.

Irwin Book Team

Executive editor: *Ralph Rieves*
Marketing manager: *Kelly Sheridan*
Manager, direct marketing: *Rebecca S. Gordon*
Production supervisor: *Pat Frederickson*
Assistant manager, desktop services: *Jon Christopher*
Project editor: *Lynn Basler*
Designer: *Matthew Baldwin*
Compositor: *ElectraGraphics, Inc.*
Typeface: *11/13 Times Roman*
Printer: *Quebecor/Fairfield*

Times Mirror
Higher Education Group

Library of Congress Cataloging-in-Publication Data

Brancato, Carolyn Kay.
　　Getting listed on Wall Street : The Irwin guide to financial reporting standards in the U.S. / Carolyn Kay Brancato.
　　　　p.　　cm.
　　Includes index.
　　ISBN 0-7863-9329-8
　　1. Securities industry—United States.　2. Securities industry—
Law and legislation—United States.　3. Securities—United States—
Listing.　4. Stock exchanges—United States.　5. Institutional
investments—United States.　6. Corporations, Foreign—United
States—Finance.　7. Corporate governance—United States.
8. Disclosure of information—United States.　I. Title.
HG4910.B72　1996
658.15—dc20　　　　　　　　　　　　　　　　　　95-32028

Printed in the United States of America
1 2 3 4 5 6 7 8 9 0 QF 2 1 0 9 8 7 6 5

For Aunt Marge

Preface

U.S. stock markets are the largest, most trusted, and most stable in the world. Although emerging securities markets, such as those in Mexico, Indonesia, and Thailand, were in vogue in the early 1990s, U.S. stock markets will continue to attract the major investors of the world. Record numbers of foreign issuers are entering U.S. securities markets; in 1994 foreign issues traded on U.S. stock exchanges rose to a historic high of $7.2 billion, a 16 percent increase over 1993. Global companies—both U.S. and foreign—that want access to U.S. markets need to understand not only what it takes to list in U.S. markets but how to attract the more than $9.5 trillion of U.S. institutional investor assets that comprise the single largest portion of these markets.

This book is intended to help both U.S. and foreign corporate executives position their companies to become listed in U.S. markets and to attract U.S. institutional investor capital. Part One, Why Enter U.S. Markets? describes the investment climate and parameters of U.S. markets and the staggering increase in listings by non-U.S. companies. Part Two, How to Enter in U.S. Markets, outlines options and filing procedures for entry into various segments of public and private U.S. securities markets. Part Three, How to Attract U.S. Investors, discusses the economic power of U.S. institutional shareholders, including different investment approaches used by pension funds, investment managers, banks, and insurance companies. It then provides insight into the key issues relating to corporate governance of most concern to U.S. institutional investors, including whether companies provide shareholder representation, whether they structure their boards of directors properly, and whether they pay appropriate levels of executive compensation. These are the critical governance factors likely to be scrutinized by U.S. institutional investors as part of their investment decision-making process.

Legal materials in Chapters 3 and 4 were drafted by Catherine T. Dixon, formerly head of the Office of Disclosure Policy at the U.S. Securities and Exchange Commission. The author is grateful for invaluable research assistance rendered by Kevin Crum, Senior Research Analyst for The Brancato Report. In addition, the following individuals provided important source materials: Jean Tobin, Joseph Kenrick, and James Cochrane of The New York Stock Exchange; John Wilcox and Juliane Keppler of Georgeson & Company Inc.; Peg O'Hara and Patrick McGurn of the Investor Responsibility Research Center; and James E. Heard, Howard Sherman and Bruce Babcock of Institutional Shareholder Services.

Carolyn Kay Brancato

Table of Contents

Introduction

By early 1995, there were 669 foreign companies representing 44 countries trading in US public securities markets. From 1990–1994 alone, 365 foreign companies raised nearly $50 billion in new capital by entering US markets to trade on the New York Stock Exchange (NYSE), the American Stock Exchange (AMEX), in the over-the-counter (OTC) market, and in the private placement market. Becoming listed in US markets is a major priority for companies in such diverse countries as Argentina (YPF Sociedad Anonima was the first Latin American oil and gas company to offer public securities on Wall Street, with 35 million shares traded on its first listed day) and China (Shanghai Petrochemical was the first Chinese company to list in US securities markets). On October 5, 1993, Daimler-Benz AG became the first German company to become listed on the NYSE, representing a breakthrough in foreign listing activity, since companies from Germany had been particularly reticent to subject themselves to the required regulatory oversight.

Foreign issuers are increasingly attracted to US markets for several reasons: These markets are the largest in the world; investors have confidence in them; the markets are efficient; alternative methods of raising capital are becoming less and less attractive and available; and the United States presents less troublesome barriers to entry by foreign issuers than do other nations, and what barriers it does have are increasingly being perceived to be worth the effort to overcome. Moreover, on April 19, 1994, Chairman Arthur Levitt Jr. of the Securities and Exchange Commission (SEC) announced a number of additional measures to further simplify and lower the cost of the registration and reporting process for foreign companies accessing US public markets.[1]

Gaining access to US securities markets carries with it the potential benefit of accessing the largest pool of money in the world. As part of this pool, there is a highly concentrated institutional investor component of US markets with assets in excess of $9.5 trillion.[2] Greenwich Associates reports that US pension funds, foundations, and endowments surveyed at the end of 1993 owned $170 billion in foreign equities and planned to increase their foreign holdings to $300 billion in just three years.[3] Foreign stocks are held by a relatively small number of institutions. The California Public Employees' Retirement System (CalPERS) is the largest statewide public pension fund; this one fund controls more than 8 percent of all foreign holdings by all US institutions. In 1994, CalPERS had an $80 billion portfolio of which $15 billion was invested in foreign securities, including equity investments of $3 billion in Japan, $1.5 billion in the United Kingdom and $500 million each in France and Germany. Early in 1995, CalPERS announced its intention to increase its foreign holdings in the next few years to $20 billion.

Despite the globalization of securities markets and investor attraction to emerging markets, institutional investors still lean heavily toward investing in securities listed for trading in US markets. Certain listing requirements, such as those imposed by the NYSE and regulated by the SEC, build in minimum levels of shareholder protection by guaranteeing minimum standards of corporate governance.

For example, the NYSE requires that each listed company have an audit committee made up entirely of outside directors to increase accountability and reduce the likelihood that company officials will act in their own interests rather than in the interests of the shareholders. There are also minimum capitalization requirements, which appeal to larger investors who cannot invest their sizeable sums in thinly capitalized or traded stock. Numerous accounting and disclosure standards associated with listing or trading in US markets give investors a certain level of confidence in the markets. Finally, listing through the US National Market System, although not mandatory, can improve access to capital. Thus, foreign companies have been increasingly tempted to run the gauntlet of regulations in the United States to position themselves for expansion into US markets.

There are, however, risks associated either with entering US markets or attempting to attract US institutional investors to foreign country markets. Either way, foreign companies have to deal with US institutional investors, which can present difficulties. For example, before June 1993, Lord James Hanson, chairman of the giant British industrial conglomerate Hanson plc, had probably never heard of the Houston Firefighters Relief and Retirement Fund. But he was certainly aware of the fund after June of 1993, for in that month, officials of the fund joined with pension fund directors from the United Mine Workers of America, the State of Wisconsin Investment Board, and leading investors from the United Kingdom to defeat an attempt Hanson was making to limit shareholders' rights. The landmark case marked the first transatlantic proxy battle waged at a British company, and shareholders emerged victorious. They forced Hanson to retract proposals that would have restricted shareholders' ability to nominate directors, to propose amendments to corporate resolutions, and even to speak at future general meetings. Days before the June 25 general meeting, Lord Hanson withdrew the proposals, saying that the company had apparently given the mistaken impression it was seeking "draconian" power over shareholders to restrict their rights.[4]

A year later, Maurice Saatchi, chairman of the British Saatchi & Saatchi Co., got his wake-up call from institutional investors. A shareholder group that included two major US institutions, the State of Wisconsin Investment Board, and the General Electric Company's pension trust forced Saatchi's dismissal in 1994 by protesting an excessive stock option package and the company's dismal performance since his installation as chairman. US institutional investors have begun to make demands in Mexico, France, and even places where shareholders' rights are notoriously circumscribed: Germany and Japan. Four cases that occurred during 1992–1993, demonstrate the emerging trend:

- Tubos de Acero de Mexico, a seamless steel pipe company, proposed a secondary stock offering that favored one large Argentine stockholder over all other stockholders. The State of Wisconsin Investment Board objected to the offering's terms.

- Perhaps the best-known activist US fund, the California Public Employees' Retirement System (CalPERS), objected to a proposal by the French food giant BSN to cap shareholders' voting rights at 6 percent of BSN's total or 12 percent if they have held registered shares for two years.

- In Germany, a CalPERS representative made what was reported to be an "impassioned speech" introducing a one-share, one-vote rule at a general meeting of RWE A.G., an electrical utility company headquartered in Essen, Germany. Approximately 60 percent of the vote was controlled by 30 percent of locally held shares.

- CalPERS sent letters suggesting that two Japanese firms in its portfolio, Nomura and Daiwa, add independent directors to their boards of directors. Neither company responded.

Shareholders did not prevail in any of these instances as they did in the Hanson case. But the activists made their point and made it to a worldwide audience.[5] Institutional investors are starting to exercise their shareholder rights aggressively as the percentage of foreign proxies they vote has increased from 24 percent in 1991 to an estimated 65 percent in 1994.[6]

Even companies that are not considering entry into US markets should be cognizant of institutional investors' concerns since US institutions are rapidly expanding into foreign markets. Certain European countries such as France have companies that are well known for being closely held, even family-oriented businesses. In these European countries, companies have been permitted to build up reserves while undervaluing assets on the books. To attract outside capital, companies in these countries may have to consider instituting governance reforms, altering their accounting, and increasing their dividend payout. Arcane voting and governance procedures that traditionally favor incumbent management may have to be restructured to accommodate the new breed of investors.

In Japan, companies are faced with similar problems. A system of subsidized capital historically encouraged plant expansion to levels of overcapacity, but new sources of capital will have to be sought, since that capacity will not last forever, and recent budget pressures will limit Japan's ability to subsidize industrial and financial market transactions. Japanese firms will therefore increasingly feel pressure to attract outside institutional money for expansion purposes. It remains to be seen whether or not they can adjust from centuries of almost feudal attitudes toward shareholders to accommodate the demands of the more activist modern institutional investor, such as employing outside auditors, electing independent directors, and establishing meaningful shareholder governance. If they wish to attract US investors, Japanese companies and their transfer agents and bank trustees will have to devise ways to ensure that proxy voting occurs and that, at the very least, they acknowledge communications from major institutional investors on corporate governance issues.

Activist institutional shareholders have continued to grow as a global force. Any US or foreign company trading in US or foreign markets that chooses to ignore them will do so at its financial peril. To attract capital from US institutional investors, companies need a map to guide them through the labyrinth of corporate governance pressures the institutions exert upon management. Moreover, they need to understand that investing institutions are not a monolithic group with a unified perspective. Institutions have vastly different investment objectives, tolerance to risk, understanding of their fiduciary mandates, and perceptions of their appropriate role in corporate governance.

Notwithstanding major differences among them, institutional investors as a group have vastly expanded their economic sphere of influence in a number of important ways. Moreover, while they may be diverse, a high concentration of economic power resides among a relatively small and extraordinarily stable group of institutions.

The term *institutional investor* refers to an investor with money under professional management organization that invests on behalf of a group of individuals, another organization, or a group of organizations. Unfortunately, it is difficult to categorize every variety of funds that flow from individuals into various poolings such as venture capital funds, partnerships, and private market transactions. Nevertheless, throughout this book, institutional investors will be grouped into a few primary categories: public pension funds, corporate pension funds, mutual funds, insurance companies, and bank trusts.

Public pension funds. Public employee pension funds — "public funds" — have tended to be the more activist of the pension funds. They have made their demands known and pursued their goals either individually or through shareholder groups such as the Council of Institutional Investors.[7]

Most of the public funds delegate significant investment authority to other fiduciaries such as banks or money managers. Although they delegate investment authority, they may still retain voting authority or may impose voting standards on their delegated managers. Some, such as the State of Wisconsin Investment Board, choose to retain all of their investing and voting authority. Even among those funds that adopt passive investment strategies and place large amounts of their portfolios in indexed funds (i.e., investing in a basket of stocks such as Standard & Poor's 500) some, such as CalPERS, have made specific companies in their indexed portfolios the focus of their activism. In the spring of 1994, at an Institutional Shareholder Services (ISS) Conference in Washington, D.C., CalPERS' general counsel, Richard Koppes, quietly but emphatically informed the institutional investor and corporate communities that, in its pursuit of governance changes, CalPERS might begin to take large holding positions in companies and pursue a kind of activist role with them called *relationship investing.*

As an example of what institutional investor activism can accomplish, a small number of public funds were actively involved in the replacements of chief executive officers (CEOs) at General Motors, IBM, American Express, Kodak, and Westinghouse.

Corporate pension funds. Pension funds of publicly[8] traded corporations — "private-trusteed funds" — have largely been silent in the media on governance issues. Corporate pension plans have been noticeably absent from the shareholder activism movement, in part because of their obvious discomfort at taking aim at managements of other companies and in part because of their general belief that corporate governance activities are generally not worth the time and effort.[9] Private pension funds also tend to delegate a large proportion of their investment and voting fiduciary responsibility to other institutions such as banks and money managers, which are even more reluctant to become involved in controversy.

In 1993, however, the $1 billion pension fund of Campbell Soup, one publicly held corporation, became one of the first corporate pension funds to take an activist stance in promoting corporate governance principles. It emerged from the traditional silence by announcing that it would vote the proxies for its stock against companies that elect more than three inside directors and for companies with compensation policies that tie pay to performance. Many regarded the Campbell pension fund initiatives as another watershed in the corporate governance movement, as institutional investor activism finally spread to corporate pension funds. The trend is likely to continue since, first of all, corporate pension funds will generally be coming under increasing pressure to meet retirement payout schedules and, second, many will be faced with shortfalls in available revenues for payout, arising from overly optimistic actuarial assumptions made in the past.

Mutual funds. Mutual funds and other investment companies are the fastest-growing segment of the institutional investor market. To date, they have had relatively little incentive to actively participate in corporate governance, unless they were voting in the context of a takeover, where their vote would carry with it a direct economic value. Some have kept away from controversial issues, lest they alienate those who allocate corporate pension fund money to them to manage. Managers of these types of institutions tend to ignore proxy voting methods of exerting pressure on companies. Instead, if they think the company is not performing well on the "fundamentals" (i.e., on the intrinsic value of the stock), they tend to sell their stock, also called "doing the Wall Street walk" or "voting with their feet."[10] Recently, however, several large managers — Fidelity and Alliance Capital — became publicly involved in the battle that ultimately led to removal of the CEO of American Express.

Insurance companies. Insurance companies tend to invest a very small percentage of their assets in equities. Prudential, one of the largest, actively manages its entire equity portfolio (i.e., it retains all authority for its equity investment decisions), while giving its fundamental security analysts free rein over proxy voting. But because most of their assets are invested in bonds, insurance companies tend to participate in corporate governance in less obvious ways. Rather than exerting pressure as shareholders, insurance companies have had extraordinary influence as bondholders in many significant cases concerning the corporate governance decisions of companies that are restructuring or are facing or emerging from bankruptcy.

Bank trusts. Bank trusts occupy a position in capital markets similar to that of mutual funds and investment companies. With significant fiduciary authority delegated to them, they manage funds far in excess of what their own asset data would suggest. When other fiduciaries delegate investment authority to banks, they tend to delegate approximately 70 percent of the voting authority as well. Recently, a press for improved portfolio returns has led a very small number of banks to begin to participate more actively in corporate governance.

Forging Relationships with Institutional Investors

Not only do these institutions have different investment objectives and governance perspectives, they may take varying approaches to activism. Some may approach a company directly to discuss the structure and composition of its board of directors, its executive compensation package, or a performance-related issue. Others will simply notify a company that they are launching a campaign to use their proxy votes to "just vote no" against management's slate of directors. It is important to understand the issues that disturb institutional investors, the style used by these institutions to communicate to managements, and the fact that these institutions are equipped not only with increasing economic clout but also with powerful new regulatory tools of communication. Also, these institutions are themselves under increasing regulatory pressure to participate more actively in corporate governance. They are, after all, fiduciaries entrusted with managing money on behalf of their beneficiaries, and thus they are subject to a variety of Department of Labor regulations and state and federal pension fund laws governing the exercise of their fiduciary responsibility.[11] These regulations require them not only to invest their assets prudently but to vote the proxies for their stock as well — both domestic and foreign. The likely direction for US institutions is to expand their role of monitoring corporate structure, shareholder voting rights, and compensation into the role of evaluating in greater detail the corporation's fundamental indicators of corporate performance.

Finally, these institutions are becoming increasingly interested in exploring new markets as they attempt to boost their own yields in the face of a demographic curve of higher pension obligations in the first part of the next century. Many of them can and will take long-term stakes in companies throughout the world if they receive assurances regarding performance and corporate governance accessibility and accountability on the part of managements and boards of directors. These institutions, given their long-term payout requirements, may in fact represent the best chance many corporations have to attract needed long-term capital to enable them to restructure and to invest for future competitiveness. Moreover, studies show that a stable block of certain growth-oriented institutional shareholders may be advantageous to companies to reduce their volatility and lower their overall cost of capital.

Forging relationships with US institutional investors is fraught with difficulties, and requires the development of new and more comprehensive measures of performance as well as a common language for corporations and institutions to discuss governance and performance criteria and results. The partners to these new relationships, therefore, have considerable incentive to work out their differences. A good deal of economic well-being for US and foreign businesses hangs in the balance.

NOTES

1. Kevin D. Cramer and Catherine M. Stavrakis, "SEC Simplifies Foreign Companies' Access to US Markets," *International Securities Regulation Report,* Buraff Publications, May 3, 1994, pp. 50–54.

2. Carolyn Kay Brancato, *The Brancato Report on Institutional Investment* 2, ed. 1 (January 1995), p. 11.

3. Greenwich Associates, "Seismic Shift in Pension Planning," *Greenwich Investment Management Report* 1994, pp. 23–24. See also *Financial Times,* March 30, 1994, p. 21.

4. Marlene Givant Star, "Hanson Bows to Pressure, Drops Resolution," *Pensions & Investments,* July 12, 1993, p. 39; and Bruce Babcock, "The Rise of Global Shareholder Activism," *ISS Issue Alert* 8, no. 7. (July–August 1993), pp. 1 and 9.

5. Leslie Wayne, "Exporting Shareholder Activism," *New York Times,* July 16, 1993, p. D-1.

6. Global Shareholder Services, "Corporate Governance: The Emerging Power of the Institutional Investor," Presentation at ISS Client Conference, Washington D.C., February 23–24, 1995, p. 8.

7. The role of shareholder advisory groups among US institutional investors should not be forgotten. Groups such as the Council of Institutional Investors (CII), Institutional Shareholder Services, Inc. (ISS), and the Investor Responsibility Research Center (IRRC) play important roles in collecting and disseminating information about proxy voting initiatives to members or subscribers. Even these groups are not monolithic, since some of them are more interventionist than others. Finally, a plethora of proxy voting service companies, such as Georgeson & Company, stand ready to assume the voting authority for a range of fiduciaries.

8. The use of the term *publicly traded* in this context refers to a corporation that has stock traded in the public securities markets. Pension funds for this type of corporation are referred to as *private* corporate pension funds. These should not be confused with the "public" pension funds that invest money on behalf of "public" employees.

9. Vineeta Arnand, "Corporate Funds Still Not Active Investors," *Pensions & Investments,* July 25, 1994, p. 4.

10. Wells Fargo Nikko Investment Advisors, the largest indexer, generally commands about 1–2 percent of the stock of its portfolio companies. Its proxy voting is handled centrally. Other funds with active managers may either centralize or decentralize their voting by delegating it to their security analysts who cover the stocks. Thus, there is no set policy in the mutual fund or investment company industry.

11. Federal regulatory oversight by the Department of Labor (DOL) through the Employee Retirement Income Security Act (ERISA) and the issuance of the "Avon letter," which required fiduciaries to vote their proxies as a matter of fiduciary responsibility, assisted this effort. Public pension funds not covered by Department of Labor regulations are most often subject to state law versions governing their fiduciary conduct, which closely track DOL regulations and case law.

WHY ENTER US MARKETS?

Chapter 1

Where the Money Is

When asked why he robbed banks, the notorious American criminal Willie Sutton is reputed to have responded, "That's where the money is." If corporations want to expand, they should also consider going where the money is—entering US capital markets, widely regarded to be the largest, most efficient, and liquid in the world.[1] The National Market System links the trading in public securities on the New York Stock Exchange (NYSE), the American Stock Exchange (AMEX), the five regional stock exchanges—the Boston, Chicago, Cincinnati, Pacific, and Philadelphia Stock Exchanges—and the over-the-counter (OTC) market. Becoming a part of the National Market System can benefit foreign companies by providing them unparalleled access to capital. Glaxo, a British company, attained the distinction of being the first foreign issuer to be the most actively traded stock on the New York Stock Exchange, when, in 1992, approximately 275 million Glaxo American Depositary Receipts (ADRs) were traded on the NYSE. Over 350,000 US investors own Glaxo ADRs, and Glaxo's market capitalization in the United States is approximately 20 billion US dollars.[2]

From 1992 to 1994, trading volume for foreign issuers trading in US public securities markets rose from an estimated $130–$140 billion to an estimated $275–$300 billion. During this same period, the numbers of foreign companies listed in London, Tokyo, Paris, and Frankfurt all declined.[3] Speaking at a conference late in 1993, former SEC Chairman Richard Breeden noted:

> In 1992, ninety-four new foreign companies entered the US market for the first time, offering US $32 billion in securities. This year so far there have been seventy-six new foreign entrants, and we have seen around US $40 billion in offerings in the first ten months . . . securities of foreign companies from forty countries trade in the public markets of the United States, representing every continent except the Antarctic.[4]

US EQUITY MARKETS DOMINATE
WORLD TRADING

US equity markets, with capitalization in 1994 of $5.1 trillion, are significantly larger than equity markets in Japan ($3.7 trillion), the United Kingdom ($1.21 trillion), and Germany ($471 billion). From 1988 to 1994, US equity market capitalization rose more than 80 percent, while total equity capitalization in global equity markets rose only 56 percent, from $9.7 trillion in 1988 to $15.2 trillion in 1994. The US share of world equity capitalization, therefore, increased from 28.7 percent in 1987, peaked at 37.2 percent in 1993 but still remained a strong 33.5 percent in 1994 (see Table 1–1).

While US markets represented 33.5 percent of 1994 world capitalization, they have consistently accounted for a much larger percent—37.3 percent in 1994—of the value of all shares traded in global markets, as shown in Table 1–2 and Figure 1–1. Table 1–2 also shows a reversal of fortune for Japanese stock market trading, as its value of shares traded dropped from a high of 43.3 percent of global value in 1988 to only 11.7 percent in 1994. US markets bounced back from the sharp market decline of 1987 to show an overall increase in share value of global trading from 28.7 percent in 1988 to 37.3 percent in 1994. Despite some fluctuations in the trend, US markets seem to be, over the long term, comparatively more resilient than many other equity markets.

Total US equity holdings of foreign corporations increased 24.4 percent from $91.5 billion in 1988 to $113.8 billion by year-end 1990. The most dramatic growth in US equity holdings for the five-year period, however, occurred during 1991–1993, with equities growing 56.5 percent, from $113.8 billion in 1990 to $178.1 billion in 1992, and then *another* 35.5 percent, to $241.4 billion in 1993 (see Table 1–3). By year-end 1994, US equity holdings had gained yet another 20 percent, rising to $288.5 billion. Despite the vagaries of the Japanese stock market, Japan's equity markets have been rather resilient in their ability to attract US investment: US equity holdings of Japanese corporations increased from $9.0 billion at year-end 1988 to $49.8 billion at the end of 1994. Western Europe continues to dominate as the favored region for US equity holdings of foreign corporations, with nearly half of the 1994 total. Latin America, however, has steadily been increasing its share of US equity investment, from 5.2 percent in 1988 to 11.0 percent at year-end 1994 (see Figure 1–2).

TABLE 1-1

Capitalization of Global Equity Markets: 1988–1994
($ Billions)

	1988		1990		1993		1994	
	Market Value	*Percentage of Total*	*Market Value*	*Percentage of Total*	*Market Value*	*Percentage of Total*	*Market Value*	*Percentage of Total*
United States	2,794	28.7%	3,090	32.8%	5,224	37.2%	5,082	33.5%
Japan	3,907	40.2%	2,918	31.0%	3,000	21.3%	3,720	24.5%
United Kingdom	771	7.9%	849	9.0%	1,152	8.2%	1,210	8.0%
Germany	252	2.6%	355	3.8%	463	3.3%	471	3.1%
France	245	2.5%	314	3.3%	456	3.2%	451	3.0%
Hong Kong	74	0.8%	83	0.9%	385	2.7%	270	1.8%
Canada	242	2.5%	242	2.6%	327	2.3%	315	2.1%
Switzerland	141	1.4%	160	1.7%	272	1.9%	284	1.9%
Australia	138	1.4%	108	1.1%	204	1.5%	219	1.4%
Netherlands	114	1.2%	120	1.3%	182	1.3%	283	1.9%
Italy	135	1.4%	149	1.6%	136	1.0%	180	1.2%
Singapore	24	0.2%	34	0.4%	133	0.9%	135	0.9%
Other developed countries	408	4.2%	390	4.1%	531	3.8%	637	4.2%
Emerging markets	483	5.0%	612	6.5%	1,591	11.3%	1,929	12.7%
World	9,728	100%	9,424	100%	14,056	100%	15,186	100%

Source: *The Brancato Report on Institutional Investment* 2, ed. 3 (September 1995).

TABLE 1–2
Value of Shares Traded in Global Equity Markets: 1988–1994
($ Billions)

	1988		1990		1993		1994	
	Market Value	Percentage of Total	Market Value	Percentage of Total	Market Value	Percentage of Total	Market Value	Percentage of Total
United States	1,720	28.7%	1,815	32.6%	3,507	47.8%	3,593	37.3%
Japan	2,598	43.3%	1,602	28.7%	954	13.0%	1,121	11.7%
United Kingdom	579	9.7%	279	5.0%	424	5.8%	928	9.6%
Germany	350	5.8%	502	9.0%	303	4.1%	461	4.8%
France	66	1.1%	117	2.1%	174	2.4%	615	6.4%
Switzerland	NA	0.0%	NA	0.0%	168	2.3%	227	2.4%
Canada	67	1.1%	71	1.3%	142	1.9%	161	1.7%
Hong Kong	23	0.4%	35	0.6%	132	1.8%	147	1.5%
Singapore	4	0.1%	20	0.4%	82	1.1%	81	0.8%
Australia	37	0.6%	39	0.7%	68	0.9%	95	1.0%
Netherlands	35	0.6%	40	0.7%	67	0.9%	171	1.8%
Italy	32	0.5%	43	0.8%	66	0.9%	118	1.2%
Other developed countries	78	1.3%	119	2.1%	186	2.5%	264	2.7%
Emerging markets	409	6.8%	894	16.0%	1,069	14.6%	1,640	17.0%
World	5,998	100%	5,576	100%	7,342	100%	9,622	100%

Source: *The Brancato Report on Institutional Investment* 2, ed. 3 (September 1995).

FIGURE 1–1
US Presence in Global Equity Markets: 1988–1994

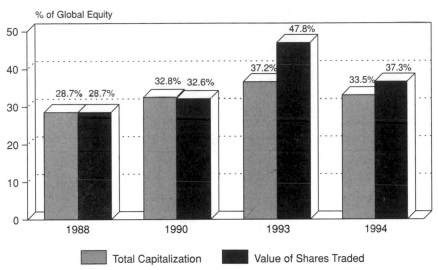

% of Global Equity

Legend: Total Capitalization · Value of Shares Traded

Data labels:
- 1988: 28.7% 28.7%
- 1990: 32.8% 32.6%
- 1993: 37.2% 47.8%
- 1994: 33.5% 37.3%

Source: *The Brancato Report on Institutional Investment* 2, ed. 3 (September 1995).

US investors' appetite for foreign equities traded in US markets has dramatically increased during the decade ending in 1994. Table 1–4 shows that gross purchases of foreign stock increased from $17 billion in 1983 to $433.2 billion in 1994. Although sales of foreign stock by US investors increased as well, net purchases (purchases minus sales) increased tenfold, from $3.7 billion in 1983 to $32.3 billion by year-end 1992, nearly doubled in 1993 alone, to $62.7 billion, then increased another $46.9 billion by year-end 1994 (see also Figure 1–3).

Figure 1–4 shows how net purchases of foreign stocks by US investors has changed according to region. Between 1983 and 1994, US investors entered the Latin American region with large investments, as net purchases increased from a negligible amount to 18.1 percent of the total. This increase actually outstripped the growth in Asian markets, which fell as a percent of total purchases from 32.1 percent in 1983 to 25.2 percent in 1994.

TABLE 1–3
US Equity Holdings of Foreign Corporations by Region: 1988–1994
($ Billions)

	Year-end 1988	Year-end 1990	Year-end 1992	Net Purchases in 1993	Year-end 1993	Net Purchases in 1994	Year-end 1994
Western Europe	43.7	58.4	91.0	31.5	122.5	16.3	138.8
Japan	9.0	10.6	28.9	6.2	35.1	14.7	49.8
Latin America	4.8	7.5	15.2	12.3	27.5	4.3	31.8
Canada	14.1	15.5	14.8	5.1	19.9	2.4	22.3
Other	19.9	21.8	28.2	8.2	36.4	9.4	45.8
Total	91.5	113.8	178.1	63.3	241.4	47.1	288.5

Source: *The Brancato Report on Institutional Investment* 2, ed. 3 (September 1995).

FIGURE 1–2
Share of US Equity Investments in Foreign Corporations by Region: 1988–94

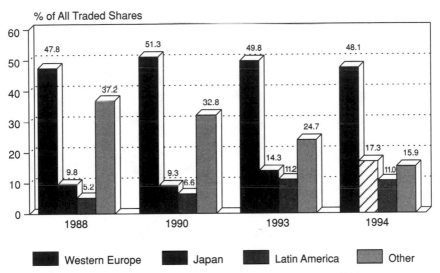

Source: *The Brancato Report on Institutional Investment* 2, ed. 3 (September 1995).

TABLE 1–4
Transactions in Foreign Stocks on US Equity Markets: 1983–1994
($ Billions)

	Purchases of Foreign Stock by Americans	Sales of Foreign Stock by Americans	Total Purchases and Sales	Net Purchases by Americans
1983	17.0	13.3	30.3	3.7
1984	15.9	14.8	30.7	1.1
1985	24.8	20.9	45.7	3.9
1986	51.0	49.1	100.1	1.9
1987	94.4	95.5	189.9	−1.1
1988	77.3	75.4	152.7	1.9
1989	122.9	109.9	232.8	13.0
1990	131.9	122.6	254.5	9.3
1991	152.6	120.6	273.2	32.0
1992	182.3	150.0	332.3	32.3
1993	308.2	245.5	553.7	62.7
1994	433.2	386.3	819.5	46.9

Source: *The Brancato Report on Institutional Investment* 2, ed. 3 (September 1995).

FIGURE 1–3
Transactions in Foreign Stocks on US Equity Markets: 1987–1994

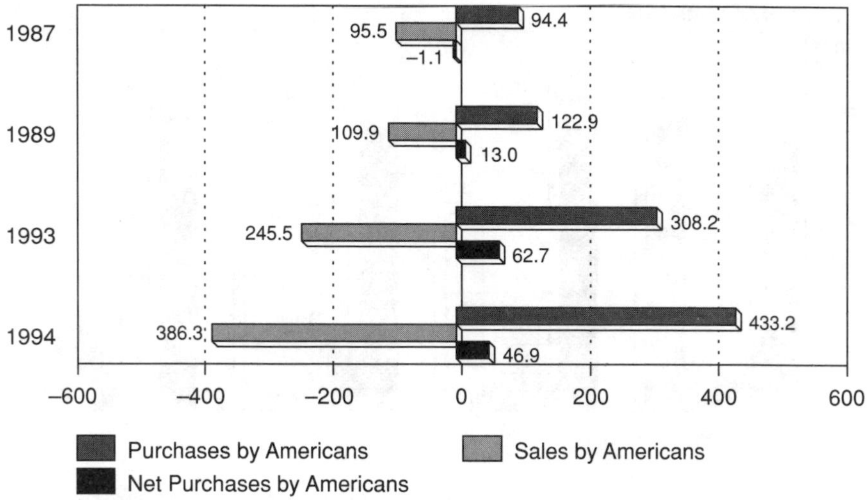

Source: *The Brancato Report on Institutional Investment* 2, ed. 3 (September 1995).

US MARKETS INSPIRE CONFIDENCE

The most attractive markets for investors—both foreign and US—are those that enjoy liquidity, depth, and stability. Despite the trend toward globalization of markets, US markets enjoy superior liquidity, relatively low political risk, a stable and low-cost trading environment, and a high degree of transparency, which inspires long-term confidence. Thus, access to US markets remains a prize that many foreign issuers strive to attain, and that US investors continue to desire, despite rapid growth in emerging markets.

M. Shane Warbrick is controller of Fletcher Challenge Limited, a diversified international paper, pulp, forestry, oil, and gas company headquartered in New Zealand, which operates throughout the world, including China, Asia, and the South Pacific. He addressed a recent conference sponsored by the Fordham University School of Law and the Graduate School of Business Administration to discuss considerations for foreign companies entering the US securities markets. Fletcher Challenge is one of those foreign issuers who considered it important to comply with the regulatory stipulations required to seek registration in US equity markets.

FIGURE 1–4
US Net Purchases of Foreign Stock by Region: 1983 and 1994

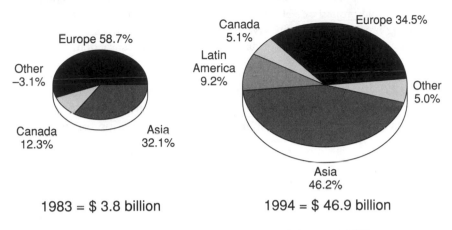

1983 = $ 3.8 billion   1994 = $ 46.9 billion

Source: *The Brancato Report on Institutional Investment* 2, ed. 3 (September 1995).

Warbrick explains the reasons by pointing out an important deficiency in New Zealand's own markets:

> Let me go through a little bit of our history. New Zealand was probably the hardest hit country following the 1987 market collapse. We probably had one of the most hyped-up equity markets around the world, having had the highest returns of any market for the last eighteen months before October 1987, and then we had the hardest crash as well, which was hardly a surprise.
>
> Following the crash, most other markets in the world recovered, but New Zealand did not. One of the reasons why the New Zealand market did not recover is that the trust and confidence in the New Zealand regulatory and accounting standards was basically shattered. . . . Once you lose trust, it is very hard to attract investors back to a market.[5]

US securities laws are based on disclosure rather than on regulatory judgment of the underlying merits of securities. The SEC has no authority to approve any security or to rule on its merits. Its sole function is to ensure that all required filings—including registration statements and annual reports—are accurate and complete. According to one legal observer:

> In the United States, we do not have, in general, a system of securities regulations that is based on the fairness or attractiveness of securities. It is not, in general, a matter of concern to the SEC whether or not a particular stock is a

good buy at US $30 or US $20, or whether a debt security is properly priced. The focus of our securities laws is on full disclosure. The theory is that if the business and prospects, management, and financial condition of a company are fully and properly disclosed in registration statements and in the accompanying prospectus, then the investor can make up his own mind regarding the appropriateness of the price and the fairness of the transaction.[6]

Arguing against SEC relaxation of standards foreign issuers must meet to enter US securities markets, former SEC Chairman Richard Breeden noted that the US disclosure system is currently superior to most others in the world because it provides the most relevant information for investors:

> When I make this statement I am not simply referring to the numbers that appear in the balance sheet, income statement, and statement of cash flows, as important as the reported numbers are. I am also referring to the footnote requirements contained in [accounting] opinions, FASB [Financial Accounting Standards Board] statements, and disclosure requirements of the SEC, such as the very useful Management Discussion & Analysis ("MD&A"). I believe that the information provided by this system is one of the primary reasons why the US capital markets are among the most liquid and efficient in the world . . .[7]
>
> Increased disclosure is the key to efficiently accessing the largest equity capital market in the world. The more information provided to the investment community, the clearer that information is presented, the more transparent the company becomes to both national and international investors, making it a more attractive investment, which in turn raises its stock price and lowers its cost of capital.[8]

Confidence stems not only from disclosure but also from enforcement—*and the perception* of rigorous enforcement—of laws against insider trading. While the United States has not been without its share of highly publicized insider trading scandals, it is also widely perceived as fostering a climate in which such abuses will be robustly prosecuted.

Examples of this enforcement include the vigorous prosecution of insider trading cases against major Wall Street financiers during the 1980s merger era. More recently, in 1994, an uproar over trading "spreads" on the NASDAQ stock market illustrated another important example of vigorous SEC investigation of allegations of trading abuse and swift correction to restore market confidence. Two professors—William G. Christie of Vanderbilt University and Paul H. Schultz of Ohio State University—conducting a study on an unrelated NASDAQ matter apparently uncovered irregularities that, they contended, showed a pattern of dealers avoiding posting of NASDAQ quotes in "odd-eights" on NASDAQ's 100 most active stocks, a tactic that apparently kept spreads—the difference between quoted buying and selling prices, or what amounts to profits for dealers—unnecessarily wide. The professors contended that spreads on the more heavily traded NASDAQ shares had been one-quarter point, or 25 cents a share, compared with the more typical one-eighth point, or 12.5 cents a share, of the New York and American stock exchanges. This triggered immediate investigations by the Justice Department, the Securities and Exchange Commission, and the National Association of Securities Dealers (NASD), the self-regulatory organization that monitors NASDAQ. Moreover, under increased scrutiny from the news media (some of the large, highly visible NASDAQ stocks such as Microsoft were involved[9]) and even as the investigations proceeded, brokers moved to narrow spreads and restore confidence in the market.

Markets in a number of other countries do not enjoy similar confidence. Legal scholars at a Fordham Law School conference discussed the perceptions that other stock markets routinely operate in a less honest atmosphere. James Silkenat observed:

> Although there have been a number of recent efforts to curb insider trading on European exchanges and European markets, such efforts have had little practical effect to date either on the insiders themselves or on the typical investor's perception of how insiders act. The common belief in Europe that certain investors have access to confidential information and regularly profit from that information may be the major reason why comparatively few Europeans actually own stock. In the United States, nearly thirty-five percent of adults own shares directly. In Germany, that number is seven percent; fourteen percent in France; and twenty percent in England. Those are sizeable differences, and partially explain why the US markets are so active and why so much money is available for those companies that seek to enter the US markets.[10]

Other participants at this conference noted that it may be irrelevant whether insider information is actually communicated among market participants; it is the *perception* that it is communicated that damages the credibility and attractiveness of certain markets as trading centers.

Another issue regarding confidence is the threat of excessive volatility, which can potentially undermine investors' confidence in markets. The organized US stock exchanges must certainly be credited with their creative design of "circuit breakers," which they instituted in an atmosphere of self-regulation to prevent sudden, excessive rushes to sell among investors. The exchanges expeditiously instituted these circuit breakers following the major fall in the market of October 1987. They bring a stop to trading when price limits—specifically a 50-point decline in the market—are exceeded. These were deemed especially necessary because institutional investors, with their great liquidity, control increasingly large block trading and because increasingly widespread use of computerized program trading can cause sudden sharp dips in the market.

For a number of years, emerging markets captured the fancy of many investors, with their promise of rapid capital appreciation, frequently from a small investment base. But the heady early days of emerging markets may have been replaced by a more mature phase, as money managers have begun to apply a more rigorous set of standards. According to Craig Torres of *The Wall Street Journal,* "The euphoria over economic reforms in Latin America and high economic growth rates in Asia is over."[11] Torres notes that, as money management globalizes, so do standards of valuation.

By mid-1994, the initial burst of growth in emerging markets seemed to have waned, and—like someone all dressed up with no place to go— institutions, with the sizeable sums they must keep invested, indicated an interest in moving back to the more familiar and less risky US markets. Despite a drop in US equity markets during the first half of 1994, the performance of emerging markets in the Asian and Pacific regions, (excluding Japan) had by July 26, 1994, declined even more substantially, by 14.9 percent from the beginning of the year, compared with a 3.1 percent decline for US markets (see Table 1–5). Some specific stock index declines recorded from January 1 to July 26, 1994, were 24.3 percent in Indonesia, 22.7 percent in Hong Kong, 14.4 percent in Thailand, and 16.2 percent in Mexico. Big global investors began pulling out of emerging markets. Again in the words of Torres:

> Money managers have sold shares in Asian markets such as Hong Kong, which is considered a play on the developing China market, as well as other emerging Asian markets, including Singapore, Malaysia and India. And in Latin America, political risk or, in some cases, high stock valuations are prompting money managers to sell Mexican and Chilean shares and to look for buys in Europe and the US.[12]

As early as mid-1994, cutbacks at major international mutual funds such as Putnam Investments were reported in the financial press. Putnam was reported to be reducing the firm's emerging market exposure to below

TABLE 1-5

Dow Jones World Stock Index

	Closing Index 7/26/94	Index Change From 12/31/93	Percentage Change	Closing Index 4/25/95	Index Change From 12/31/94	Percentage Change
Americas	108.19	−3.98	−3.55	119.88	+11.35	+10.46
US	428.68	−13.51	−3.06	482.68	+49.61	+3.75
Mexico	153.24	−29.64	−16.21	76.62	−30.44	−28.43
Canada	93.6	−6.76	−6.73	98.81	+3.58	+11.46
Europe	117.36	+1.28	+1.10	125.56	+9.86	+8.53
Austria	106.67	+1.85	+1.77	108.25	+3.89	+3.72
Belgium	119.5	+7.96	+7.13	133.08	+17.34	+14.98
Denmark	105.47	+9.74	+10.18	105.65	+7.49	+7.63
Finland	179.62	+40.95	+29.53	219.05	+13.14	+6.38
France	118.52	+0.73	+0.62	125.24	+16.08	+14.73
Germany	122.46	+3.53	+2.97	130.95	+8.38	+6.83
Ireland	117.5	+5.55	+4.95	133.14	+10.55	+8.61
Italy	126.91	+27.80	+28.05	104.48	−5.05	−4.61
Netherlands	130.91	+5.17	+4.12	148.88	+15.01	+11.21
Norway	118.19	+14.91	+14.44	128.20	+5.61	+4.57
Spain	97.83	+2.95	+3.11	93.37	+4.04	+4.52
Sweden	114.97	+10.91	+10.48	127.77	+8.35	+6.99
Switzerland	156.04	−2.24	−1.42	183.95	+20.96	+12.86
United Kingdom	107.07	−5.23	−4.66	115.22	+7.89	+7.35
Asia/Pacific	124.75	+17.99	+16.85	123.89	+4.41	+3.69
Australia	116.24	+2.95	+2.61	113.48	−1.41	−1.22
Hong Kong	208.95	−61.40	−22.71	191.30	+7.36	+4.00
Indonesia	177.17	−56.75	−24.26	152.63	−23.07	−13.13
Japan	121.31	+25.60	+26.74	121.41	+5.20	+4.48
Malaysia	219.59	−50.40	−18.67	225.79	+9.10	+4.20
New Zealand	152.03	+0.51	+0.33	184.77	+28.91	+18.55
Singapore	165.85	−13.37	−7.46	178.50	+0.44	+.25
Thailand	208.78	−35.13	−14.40	171.76	−35.9	−17.29
Asia/Pacific (excluding Japan)	164.67	−28.93	−14.94	157.91	+0.35	+0.22
World (excluding U.S.)	120.71	+10.19	+9.22	122.68	+6.10	+5.23
DJ World Stock Index	116.03	+4.96	+4.46	122.5	+8.56	+7.51

Source: *The Wall Street Journal.* July 27, 1994, and April 26, 1995.

10 percent from about 30 percent the previous year. At the same time, Janus Funds in Denver reported sharp reductions in emerging market exposure to 12 percent, down from more than 20 percent the previous year.[13]

On October 31, 1994, *Pensions & Investments* ran a lead article by Margaret Price, entitled "Global Managers Turning Defensive," which surveyed several international money managers concerned that rising interest rates in many countries were burying hopes that struggling stock markets could soon resume their gains. Michael Perelstein, managing director of international investments at MacKay-Shields, was among those who saw emerging markets as a danger spot. According to Perelstein, interest in emerging markets has become "excessive." He notes, "A number of other managers say although they are bullish [for the] long term on emerging markets, the current climate looks questionable, perhaps especially in Southeast Asia and in some Latin American markets that rallied this year."[14] Table 1–5 also shows that, in 1995, stocks in many of these emerging markets—especially Mexico, Indonesia, and Thailand—have continued their sharp declines, bearing out the 1994 warnings that investors should return to the long-run safety of US markets.

Not only is volatility in emerging markets a deterrent to some investors but the myriad of arcane requirements that foreigners must observe simply to put their money into these markets can be daunting and expensive. Box 1–1 summarizes some of the more notable problems in trading directly in emerging markets. It is based on a September 1994 report by *Pensions & Investments* in association with Buttonwood International Group, New York, surveying 13 major global custodian banks and interviewing five global custodial executives. The report notes that a host of difficulties confront investors and their global custodians participating in non-US markets, particularly in emerging markets. This is why US institutional investors have tended to invest in the United States in the ADRs of foreign issuers rather than in the companies' underlying stocks in their host countries.

The *Pensions & Investments*/Buttonwood global survey reports six major areas of difficulty of investing in non-US markets:

1. Local regulations
2. Valuation problems
3. Liquidity concerns
4. Risk assessment
5. Operating procedures
6. Corporate governance variations

Box 1–1

Operational Difficulties in Foreign Markets: Summary of the 1994 Pensions & Investments/Buttonwood International Global Custody Survey

Argentina

One custodian employs its own branch in Argentina where true delivery vs. payment [DVP] does not exist, as the securities settlement system at the Caja de Valores is totally separate from the cash settlement bank. The custodian established a procedure to pay on settlement date against a certified transfer (stamped by the Caja de Valores), thus instituting a most reasonable facsimile of DVP.

Bangladesh, India, Pakistan

Short-term money market instruments, which require same-day settlement, represent the most problematic securities to US investors. Bangladesh, India and Pakistan have a lengthy settlement and registration process. In addition, the level of US investor interest in these markets is straining the capabilities of the limited number of service providers to settle, process, and even vault the securities.

The very large volume of trading in India, which operates on a labor-intensive, certificate-oriented system, has caused registration delays extending over several months. Because certificates cannot be sold until they are immediately available for delivery, investors must be aware that their investments are very illiquid until the registration process is complete.

In addition, most certificates are held in small denominations. The average lot is between 10 and 50 shares, and each certificate must be signed and have a transfer form attached. Further, each transfer form must be stamped, often more than once, and the shares must be sent to the registrar for processing before they can be sold. All of these rules burden the trading system.

"India and the Philippines have been most problematic to US investors," said one custodian. Another cited security registration delays, application of stamp duties, and foreign ownership limits.

"Markets such as India (and Malaysia), where there is physical registration of certificates, can pose significant challenges for investors. In these markets, foreign investors must take into account delays in registering ownership in order to insure that they do not cause settlement problems when selling securities," another custodian warned.

Box 1–1 (continued)

Brazil

Brazil recently prohibited foreign investors from buying debt, and those owning debt instruments were forced to sell. Selling under such conditions depresses the price of these instruments.

One custodian mentioned several investment barriers in this market, namely, investor ID requirements, inflation, and currency conversion.

Chile

Chile has one of the most extensive application processes for foreign investors. The process is so complicated, it actually has deterred direct investment.

In addition, selecting the appropriate tax rate (fixed or variable) is a difficult and confusing area for foreign investors.

Even in a sophisticated market such as Chile, with private sector funds worth $16 billion, investing directly in the Santiago market is very complicated. Foreign investors must register either with the Central Bank or the Republic of Chile and appoint a Chilean local administrator to serve as legal representative. Registration can take from one to three months—depending on which of the three investment modes the investor chooses.

China

The regulation of foreign shares creates settlement problems. Also, the varied settlement practices at China's two depositories of Shanghai and Shenzhen create difficulties. For example, in Shanghai securities settlements are against US dollars, while in Shenzhen securities settlements are against Hong Kong dollars.

France

Because of double-taxation treaty problems, US investors (even those normally accepted as tax-exempt institutions) cannot reclaim the *avoir fiscal,* a tax levied on dividend payments. This effectively puts US investors at a yield disadvantage. Custodians also reported difficulty with proxy voting requirements.

Indonesia

Investors can expect to encounter problems with ownership laws in Indonesia. There, the regulatory agency typically requires some form of power of attorney or other legal agreement for a foreign investor to easily navigate the local securities market. The major question typically raised in

Box 1–1 (continued)

a market such as Indonesia is how investors can guarantee the ownership of securities if they are not holding the securities.

The Philippines
The sudden increase in the trading volume in the Philippines between September and December 1993 caused the Makati Stock Exchange's clearinghouse to collapse and continues to delay the transfer of ownership of securities.

Peru
In Peru, settlement of equity business is handled by the Lima Stock Exchange and its offshoots, Caja de Valores and Caja de Liquidaciones, which collect and disburse payments. Under current law, only brokers can be directly involved in the clearing procedure. One custodian has won the right to have access to client records at the Caja de Valores—provided clients give it power of attorney. This allows the bank to verify client positions on a regular basis and to collect dividends and review transaction statements on their behalf.

Russia
Russia has no central regulator to supervise issuance—trading or clearing—according to respondents. No centralized stock exchange exists, and there are no commercial or securities laws governing the marketplace. The Moscow Interbank Currency Exchange (which trades only in short-term government bonds) has put a custody and clearing system in place, and the Central Bank recently produced a regulatory framework for the issuance of new shares in banks. But the emergence of a well-regulated exchange backed by a viable clearing infrastructure appears to be some way off.

Taiwan
Taiwan has aggregate foreign ownership limits and quotas assigned to each foreign investor. This is preceded by an extensive application process. Additionally, there are limitations on repatriating capital. These present difficulties and challenges to clients, not to mention risks.

United Kingdom
US investors often are discriminated against when it comes to capital reorganizations, said one global custodian, although companies still are pleased

Box 1–1 (continued)

to attract their investment. This applies particularly (but not exclusively) to the UK market, where US institutional shareholders often cannot subscribe for new shares.

Venezuela
Venezuela has a particularly cumbersome physical settlement process, requiring a number of sign-offs and a huge paper trail that leads to a very long settlement period regardless of contractual settlement date. It also exposes the investor to substantial risk.

One custodian bank in Caracas with 17(f)5 qualification, a mutual fund requirement, has created a delivery versus payment environment for foreign investors that is based on the presentation of a certified *transposo* (e.g. stock transfer certificate) and a stock exchange transaction payment note. It also has set up procedures to reduce fails and, in a market where transactions settle on schedules ranging from T+0 [T=Trade date+number of days to settlement] to T+90, recommends investors negotiate a T+5 settlement cycle.

Source: John Giudice, "Custodians Meeting New Challenges," *Pensions & Investments*, September 19, 1994, p. 26, 28.

Local regulations.   David Bilbe, managing director of Chemical Bank Global Security Services, notes that in many markets nondomestic investors cannot invest until "approved" by the local authorities. Moreover, investors can experience problems in markets requiring some form of registration prior to investing, such as in Chile, Colombia, India, Korea, and Taiwan. While foreign investment is allowed in these countries, there are numerous regulations governing which foreigners may register for investment and how the registration may be accomplished. As Box 1–1 points out, even in a sophisticated market such as Chile, the obstacles can be formidable.[15]

Valuation problems.   Another major difficulty of investing in foreign markets, according to Patti L. Smith, vice president of Bankers Trust Company, New York, is the problem US investors may have in acquiring useful pricing and valuation information. Methodologies of pricing and valuation may vary among performance measurement providers, custodian banks, and investment managers. In some instances, global custodians are known to use more than 80 different pricing sources to provide comprehensive and accurate information. Bilbe (from Chemical Bank) notes that while most US securities can be priced accurately at the close of business every day by any custodian, foreign securities are quite different. Even the world's best international data vendors cannot accurately price all securities in all markets since coverage may be as low as 50 percent. The efficiency of data maintenance also determines how soon month- and/or quarter-end evaluation can be provided. The *Pensions & Investments*/Buttonwood survey found that all global custodians use one or more primary vendors and one or more secondary vendors to determine the most accurate and timely price. They also use other price sources including local brokers, agent banks, and local branches of their own custodial banks.

In Korea, for example, foreign investment limits have been imposed on equity shares and as a result there is a separate market for registered foreigners, where all trading is done over the counter. Pricing data, therefore, cannot be obtained from either vendors or brokers. Bankers Trust has introduced a sophisticated internal price-estimating system for foreign-registered shares on the Korean market, where brokers' estimates of premiums applicable to these shares are used to produce estimates on a daily basis.[16] In Thailand and Indonesia as well, because foreign investment limits have also resulted in a separate market, prices can typically become stale if no trades are effected for a period of time, as is frequently the case for alien shares (shares held by foreigners). In India, with Bombay the main exchange and the only one supported by most data vendors, pricing is infrequent. Pricing for any stock trading on any of the other Indian exchanges is even more difficult to obtain.

Liquidity concerns. The same lack of frequent trading that gives rise to valuation problems also leads to the third area of difficulty in trading directly in host country equities: liquidity concerns arising from the fear that institutional investors will not be able to sell on a timely basis foreign securities purchased in non-US markets. Concern over potential lack of trading, coupled with severe regulations by local authorities can create operational difficulties for investors that may reduce the liquidity of their equities. For example, as John Giudice comments to the *Pensions & Investments*/Buttonwood Group team survey:

In certain markets, investors are not able to repatriate sales proceeds or income unless they can produce documentation proving prior purchase of the related security with hard currency. This can be a daunting task. The investor must first produce documentation showing the foreign exchange transaction by which the local currency was purchased. If the foreign exchange was transacted with a third party and not the investor's custodian or the custodians local agent, the investor also must prove the cash was moved to the custodian and used for purchase of the security in question.[17]

Giudice notes that investment is most problematic in countries where restrictions are plentiful and the mechanisms to exchange securities for cash and vice versa are not well suited for non-resident investors. Restrictions, he says, vary depending on market infrastructure and central bank regulations that control flows into and out of the market. For example, such restrictions include the appointment of local administrators prior to regulatory approval to begin trading in Brazil, application for a trade identification, and deposits of funds in advance in Korea, and foreign exchange controls in Latin America, which require investors to prefund the trade and restrict repatriation of investment.

Risk assessment. In entering overseas markets, the most obvious risks investors need to assess are the currency and political risks. But these are not the only risks they need to consider. According to Bilbe, investors should examine counterpart (credit) risk and settlement, or custodian, risk. Custodians often provide some sort of indemnity that covers fraud, negligence, default, and other risks. Although many will so do on behalf of their subcustodians, a custodian will not necessarily offer a blanket indemnity and most certainly will offer little indemnity in the newly emerging markets. A number of markets have changed certain operational procedures that increase investor risk. For example, early in 1994, Korea introduced rules requiring foreign investors to pay 20 percent of the value of an investment on trade date and the remaining 80 percent on settlement date. The same year, Venezuela introduced a tax of 0.75 percent on certain transactions.

Operating procedures. Trade processing, delivery, and payment can become extremely complicated in foreign and emerging markets. Difficulties include the lack of rate matching or affirmation procedures and confusion about where the cash and securities settle in many countries. Mark C. Aprahamian, director, global broker-dealer, and business manager of Barclays Bank plc, notes that poor procedures to notify buyers or sellers if trades are not settled can increase the uncertainty of the completion of trade in certain markets. With respect to delivery versus payment (DVP), most of the custodians note a potential for risk, but most indicate that, because this is an area where they focus a great deal of their attention, they have been able to bring issues under control. One custodian employs its own branch in Argentina, where true DVP does not exist because the securities settlement system at the Caja de Valores, the central depository, is separate from the cash settlement bank. This custodian established a procedure to pay on settlement date against a certified transfer, stamped by the Caja de Valores, thus instituting a reasonable facsimile of DVP. The Mexican depository, Indeval, does not offer a cash facility to effect either DVP or receipt versus payment (RVP). Customers are left to contract with local banks. Coordinating and tracking cash would be difficult for transactions off the Mexican Stock Exchange. Robert Mancuso, vice president and director of marketing for Investors Bank and Trust Company, notes that many emerging markets such as China, Sri Lanka, and Peru have developed very efficient settlement practices and have full-book entry processing via central depositories. These markets have recognized that settlement efficiency will help attract additional foreign investment. Other markets, such as India, Pakistan, and Africa, are still bogged down with paper and are inefficient.[18]

Corporate governance variations. Many US institutional investors are under increasing pressure to cast their proxy not only for their domestic shares but for their foreign shares as well. Proxy voting will be discussed in detail subsequently, but it should be noted at this point that the ability or inability to vote foreign shares will increasingly become an aspect of institutional investors' fiduciary responsibility and will therefore, in all probability, influence where institutions direct their assets, as they look for areas where voting can go smoothly at low cost. Finally, US institutional investors and foreign issuers will often have different ideas of the role of investors in corporate governance; later chapters of this book will explore the differences in depth.

AN EFFICIENT US NATIONAL MARKET TRADING SYSTEM

It has been more than 60 years since enactment of the major legislation setting up the complex mechanisms of regulatory oversight governing the securities markets in the United States. Through a combination of the Securities and Exchange Acts of 1933 and 1934 and important 1975 amendments to Section 11A of the 1934 Act, the United States now operates under an efficient and broadly reaching National Market System (NMS). The US equity markets are considered an important national asset, which enables the nation to raise capital, provide investment opportunities, and promote entrepreneurship. Confidence is the key element as the Securities and Exchange Commission works to ensure that equity markets remain vibrant and efficient and that regulation protects investors, aids raising capital, and keeps pace with the changing dynamics of these markets.

Improvements to the governing US securities market regulatory structure were triggered by the SEC's 1971 Institutional Investor Study.[19] This study found that, since the 1930s, securities markets had become increasingly active, complex, and susceptible to various practices that raised structural and efficiency questions. The study, recalled in the SEC's *Market 2000* report of 1994, detailed numerous developments that threatened the viability of the markets, including unstructured trading by the growing institutional investor sector and processing capacity overload:

> [B]y 1972, New York Stock Exchange ("NYSE") volume had more than quadrupled over the past decade to the then dizzying figure of 16 million shares per day. The growing presence of institutional investors was reflected by the increase in block volume in NYSE stocks from 1% to 18.5% of trading during the same period. In the OTC [over the counter] market, the National Association of Securities Dealers ("NASD") had modernized trading with the introduction of NASDAQ [the National Association of Securities Dealers Automated Quotation system] a year earlier. The markets were only a few years past the "paperwork crisis" during which a surge of volume nearly overloaded the securities processing capabilities of the major broker-dealers. Perhaps most importantly, institutional investors had developed arrangements and relationships with brokers on the regional exchanges and OTC market to avoid paying the NYSE's fixed commission schedule. These relationships raised the specter of a fragmented market structure in which multiple markets offering limited access traded the same securities without publicly disseminating quote and trade information.[20]

In response to these concerns, Congress adopted the Securities Acts Amendments of 1975, establishing the National Market System for securities (NMS) to strengthen US securities markets, protect investors, and maintain fair and orderly markets. The goals were essentially to rein in all the various trading systems springing up yet permit flexibility for large and small investors to obtain information and to execute trades in an atmosphere of confidence. The 1975 amendments were enacted to ensure the following:

- Economically efficient execution of securities transactions.
- Fair competition among brokers and dealers, among exchange markets, and between exchange markets and markets other than exchange markets.
- The availability to brokers, dealers, and investors of information with respect to quotations for and transactions in securities.
- The practicability of brokers executing investors' orders in the best market.
- An opportunity, consistent with the above, for investors' orders to be executed without the participation of a dealer.

Establishing the NMS led to significant improvements in market operations. For example, the SEC abolished fixed commission rates, and the markets established a consolidated quotation system, consolidated transaction tape, and the Intermarket Trading System (ITS) to link markets for listed securities. The SEC believes that investors have benefitted directly from these efforts: Trading costs have been reduced, particularly as fixed commission rates were eliminated, and increased market transparency has enabled investors to monitor the quality of trade executions. In addition, investors have benefitted as higher levels of transparency and lower costs have contributed to greater liquidity.

There are now approximately 3,300 stocks listed on the major exchanges (the NYSE and the AMEX) and another nearly 5,000 unlisted companies trading on NASDAQ. (Figure 1–5 illustrates the growth in listed stocks from 1985 through 1994.) The New York Stock Exchange is considered by many to be the key equity market when choosing where to list in the United States. As Figures 1–5 through 1–7 show, the NYSE may not be the market with the greatest number of companies listed (there are more companies listed on NASDAQ), but the NYSE clearly dominates average dollar trading (the NYSE accounts for approximately 58 percent of daily trading volume), as well as market capitalization (the NYSE accounts for more than 83 percent of total US equity market capitalization).

The primary exchanges have traditionally operated as modified auction markets, where order flow for a stock is directed to a central location: the trading post for the specialist in the stock. At one time, orders used to in-

FIGURE 1–5
Number of Companies Listed on US Equity Markets: 1985–1994

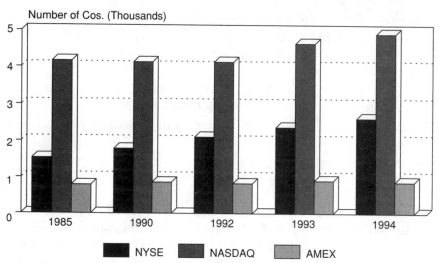

Source: Securities Industry Association.

teract to the maximum extent possible on the specialist's book, with the specialist acting as a market maker by trading for his own account to ameliorate temporary disparities in supply and demand. The increase in large block trading, however, in the late 1960s and early 1970s rendered this trading floor structure inadequate. Table 1–6 shows large block NYSE trading in excess of 10,000 shares. The level of block trading is widely regarded as a surrogate measure for large institutional investor trading on the NYSE. In 1994, block trading accounted for 52.7 percent of the value of trades and 55.5 percent of the volume of trades. This level of "institutional" trading has increased substantially from 1970, when it was only 13.0 percent of the value of trades and 15.4 percent of the volume of trades.

The growth in block trading plus the expansion of trading listed stocks *off the exchanges* has led to a very creative linkage of trading options.[21] Table 1–7 illustrates how trading activity has become dispersed for NYSE listed stocks. The NYSE accounted for only 70.5 percent of the total first-half 1993 orders and 78.5 percent of the volume in NYSE-listed stocks. The remaining portion of trading activity in NYSE-listed stocks is broken

FIGURE 1–6

Average Daily Trading Volume on US Stock Markets: 1985–1994

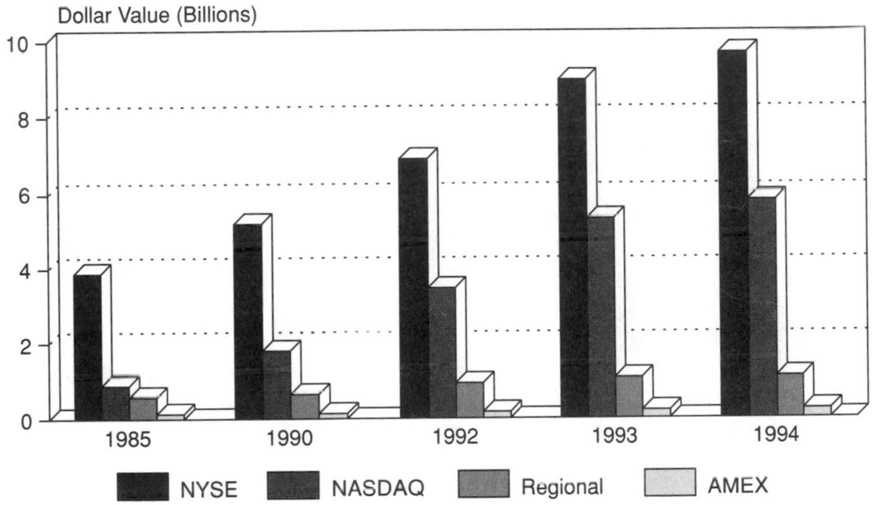

Dollar Value (Billions)

NYSE   NASDAQ   Regional   AMEX

Source: Based on Securities Industry Association Data.

down into off-exchange trading, regional stock exchange trading, third market trading, NASDAQ trading, proprietary trading systems (PTS) trading, and fourth market trading.

• **Off-exchange trading that occurs "upstairs."** A negotiated price for a block is established "upstairs" off the exchange *in a crossing session,* and the transaction is then brought down to the trading post on the trading floor and exposed to the buyers and sellers and to any limit order book maintained by the specialist. About 1.36 percent of NYSE shares are traded in crossing sessions.

• **Regional stock exchange trading.** At an earlier point in their history, the regional exchanges served as "incubator" markets for small, local companies. The SEC reports, however, that during the past 20 years, the overwhelming proportion of regional stock exchange business has been in the stocks of NYSE- and Amex-listed companies that the regional exchanges trade pursuant to grants of unlisted trading privileges (UTP). In 1992, this trading accounted for over 97 percent of the regional stock exchanges' volume. And, for the first half of 1993, regional exchanges accounted for 10.17 percent of the volume of NYSE stocks traded and

FIGURE 1–7
Capitalization of US Equity Markets: 1985–1994

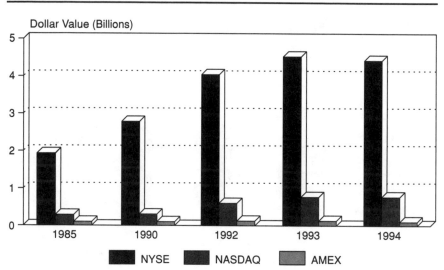

Source: Based on Securities Industry Association Data.

close to 20 percent of the orders placed. The regional exchanges are linked with the primary markets in UTP issues through the Intermarket Trading System (ITS), the Consolidated Quotation System (CQS) and a consolidated tape that records all transactions.

• **Third market trading.** Over-the-counter (OTC) trading in exchange-listed securities is commonly known as *third-market* trading. Third-market activity is concentrated in only the 400 most active NYSE stocks and a much smaller number of Amex stocks; the remainder of the listed stocks are not traded actively enough to be included in third-market operations. The third-market makers handle order flow sent to them by other broker-dealers. They act much like NASDAQ market makers in that they accept orders of up to a few thousand shares and execute these orders against the best bid or offer on ITS. The SEC reports that in 1989, the third market garnered 3.2 percent of reported NYSE volume and 5 percent of the reported trades; by 1993, this percentage had increased to 7.4 percent of reported NYSE volume and 9.3 percent of the reported trades.

• **NASDAQ trading.** This is the interdealer quotation system operated by the National Association of Securities Dealers (NASD). NASD

TABLE 1-6
New York Stock Exchange Large Block Transactions: 1970–1994

Year	# of Block Trades	Block Trade Shares (millions)	Reported Share Volume (millions)	% of Reported Volume	$ Value Block Trades (millions)	$ Volume Trading (millions)	% Total $ Value
1970	17,217	0.451	2.937	15.4%	13,354	102,494	13.0%
1975	34,420	0.779	4.693	16.6%	19,408	131,705	14.7%
1980	133,597	3.311	11.352	29.2%	N.A.	382,447	N.A.
1985	539,039	14.222	27.511	51.7%	N.A.	980,772	N.A.
1990	843,365	19.681	39.664	49.6%	N.A.	1,336,229	N.A.
1991	981,077	22.474	45.266	49.6%	678,408	1,533,578	44.2%
1992	1,134,832	26.069	51.375	50.7%	815,148	1,764,590	46.2%
1993	1,477,859	35.959	66.923	53.7%	1,144,771	2,283,400	50.1%
1994	1,654,505	40.758	73.420	55.5%	1,293,054	2,454,242	52.7%

Note: Large block transactions are 10,000+ shares.

Source: New York Stock Exchange.

TABLE 1–7
Illustration of Trading Flows for NYSE-Listed Stocks

	Average Shares* Per Day ($Millions)	Average Shares Per Day (%)	Average Transactions Per Day	Average Transactions Per Day (%)
NYSE				
Regular hours	264.8	78.53%	186,410	70.48%
Crossing session I	0.2	0.06%		
Crossing session II	4.4	1.30%		
All Regional Stock Exchanges	34.3	10.17%	52,699	19.92%
Boston	4.2	1.25%	6,941	2.62%
Chicago	13.1	3.88%	16,202	6.13%
Philadelphia	4.8	1.42%	7,609	2.88%
Pacific	8.4	2.49%	15,602	5.90%
Cincinnati	3.8	1.13%	6,345	2.40%
Third Market				
Regular hours	19.6	5.81%	24,847	9.39%
PTS After hours	0.9	0.27%		
Proprietary Trading Systems				
Regular Hours	3.6	1.07%	543	0.21%
PTS After Hours	1.1	0.33%	n.a.	n.a.
Overseas by NYSE Firms				
Program trades	5.9	1.75%	n.a.	n.a.
Over the counter (nonprogram)	1.7	0.50%	n.a.	n.a.
Foreign Exchanges (nonprogram)	0.7	0.21%	n.a.	n.a.
Total	337.2	100.00%	264,499	100.00%

Notes: * These figures are for the first six months of 1993 (125 trading days) except for non program foreign data, which uses a daily average from May, June, and July 1993. The figures do not include trades executed in the fourth market, such as trades directly between institutions without using an exchange or a broker-dealer.

n.a. = not available

Source: SEC *Market 2000 Report,* January 1994, Exhibit 11.

is regulated in ways that are substantively similar to the regulation for national securities exchanges. In 1971, NASDAQ replaced the mimeographed *pink sheets* that provided data on trades although this segment of the market is still referred to as the *pink sheet market.* Since then, NASDAQ has revolutionized over-the-counter trading by increasing the availability of quotes for OTC securities, thereby increasing the efficiency and transparency of the OTC market.[22]

- **Proprietary trading systems.** Automated trading systems offer institutions and broker-dealers the opportunity to trade away from both the exchanges and NASDAQ. The primary automated systems are proprietary trading systems (PTSs), which are screen-based automated trading systems typically sponsored by broker-dealers. They have been used primarily by institutional investors to reduce execution costs, avoid the market-maker spread, and trade in large volume without incurring the market impact costs that could result if orders were handled on the organized markets.[23] For the first half of 1993, the total share volume on PTSs was 4.7 billion shares, which was almost equal to the entire volume in 1992. The total share volume for 1992 was nearly 4.9 billion, an increase of more than 60 percent from the 1991 volume of 2.9 billion. Trading in NASDAQ stocks represented 87 percent of PTS volume in the first half of 1993; during the same period, listed stocks were only 13 percent of PTS volume.

- **Fourth-market trading.** The fourth market is the trading of shares directly between institutional investors without the intermediation of a broker-dealer. Unlike trading through PTSs, fourth-market trading does not require one of the parties to register as a broker-dealer to process and guarantee the trades; thus, fourth-market trades are not, for the most part, subject to transparency rules or oversight by the NASD. According to the SEC, the fourth market consists of internal crosses of orders between different accounts of the same institution or money manager. A few large institutions or money managers use this technique to avoid brokerage commissions. The SEC believes it is impossible to quantify the amount of fourth-market trading, although it estimates that it averages several million shares per day. In addition, some trading may be conducted in what is referred to as the *rolodex market* of institutions that call one another to solicit interest in an order; the SEC does not believe this activity generates significant volume.

INTERNATIONAL AVENUES OF TRADING

Certainly not all international securities trading takes place in the United States. Advances in technology coupled with the growing presence of institutional investors with large resources to trade wherever they choose has led to an unprecedented openness to new methods of trading. An article by Peter Lee in *Euromoney* explains the proliferation of international avenues for trading:

> International equity trading is growing big and rich, and everybody wants market share. Players who are hoping to win some of the cross-border flows from the world's institutional investors include the major and minor stock exchanges, leading international brokerage firms, automatic clearing houses, and even private trading systems. But no one knows for sure what channels the investors will favor as their needs get bigger . . .[24]

It has been estimated that between 750 and 1,000 institutions around the world invest in equity across borders, while only about 20 brokers, often members of the larger national stock exchanges around the world, serve these institutions.[25] Together, these institutions and brokers will have significant influence over how international equity will change hands.

The following are among the mechanisms for this trading:

- **The NYSE.** The New York Stock Exchange is aggressively seeking foreign issuers to enhance its ADR volume. James Cochrane, senior vice president and chief economist, estimates that, depending on whether a "world class" of foreign companies can receive favored-listing treatment, there are about 2,000 foreign companies waiting to be listed.

- **Seaq International.** *Euromoney* reports there are over 45 market markets that quote prices in approximately 600 global stocks on a computer system referred to as *Seaq.* Turnover in these foreign stocks is more than twice that on the NYSE, the next largest competitor. The highest volumes are, however, in European stocks, and bourses on the continent are fighting to win back that business.

- **Local markets.** Small national stock exchanges throughout the world are improving their settlement systems, upgrading their trading mechanisms, and encouraging more strongly capitalized local brokers.

- **Large international brokers.** *Euromoney* reports that several of the largest American, British, European, and Asian brokers are beginning to make a market in leading stocks around the world 24 hours a day. They will quote prices to customers even when home stock markets are closed.

- **Private electronic markets.** The potential is unlimited and diminished only by custom and convenience of the international institutional investors.

No one can be sure what future technology will afford in the way of access to cross-border markets. Currently, international equity investors, because of the sheer size of their orders, have substantial choice in when and how to trade. As the institutional investors become more comfortable with cross-border trading, and if their own regulations permit it, they could easily move capital like liquid mercury. But confidence and efficiency are still the paramount considerations; for the time being, entering the US capital market will continue to be seductive for an increasing number of foreign issuers.

NOTES

1. US Securities and Exchange Commission. Division of Market Regulation, *Market 2000: An examination of Current Equity Market Developments,* January 1994, Executive Summary, p. 1 (hereinafter cited as SEC *Market 2000* Report).

2. Joseph Velli, "American Depositary Receipts: An Overview," *Fordham International Law Journal* 17 (1994), p. 38.

3. Richard C. Breeden, "Foreign Companies and US Securities Markets in a Time of Economic Transformation," *Fordham International Law Journal* 17 (1994), p. 77.

4. *Ibid.,* p. 83.

5. M. Shane Warbrick, "Practical Company Experience in Entering US Markets: Significant Issues and Hurdles from the Issuer's Perspective," *Fordham International Law Journal* 17 (1994), p. 112.

6. Frode Jensen, "The Attractions of the US Securities Markets to Foreign Issuers and the Alternative Methods of Accessing the US Markets: From A Legal Perspective," *Fordham International Law Journal* 17 (1994), p. 27.

7. Breeden, p. 122.

8. *Ibid.,* p. 127.

9. Warren Getler and William Power, "Nasdaq Critic Vows He Isn't Taking Sides: Small Stock Focus," *The Wall Street Journal,* November 21, 1994, pp. C1 and C7.

10. James R. Silkenat, "Overview of US Securities Markets and Foreign Issuers Entering the US Securities Markets: Opportunities and Risks for Foreign Companies," *Fordham International Law Journal,* 17 (1994), p. 6.

11. Craig Torres, "Overseas Investors Are Cutting Exposure to Emerging Markets," *The Wall Street Journal,* July 27, 1994, p. C1.

12. *Ibid.*

13. *Ibid.*

14. Margaret Price, "Global Managers Turning Defensive," *Pensions & Investments,* October 31, 1994, p. 46.

15. John Giudice, "Custodians Meeting New Challenges," *Pensions & Investments,* September 19, 1994, p. 26, 28. (See Box 1–1 for a country-by-country discussion of variations in local regulations and operating procedures.)

16. *Ibid.,* p. 20.

17. *Ibid.*, p. 22.

18. *Ibid.*, p. 24.

19. SEC Institutional Investor Study Report, H.R. Doc. No. 64. 92nd Cong., 1st Sess. (1971).

20. SEC *Market 2000* Report, p. II-4.

21. See SEC *Market 2000* Report, pp. II-7–II-14.

22. NASDAQ has made tremendous strides in automating OTC market making including (1) the display of all market makers' quotes, (2) the implementation of real-time trade reporting for NASDAQ/NMS securities in 1982 and NASDAQ small-cap stocks in 1992, (3) the display of market-maker quote size, (4) the introduction of its Automated Confirmation Transaction Service, and (5) the development of SelectNet. In addition, all NASDAQ/NMS securities have been marginable in accordance with Federal Reserve Board guidelines since 1984. They are also exempt from state blue-sky registration provisions in most states. SEC *Market 2000* Report, p. II-11.

23. According to the SEC, the popularity of PTSs has been fueled by two phenomena. "For listed securities, they are attractive to passive managers or other patient investors who are sensitive to transaction costs, but do not need the instant liquidity that the exchanges provide and do not want to pay the market spread. For NASDAQ securities, they are used by institutional investors who do not want to go through NAS-DAQ market makers to enter an order or who want to avoid paying the bid-ask spread, but instead prefer to seek liquidity through interaction with other institutional investors." SEC *Market 2000* Report, p. II-12.

24. Peter Lee, "The Fight to Gain Control of World Equities," *Euromoney,* July 1, 1993, p. 5.

25. *Ibid.*

Chapter 2

Foreign Access to US Markets

The immense liquidity of the US securities market is absorbing issuances of new securities from all domestic and foreign sources with a value of more than $1 trillion per year. According to former SEC Chairman Richard Breeden, capital being raised in the US market through securities offerings undoubtedly exceeds the total of all primary offerings taking place in every other market in the world put together. Breeden observes:

> Now, it is true that many markets are very active and successful secondary trading markets. The US markets have plenty of strong competition when it comes to markets for secondary trading. But if you look at the capital markets picture from the perspective of primary offerings and where capital is actually raised by companies for productive purposes on an annual basis, there the US lead—the reason why the US markets are attractive, because of the ready availability of capital—is quite dramatic.[1]

It is not only the size of the US capital markets that lures foreign issuers; merely being a part of them can increase the visibility and marketability of a foreign issuer. Foreign issuers can enter US markets in several ways: through private placements, through unlisted or listed secondary trading (in secondary trading, stock is traded in securities markets, but new capital is not raised), or by making a primary offering of new securities (in a primary offering, new capital is raised). Although foreign issuers recognize the attractiveness of US markets, they may be reluctant to enter these markets because they do not know which of the various financial vehicles suits them best or how to position themselves to attract US capital. This chapter explores the various methods of entering US markets, either on an unlisted or listed basis, the reasons foreign issuers might seek capital beyond their home-country markets, and the steps recently taken by US regulators to simplify the process and reduce barriers for foreign issuer entry into US securities markets. Chapters 3 and 4 provide filing requirements for the various routes discussed in this chapter, while Chapters 5 and 6 discuss the US institutional investor pool of money and how to position a company to meet institutional investment criteria.

AMERICAN DEPOSITARY RECEIPTS

As of late April 1995, the securities of a total of 669 foreign companies, representing 44 countries, were traded in the US public markets.[2] Since January 1, 1993, 191 foreign companies from 26 countries have entered the US reporting system, among them companies from Argentina, China, Germany, Indonesia, and Korea. Recent entrants through the listing of American Depositary Receipts (ADRs) on the NYSE include Daimler-Benz of Germany and China's Huaneng Power International Inc. ADRs are the key trading instruments foreign companies use to enter whatever segment of the US securities markets they choose (see Box 2–1 for an explanation of the various types of ADRs). Peter Lee of the financial magazine *Euromoney* observes:

> American investors are now the dominant buyers of international equity. Leading companies from around the world are keen to list on the NYSE to gain access to the world's largest pool of capital. ADR [American depositary receipt] volume is growing. It sometimes exceeds home market trading.[3]

Numerous foreign companies are approaching US investors in one or more of the following manners: by listing on various exchanges and in the listed portion of the over-the-counter markets; by entering the unlisted over-the-counter markets (often referred to as "pink sheet" markets because bid-and-ask quotes for these over-the-counter stocks used to be printed on pink mimeograph paper and circulated by messenger or mail— trades are currently electronically matched, although the historic name endures); and by making a Rule 144A private placement (which will be explained shortly). Some companies that make private placements qualify to trade in the public markets and go on to make public offerings. Box 2–1 briefly describes the ADR options available to overseas companies.

Joseph Velli, executive vice president of the Bank of New York, was one of the pioneers in the ADR field; he established his bank's depositary receipt business in 1984. According to Velli, the ADR trades as if it were

Box 2–1

Foreign Issuers Enter US Markets

ADRs
The only way for foreign issuers to enter US markets is to use one of various levels of ADRs—American Depositary Receipts. These are receipts issued by a US depositary bank. The receipts represent shares that are held overseas. Trading and payment of dividends are in US dollars. ADRs are sometimes also called GDRs, or global depositary receipts. They are traded exactly like US shares, except that actual shares are held overseas in the home country. Many US institutional investors must hold ADRs rather than home-country shares of foreign issuers.

Level 1: Pink Sheet Unlisted OTC Trading in ADRs
The ADR is traded over the counter. It is unlisted and unregistered by the Securities and Exchange Commission (SEC). Trades are electronically matched, but volume is not reported and no real-time quotes are available.

Level 2: Listing in Public Markets
To issue a level 2 ADR, a company registers with the SEC to have its existing shares listed on US exchange or in listed OTC markets through NASDAQ (National Association of Securities Dealers' Automated Quotation System). The company must go through the SEC registration process, conforming with US GAAP and other accounting and disclosure requirements. This positions a company to rise to the next level: to enter the public markets with a public offering.

Level 3: Making a Public Offering
The level 3 ADR is an instrument through which a foreign company raises money directly in US capital markets. The company files a prospectus with the SEC, which requires not only reconciliation of its financial statements with US standards, but mandatory disclosure pertaining to material aspects of the business, legal actions, and risk factors. The company must then conform to SEC disclosure requirements to report as required and to announce material changes in its business.

Rule 144A Private Placements
A company may offer a private placement ADR to take advantage of the SEC's Rule 144A, which allows private placement of offerings to qualified

---

Box 2–1 (continued)

institutional buyers (QIBs) for a restricted two-year period. No listing under SEC rules takes place; rather, the financial requirements are negotiated between the investment banker and the company offering the securities. Financial statements can be in accordance with the home country's accounting principles but will frequently include a narrative description of the differences between these principles and US generally accepted accounting principles (US GAAP). Many companies first raise money in the Rule 144A private placement market and then go on to list their securities in public markets.

---

a US security—in dollars, with dividends paid in dollars as well. According to Velli, "There is no difference between buying Glaxo ADRs and buying IBM, AT&T, or General Motors stock."[4] Much to the chagrin of officials of bourses overseas, many companies are more actively traded through ADRs in US markets than they are through common stock traded in their home countries. Hong Kong Telecom trading in Hong Kong, Repsol trading in Spain, and Telefonos de Mexico trading in Mexico are three examples of companies having more trading volume, both in share terms and in dollar terms as ADRs, in the US than in their respective home countries.[5] Other examples are offered by financial reporter Peter Lee:

> At times, certain ADRs will offer greater liquidity in New York than the underlying stock. Reuters share price in Britain has often been driven by trading on Nasdaq. In much the same way, Glaxo traded more heavily, or as heavily, through ADRs on the NYSE than on London, for two or three years. The price of shares in Jaguar, before it was taken over by Ford, used to be set by American buyers. More recently, there have been days when BP has been turned over in tremendous volume in New York—seven to eight million shares a day—while the stock has been much quieter in Britain.[6]

The ADR is the preferred method for entering US markets, although there are several, infrequently used, alternatives. A few Chinese companies have formed shell companies in Bermuda and then listed their shares—not their ADRs—directly in the United States; several European companies have done something similar. But in each case, the overseas companies are not being directly listed; they are forming separate US

TABLE 2-1

Summary of the Public and Private ADR Market: 1992–1994

	1992	1993	1994
Public Market			
Total public depositary receipt programs	922	988	1,129
Total number of listed companies offering ADRs	213	258	322
NYSE	118	153	210
NASDAQ	87	97	104
AMEX	8	8	8
Total number of OTC companies (pink sheet)	709	730	807
$ Volume of trading of all public ADRs	$130–140 billion	210–220 billion	$273–298 billion
$ Volume of trading for listed ADRs	$125 billion	$201 billion	$248 billion
NYSE	NA	$169.2 billion	$212.7 billion
NASDAQ	NA	$29.3 billion	$33.3 billion
AMEX	NA	$2.2 billion	$2.0 billion
$ Volume of trading for pink sheet ADRs	$5–10 billion	$10–20 billion	$25–50 billion
Capital raised through depositary receipt new public offerings			
Number	23	49	64
Total capital raised	$5.3 billion	$9.5 billion	$11.0 billion
Private Market			
Private Placement ADRs # of 144A filings	25	33	102
$ Volume of 144A filings	$3.8 billion	$2.1 billion	$8.3 billion

Source: The Bank of New York; NYSE Research and Planning Division and 1994 Fact Book; 1994 NASDAQ Fact Book and company directory; *Business Week,* September 19, 1994; and *Brancato Report* estimates.

companies and listing those companies in the United States. Moreover, according to Velli, some pension funds and investment managers may be legally required to invest in ADRs when they invest in non-US securities.

FIGURE 2–1A
Percentage of Total Depositary Receipt Programs by Country: 1994

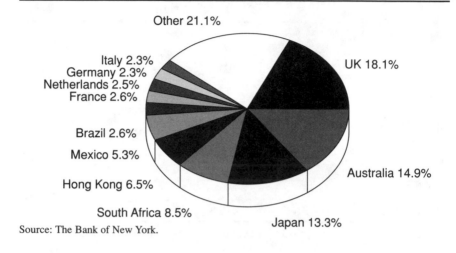

Source: The Bank of New York.

FIGURE 2–1B
Depositary Receipt Share Trading Volume by Country: 1994

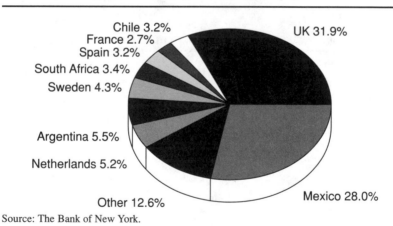

Source: The Bank of New York.

The growth in ADRs attests to their popularity as a means for access-ing US capital markets. ADR volume for US exchange-listed stocks is growing astronomically: from $75 billion in 1990 to $94 billion in 1991,

FIGURE 2–1C
Depositary Receipt Dollar Trading Volume by Country: 1994

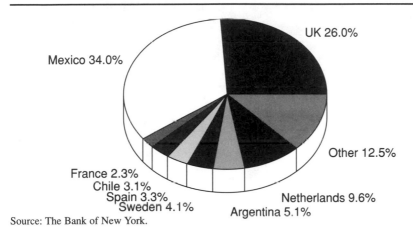

UK 26.0%

Mexico 34.0%

Other 12.5%

France 2.3%
Chile 3.1%
Spain 3.3%
Sweden 4.1%   Netherlands 9.6%
                        Argentina 5.1%
Source: The Bank of New York.

$125 billion in 1992, $201 billion in 1993, and an estimated $248 billion in 1994. Exchange listed trading in ADRs, therefore, has virtually doubled from 1992 to the end of 1994. Add to this the volume of unlisted "pink sheet" over-the-counter ADRs, traded among brokers via electronic bulletin boards ($5–$10 billion in 1992, growing to an estimated $25–$50 billion in 1994), and the total ADR market for listed and unlisted ADRs, approached $300 billion by the end of 1994 (see Table 2–1). By far, the largest number of ADR issues are traded in the OTC markets, including such popular unlisted ADRs as Nestlé, Deutsche Bank, and the Mexican retailer Cifra. In 1994, the total number of companies offering ADRs climbed to 1,124, of which only 322 were listed company ADRs and 807 were over-the-counter ADRs.

Figure 2–1 shows the countries with the largest number of ADR programs in 1994; the United Kingdom accounted for 18.1 percent of all ADR programs, with Australia in second place at 14.9 percent and Japan a close third at 13.3 percent of all 1994 ADR programs. In terms of both share ADR trading volume and dollar ADR trading volume, the United Kingdom and Mexico take the lead (the United Kingdom accounted for 31.9 percent of all ADR shares traded and 26 percent of dollar ADR volume in 1994, while Mexico accounted for 28 percent of ADR trading volume and 34 percent of ADR dollar volume in 1994).

TABLE 2–2
Worldwide Distribution of NYSE ADR Issuers: 1993 and 1994

| Country/Territory | Number of Non-U.S Companies Listed on the NYSE: 1993 and 1994 | | | |
| | 1993* | | 1994** | |
	Companies	Issues	Companies	Issues
Argentina	3	3	6	6
Australia	8	8	9	9
Bermuda	2	2	2	2
Brazil	1	1	1	1
British W.I.	1	1	1	1
Canada	28	29	32	33
Cayman Is.	0	0	5	7
Chile	5	5	15	15
Colombia	0	0	1	1
Denmark	1	1	3	3
Finland	0	0	1	1
France	4	4	5	6
Germany	1	1	1	1
Hong Kong	6	6	6	6
Indonesia	0	0	1	1
Ireland	1	1	1	2
Israel	2	2	2	2
Italy	6	6	8	11
Japan	9	9	11	11
Korea	0	0	2	2
Liberia	1	1	1	1
Luxembourg	1	1	1	1
Mexico	13	15	21	26
Netherlands	8	8	9	9
Netherlands Antilles	2	2	2	2
New Zealand	2	3	2	3
Norway	2	2	3	3
Panama	2	2	2	2
People's Republic of China	1	1	3	3
Peru	0	0	1	1
Philippines	1	1	2	2
Portugal	1	1	1	1
South Africa	1	1	1	1
Spain	7	7	8	10
Sweden	0	0	1	1
Turks & Caicos	0	0	1	1
United Kingdom	32	34	35	49
Venezuela	1	1	1	1
Total	153	159	208	238

Notes: * As of December 31st.

    ** As of November 18th. Total for 1994 = 210.

Source: New York Stock Exchange, Research & Planning Division.

FIGURE 2–2A
Depositary Receipt Share Volume by Exchange: 1994

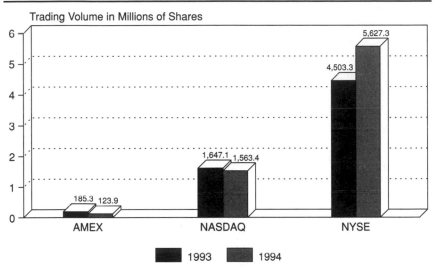

Source: The Bank of New York.

FIGURE 2–2B
Depositary Receipt Dollar Volume by Exchange: 1994

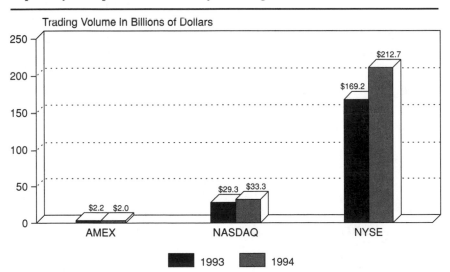

Source: The Bank of New York.

Notes: Trading in listed ADRs represented 4.8 percent of all shares traded in 1994 on AMEX, NASDAQ & NYSE and 6.3 percent of total dollar trading volume.

In terms of sheer volume as well as numbers, however, the largest exchange, the NYSE, is recording impressive competitive growth in ADRs (see Table 2–1 for total numbers of NYSE ADRs and Table 2–2 for country of origin for NYSE ADRs). By the end of 1992, 118 foreign companies had registered ADRs on the NYSE; that number grew to 210 companies by the end of 1994. Figure 2–2 compares share volume and dollar volume of ADRs traded on the NYSE, the NASDAQ, and the AMEX and clearly shows the predominant position of the NYSE, which provided the trading opportunity covering 86 percent of the 1994 dollar volume of all ADR issues.

Table 2–1 also shows the dollar volume of new capital raised through new public offerings of ADRs. In 1992, there were 23 new public offerings, which raised a total of $5.3 billion; by 1994 the total of new public offerings increased to 64 while the capital raised grew to $11.0 billion. Over the three-year period from 1992 through the end of 1994, therefore, overseas companies raised a total of $25.8 billion in new capital through public offerings of ADRs in US markets; over the five-year period from 1990 through the end of 1994, approximately $32.1 billion was raised.

PRIVATE PLACEMENTS OF FOREIGN SECURITIES

An attractive method for entering US markets involves a private placement offering under SEC's Rule 144A. In April 1990, the SEC approved Rule 144A to enable issuers to offer private placements to qualified institutional buyers (QIBs) without the company undergoing the kind of stringent regulatory, financial, and accounting requirements necessary to trade either in listed or unlisted public markets. The rule had the dual purpose of attracting foreign issuers to the US market and providing US issuers an alternative to public markets in the form of private offerings. Frequently companies enter the private placement Rule 144A market to gain exposure to US investors, and then, if successful, they will step up their participation to file as an unlisted ADR company trading in the over-the-counter markets. If that is successful, they may further move up to becoming listed on one of the exchanges; the final stage is to make a public offering for securities in US markets. One noted company that tested the market in the 144A market, later sought a public listing, and then sought a stock offering is the Mexican company Telefonos de Mexico.

According to the most recent SEC staff report filed with the US Congress on Rule 144A placements, there were 211 foreign and US Rule 144A placements from April 1990 through November 1992 totaling $24.8 billion. The countries of origin for the 211 offerings included 33 from the United Kingdom, 23 from Mexico, 9 from Australia, 8 from Canada, 6 each from Venezuela and Argentina, 5 from France, and 3 each from Italy, the Netherlands, and Sweden. Seven from among the foreign issuers later entered the US public market.[7]

Table 2–1 above also shows how total depositary receipt private offerings under Rule 144A have grown in the past few years. During 1994, there were 102 private offerings, which raised $8.3 billion in new capital for foreign issuers; this represented a substantial increase from the $2.1 billion in new capital raised through 33 private offerings in 1993. From the inception of the Rule 144A program in 1990, foreign issuers have raised a total of $17.4 billion in private offerings. Added to the $32.1 billion in public new offerings discussed above, foreign issuers have raised a total of $49.5 billion in public and private new offerings from 1990 through the end of 1994.

FOREIGN COMPANIES SEARCH FOR GLOBAL EQUITY

Corporations derive their financing from a number of sources, including retained earnings, borrowings from banks, floating bonds in the bond market, and issuing stock either on a first-time, new-issue basis or by selling additional shares in the market. The finance literature is replete with debate over how essential the stock market is in bringing capital to businesses, with some arguing that most external financing is done through the stock market, while others argue that other forms of financing, such as retained earnings, are most prevalent.[8] It would appear that, depending on the period under study and the nature of the business, different firms obtain their funding through different combinations of methods. Firms in mature industries may use internal financing (such as, for example, when interest rates are high), while rapidly expanding electronics firms, for example, may sell issues in the market at more frequent intervals.

Regardless of whether a firm contemplates issuing more stock than just its initial new offering, the stock market plays an important role as a price market for secondary sales to ensure liquidity and give the potential for sustained bolstering of the value of the initial offering. Thus, stock markets carry out several interrelated functions. In the primary market, companies sell initial offerings of shares to finance capital expansion. The secondary market, on the other hand, provides a forum in which investors can buy and sell outstanding shares. According to economist Paul Marsh, "These two functions are, of course, inextricably linked, since investors would be far less willing to provide cash to companies via the primary market if there were no secondary market in which they could subsequently sell their shares."[9]

When confronted with sudden drops in the market—or market "breaks" —and rapid up and down swings that bear very little resemblance to either the underlying value of plant and equipment or the expected future returns stemming from company operations, some observers might question the validity of pricing through stock markets at all. Moreover, some companies wish to expand without "hindrance" from shareholders and therefore seek private market financing. But determining how and when to enter securities markets in order to attract needed capital depends on the price companies are willing to pay in additional risk and exposure to greater shareholder accountability.

Some companies may well find it appropriate to raise their funds through banks and remain privately held. However, if additional expansion is required, a strategy for entering the public equity markets is also generally required. (Although, according to James Cochrane, senior vice president of the New York Stock Exchange, some companies enter US public markets not to raise equity capital, but to improve their credit rating to enable them to raise debt capital.) Starting in the mid 1980s, capital markets in many countries throughout the world underwent major shifts. Equity markets, now dominated by large institutional investors, have supplanted a considerable amount of traditional bank-related finance not only in the United States, but in Germany and Japan as well. In the United States, credit is increasingly channeled through open capital markets rather than through an intermediate credit decision by a lender such as a bank. Former SEC Chairman Richard Breeden notes that commercial and industrial (C&I) bank loans were generally discontinued after early 1989. With virtually no lending to the corporate sector coming from the C&I bank loan conduit, all of the financing in the aggregate for running major US corporations is now done through the capital markets. This does not mean, according to Breeden, that banks are not participating just as actively in the area; they are merely participating in a different form, providing credit through the purchase of securities rather than through the more traditional commercial loan. Thus, the "loan department" has become the "capital markets group," not only in the United States but throughout the world. The role of institutional investors in this new capital market structure (see Chapter 5 for a more complete discussion of the economic power of US institutional investors) becomes paramount, as they supplant the traditional role banks have played as providers of debt. As Breeden points out:

> Even in Germany and Japan (though for very different reasons), the traditional system of relationships is changing between a universal bank in Germany, and the companies in which it holds equity stakes, and the "main bank" in Japan and its relationship to a group of companies within a keiretsu. The German banks have been fairly quiet about it, but nonetheless the steps of Deutsche Bank and others to reduce the size of their industrial equity holdings suggests the beginning of a profound change in the capital market systems of Germany.[10]

This change is clearly signaled by a momentous event. In early October of 1993, Daimler-Benz AG became the first German company to become listed on the NYSE. The traditionally strong linkages between German companies and German banks, coupled with historically high savings rates in Germany compared with those in the United States, generally meant that most German companies had access to abundant quantities of capital within Germany. That may explain why there are only about 600 publicly traded companies in Germany. Daimler-Benz's bold departure from tradition presented a threat and a challenge to European banks. David Fairlamb described their predicament in a 1994 article in *Institutional Investor*:

> Like the biblical apple proffered to Eve, US capital markets are as dangerous as they are enticing—so European bankers have learned. . . . Spurred on by the globalization of capital markets, the Europeans are now busily rethinking and reorganizing their US operations . . . Unlike Eve, the Europeans have little choice. Their biggest corporate customers need access to the US markets. The European banks also need to fight a rear-guard action against US banks that are making inroads into Europe. "To be in investment banking but not to be in the US means that the US houses will have the upper hand [globally]," points out Giorgio Questa, chairman of IMI Capital Markets and vice chairman of Mabon Securities, a subsidiary of Italy's partly privatized merchant bank Istituto Mobiliare Italiano.[11]

European banks are clearly responding by shifting into new investment strategies, as can be seen by the unprecedented alliance between Deutsche Bank, on behalf of its European clients, and US investment banking firms for the underwriting of the Daimler-Benz ADR listing in the United States. This arrangement between German banks and Wall Street has heralded a new age in the globalization of US securities markets.

There is, however, considerable debate about the need and extent to which Japanese corporations will attempt to access US capital markets. Certainly, it is widely believed that the closely knit cross-shareholding system in Japan and the presence of a main bank in the "keiretsu"—or trading group—has produced many advantages to Japanese companies during the expansionary 30-year period from the early 1960s until the early 1990s. Traditionally, capital has been relatively cheap in Japan so that firms were encouraged to use it abundantly. Until 1979, exchange controls kept savings from leaving the country in large amounts. The controls produced a more dramatic effect in Japan than similar controls had in other countries, given Japan's relatively high savings rate. In 1975, Japan saved nearly a third of its gross national product (GNP), twice as large a proportion as in Britain and the United States, and one-and-a-half times that in France and Germany. Plentiful and captive savings, it is argued, lowered Japan's real interest rates and thus its capital costs.[12] The historic Japanese model of cross-shareholdings in which there is reciprocal ownership of shares by companies in trading groups produces complex interlinkages of share ownership and a certain stability. Finally, Japanese industry also benefitted from a system whereby Japanese government banks provided strategic companies with subsidized loans and tax breaks. According to the *Economist:*

> [I]n 1973 the shipping industry alone [benefitted in the amount of] Y92 billion, according to Naoyuki Yoshino of Keio University in Tokyo. Private banks lent cheaply to officially favored firms; this was possible because regulations held down banks' cost of funds. Kazuo Ueda of Tokyo University calculates that the total value of interest-rate subsidies to banks (including regulated interest rates on savers' deposits, cheap funds from government banks and a regulated bond market) rose from Y180 billion in 1970 to Y650 billion by 1980: [an amount that was] not much as a proportion of GNP, but still important at the margin.[14]

Loans from Japanese banks also involved little risk, since a firm's main bank might well provide funds with the knowledge that it would be compensated in the event of default by inexpensive funds from the government. Cheap capital thus encouraged lavish investment, frequently in search of additional market share without a necessarily corresponding improvement in rates of return. For example, as Japanese corporate returns for the year ending March 1994 were being reported early in the summer of 1994, the *Economist* reported that one statistic was especially dramatic: The return on equity earned by firms listed on the Tokyo Stock Exchange (TSE) had fallen below 2.5 percent, compared with a 4.0 percent yield on risk-free government bonds. The report went on to criticize Japanese return on equity in general:

> In 1971–80 TSE firms made a pitifully low 0.5% a year return on equity, after adjustment for inflation. In 1981–85 they managed 5.4%, but over the next five years the real return fell back to 4.2%. So even when they were at their most profitable, Japan's firms have produced comparatively poor returns.[15]

Figure 2–3 shows how much less favorable shareholders' return on equity is in Japan than in other major stock market countries in the world. The cross-shareholding system so prevalent in Japan is more of an advantage in cementing relationships between suppliers and other keiretsu member companies than a means of producing competitive returns to outside shareholders. (It has, however, also afforded Japanese industry the ability to plan over longer-term horizons than many firms in other countries such as the United States.)

It is true that Japanese companies may have sizeable capital investment capacity left over from their expansionary days, and they may still have strong self-correcting mechanisms within their keiretsu system. But a rather iconoclastic report has been released from the Pacific Institute and the Asia Institute called "Japanese Corporate Governance"—a title some consider a contradiction in terms. Under the direction of its chairman, Dr. Kiichi Mochizuki, the Pacific Institute held a series of meetings in New York, Washington, and Tokyo, with noted leaders of Japanese businesses as well as practitioners and scholars from the United States working in the field of corporate governance. These meetings produced a chronicle of the debate over whether the Japanese corporate governance system needed to be changed and, if so, how it should be improved to accommodate the demands of global investors. One view emerging from the debate suggests that Japan's need for new capital—especially from US institutional investors—is great, despite Japanese industry's overinvestment of the past:

FIGURE 2–3
Prospective Return on Equity: 1994

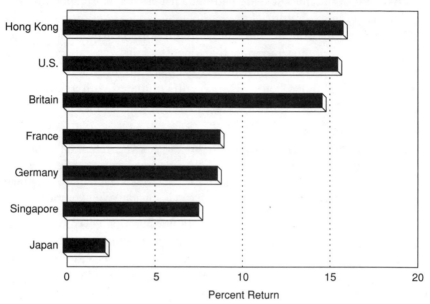

Source: The *Economist,* July 9, 1994.

[T]his view suggests that the depth of the Japanese economic crisis has yet to be realized. The massive expansion of the 1980s allowed Japanese corporations to finance themselves on the cheap. This led to undisciplined spending and capital investment, the effects of which are only now manifesting themselves. In addition, the Japan economy faces increasing pressure from the more buoyant economies of Taiwan, Hong Kong, South Korea, and Singapore, not to mention the potential threats posed by China, Indonesia, and Vietnam. To sustain themselves through what may be an extended period of slow growth at home, together with intense regional and international competition, and to overcome the excessive capital expenditures of the 1980s, Japanese corporations will need fresh sources of capital. In all likelihood, the international capital market, and in particular, institutional investors will be significant sources of this new equity. . . .

The proponents of this view further contend that internal sources of funds are not as plentiful as they would appear. The earnings of many Japanese companies have decreased to the point where little or no internal funds are available. Other sources of domestic capital are capable of seeking higher returns abroad, and, therefore, can no longer be counted on as a captive resource. The

FIGURE 2–4
Japanese Manufacturers' Sources of Capital: 1982 and 1992

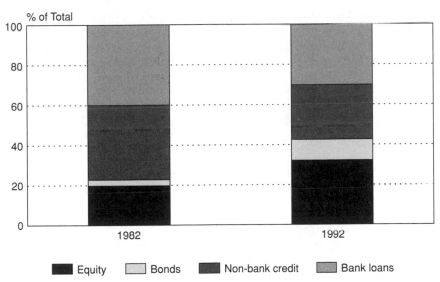

Source: The *Economist,* July 9, 1994.

need of Japanese companies to appeal to the world and, in particular, the United States and European investment community is genuine, and reform of the corporate governance system is an essential feature of that appeal.[15]

There can be no doubt that numerous traditional and stable relationships between corporations, banks, and the Japanese government have been eroding in recent years. As the Japanese stock market has declined, exchange rates have pushed the yen to all-time lows against the dollar, and the government has signaled to the markets that its budgetary deficit problems may not permit it to continue with its historic price support functions for business and financial market transactions. At the same time, there has been a shrinking reliance on bank loans to finance businesses (see Figure 2–4). These trends signal a fundamental change in Japanese capital formation, as Japanese companies become less reliant on banks and turn more to equity markets—and eventually to "outside" global equity markets. This will bring the issue of comparatively low shareholder returns to the forefront, as institutional investors will demand competitive returns and a role in corporate governance issues as well.

Finally, in other parts of the world, withdrawal of traditional sources of government funding will continue to put pressure on capital markets as newly privatized companies in the former Soviet Union and Eastern bloc countries attempt to enter global securities markets. A former SEC Commissioner, Professor Roberta Karmel, notes:

> It seems government funding is not in the cards anywhere in the world in the near future. The financial collapse of former Communist and Socialist countries and the huge budget deficits all over the Western world make it very difficult, if not impossible, for economic enterprises to continue to be financed through government grants almost everywhere. This has led to privatizations in developed Western countries and in emerging countries. These privatizations have been the driving force behind much of the internationalization of the securities markets, and in particular behind the decisions of various foreign issuers to enter the US markets.[16]

REDUCING BARRIERS TO FOREIGN ISSUERS ENTERING US MARKETS

Despite the plethora of other avenues of trading available to them, foreign issuers are finding listing, or at least partial Rule 144A private market access, desirable enough to surmount the considerable obstacles to entry. Furthermore, barriers to foreign issuers, while still substantial, have been declining. There has been considerable debate about whether and how to relax US standards. On one side is the desire to attract foreign issuers, and on the other is the need to preserve the integrity and efficiency of the US capital market.

The primary obstacles facing the foreign issuer involve US disclosure and accounting requirements; these issues will be described in greater detail in Chapters 3 and 4. The main accounting issue involves the need to reconcile home country accounting standards with US generally accepted accounting principles (US GAAP). Indeed, the issue of how to treat reserves was almost the main obstacle for the recent Daimler-Benz ADR issue. In both Germany and Japan, as well as in certain other countries such as France, companies have traditionally kept high levels of reserves for a variety of reasons, including preparing for special contingencies. Shareholders may object to these reserves—assuming they are even disclosed—as lowering allocations to them through lower dividend payout. In addition, treatment of items such as goodwill on the balance sheet can give rise to a controversial accounting discrepancy.

As will be discussed in more detail in subsequent chapters, SEC rules for listing securities require extensive disclosure and reconciliation of accounting differences, including estimates of how the issuer's bottom line would have been revised if full conformance with US GAAP had been established. Companies may face substantial costs in reworking their accounting systems, although some new companies may determine that, as long as they are establishing accounting systems, it might be in their best interests to conform to US standards for listing since investors in the US markets have come to trust and rely on the panoply of disclosure and accounting regularly provided them by companies utilizing US capital markets.

Pat McConnell, speaking at a conference at Fordham Law School, lists the major questions foreign issuers should address as they consider entering US markets:[17]

- How does home-country accounting differ from US standards? More important, why are there differences? Are these differences likely to concern investors?
- What industry-specific practices does the company use that will have to be disclosed as "material" to the business in its home country? Do these differ from similar industry practices in the United States? Why?
- Is the company engaged in transactions for which US accounting rules and/or home-country accounting rules do not exist or that US investors are unfamiliar with?
- How difficult, in terms of both time and cost, will it be for the company to gather the information necessary to fulfill the US accounting and disclosure requirements?
- Can a foreign-issuer management that may not be used to much disclosure become comfortable about providing the types of information normally disclosed in the United States, especially if that management fears that the disclosure rules may lead to dissemination of sensitive information?

McConnell also points out that there is a benefit side to the strict accounting and disclosure requirements:

For a foreign company thinking of issuing securities in the United States for the first time, the initial step is to understand the US markets—not just the regulatory requirements, but what makes the markets tick, what makes them liquid and efficient. A significant part of what makes the market tick is the accounting and disclosure system.[18]

That is, these requirements are responsible for the investor confidence that is unique in US markets.

On April 19, 1994 the SEC adopted a series of initiatives designed to simplify the registration and reporting process for foreign companies accessing the US capital markets. The rules demonstrate the SEC's commitment to enhancing the competitiveness of the US capital markets while at the same time honoring its regulatory mandate to protect US investors and markets. Then SEC Commissioner J. Carter Beese Jr. summarized the initiatives in this way: "What we are doing today is lowering impediments, not lowering thresholds."

The new rules accomplish the following:

1. Relax certain of the financial statement burdens on foreign issuers seeking access to the US capital markets through public offerings or seeking listings on US stock exchanges or NASDAQ.[19]
2. Ease the eligibility requirements for these potential foreign issuers.[20]

The SEC estimates that the number of currently reporting foreign issuers that will satisfy the new eligibility criteria will increase by approximately one-third. In addition, the SEC also extended certain aspects of its registration process to foreign companies. This action will enable eligible foreign companies to use one registration statement to register debt, equity, and other securities, without specifying in advance the amount of each class of securities to be offered. Consequently, foreign corporate treasurers will enjoy the same degree of financing flexibility as US companies in meeting the short-term and long-term capital needs of their businesses.[21]

Observers credit various efforts by the International Accounting Standards Committee (IASC) and other organizations to pave the way for reconciliation of accounting differences among countries. The SEC's April 1994 ruling recognizing as authoritative the International Accounting Standard (IAS) pertaining to cash flow is regarded as an important event: "Acceptance of International Standards is going to be the route both to international harmonization and mutual recognition."[22]

As was discussed earlier in this chapter, the Daimler-Benz case (for a chronology see Box 2–2) is historic in that it represents the immense effort undertaken by the first German company to attain entry into a US equity market whose principles of disclosure and investor protection are widely regarded as being at the opposite end of the spectrum from those

Box 2–2

Daimler-Benz Decides to List in US Markets

Though its sales had plummeted in the face of a steep downturn in Germany's economy, for the first half of 1993 Daimler-Benz reported a profit under German GAAP of almost DM200 million, a terrific result given the state of the German economy. However, this reported DM200 million profit came after an undisclosed release of more than DM1.5 billion in provisions into income. Under German GAAP, the story for investors would have ended at the DM200 million profit, though its board members and its largest shareholder, the Deutsche Bank, would have known about the results before adding back the provisions from prior years.

For the same period under US GAAP, the company reported a loss of just under DM1 billion. That fact is clearly shown in a two-page reconciliation to US GAAP, where the addition of reserves earned in prior periods is simply backed out of the current year's results, along with other changes. Thus, all the investors in Daimler-Benz . . . are now able to evaluate the company's current performance without the considerable layer of camouflage that other German companies are allowed to use to smooth out their reported earnings. Since the top managers of German banks routinely sit as board members of German companies, the banks have access to far superior financial information than non-insiders. Once Germany enacts legislation outlawing insider trading, having such a disparity of information and being major players in securities trading markets may create considerable exposure for Germany's banks that would be reduced by better public disclosure.

Interestingly, the announcement by Daimler-Benz that it was going to reconcile its financial statements to US GAAP seems to have caused its stock to rise in comparison with other German companies, providing an interesting demonstration of the value the market places on openness and transparency. Indeed, from the announcement by Daimler-Benz that it would list in the United States until the actual secondary offering, Daimler-Benz's stock out-performed the DAX average in Germany by almost 5%, and if you back Daimler-Benz out of the DAX, by even more. That represents billions of dollars in additional market capitalization that may be directly attributable to its willingness to remove the camouflage from its financial results. Daimler-Benz has been subjected to criticism in some quarters for this decision to break the united front of German companies and to "give in" to the SEC. This is both untrue and quite farfetched.

Daimler-Benz approached this issue not as some sort of hockey game

Box 2–2 (continued)

between the United States and Germany, but as an important business issue that is directly related to its overall global business strategy. . . . Just
as any prudent company would arrange multiple sources of supply for in-
dispensable raw materials or component parts, Daimler-Benz sees considerable value in assuring that the company has the capacity to finance its activities in multiple markets around the world. . . . Underlying the decision
of Daimler-Benz was a fundamental long-term view that a truly global
company must not only sell its products around the world, but it also must
develop a global ownership base. Daimler-Benz saw the existence of an
informed international investor base with confidence in its understanding
of the company's financial picture as a significant corporate asset.

Source: Former SEC Chairman, Richard C. Breeden, "Foreign Companies and US Securities Markets in a Time of Economic Transformation," *Fordham International Law Journal,*
17 (1994), pp. 91–93.

in Germany.[23] The controversy surrounding the listing application was a
landmark in regulatory and accounting circles, and it took on a serious
political dimension as German government officials pressed for "reciprocity" to allow Daimler-Benz to maintain its own accounting system.
The SEC held fast and refused to give in on the grounds that foreign companies seeking to sell securities in the United States should provide the
investing public with the same information as US companies, lest the foreign company have an advantage in raising capital. Proponents for the
reciprocity accounting allowance argued that such a world-class company
has extensive reporting available to those investors who seek such information and that, furthermore, most sophisticated global investors are
more than capable of understanding the accounting differences. To deny
the company access, they argued, was to foreclose a major segment of the
world from entering US markets. The SEC was not persuaded, and the
listing went forward under US regulations.

During the listing process, variations in German and US accounting
standards were extensively reviewed. Under German accounting policies, companies are afforded considerable discretion in either reporting
income through to the bottom line or placing earnings into reserves. In
the United States, reserves under US GAAP can be diverted from income

only to provide for an adverse event that must be probable and estimable in amount. German companies may record reserves without such a stringent restriction, and they can later release them to improve sagging earnings. Former SEC Chairman Richard Breeden notes that, at one time, roughly 40 percent of the entire balance sheet of Daimler-Benz was represented by the single line item "provisions." The so-called hidden reserves so notoriously associated with German companies turned out, unexpectedly, to be reconciled with accounting methods that produced lower rather than higher reported earnings. (Most investors had assumed that the reserves would have produced a surplus for earnings, not a deficit.) Yet the markets reacted favorably and, ultimately, Dr. Gerhard Liener, the chief financial officer of Daimler-Benz, was reported to have indicated that, during the preparation of the SEC filing materials, Daimler-Benz found out that, apart from the reserve issue, some of the other differences between the two accounting systems were not as striking as they had been perceived to be. The percentage of completion method used in the United States is fairly well duplicated by the German milestone system; a good guideline for setting up reserves under GAAP is given by the German tax accounting rules; and leasing, depreciation, manufacturing cost, and pension provisions were areas where Daimler was able to keep its procedures or where the differences in calculations were immaterial.[24] In any event, Daimler–Benz clearly thought the effort was worth the price.

NOTES

1. Richard C. Breeden, "Foreign Companies and U.S. Securities Markets in a Time of Economic Transformation," *Fordham International Law Review* 17 (1994), p. 80.

2. Data obtained from the SEC's Division of Corporation Finance, current as of April 28, 1995. Securities of these issuers are traded on the NYSE, the AMEX and regional exchanges, through the facilities of NASDAQ's NMS and small cap markets, and in the over-the-counter markets made up of the NASD's Electronic Bulletin Board Service and the so-called *pink sheets.*

3. Peter Lee, "The Fight to Gain Control of World Equities," *Euromoney,* July 1, 1993, p. 5.

4. Joseph Velli, "American Depositary Receipts: An Overview," *Fordham International Law Journal* 17 (1994), p. 38.

5. *Ibid.*

6. Lee, p. 5.

7. Cover letter from Richard C. Breeden, chairman, U.S. Securities and Exchange Com-

mission to the Hon. John D. Dingell and the Hon. Edward J. Markey, dated February 19, 1993, to accompany SEC Staff Report on Rule 144A, January 27, 1993.

8. See, for example, Colin Mayer, "Stock-Markets, Financial Institutions, and Corporate Performance" and Allen Sykes, "Proposals for a Reformed System of Corporate Governance to Achieve Internationally Competitive Long-Term Performance," both in *Capital Markets and Corporate Governance,* eds. Nicholas Dimsdale and Martha Prevezer (Oxford: Clarendon Press, 1994). Mayer argues that stock markets are not a major source of external financing for industry, while Sykes argues that, under the British/U.S. system most external long-term funds are raised from the stock market.

9. For further discussion of the role of stock markets in capital formation see Paul Marsh, "Market Assessment of Company Performance," *Capital Markets and Corporate Governance,* eds. Nicholas Dimsdale and Martha Prevezer (Oxford: Clarendon Press, 1994), p. 67.

10. Breeden, pp. 79–80.

11. David Fairlamb, "The American Imperative," *Institutional Investor,* July 1994, p. 186.

12. Japan Survey, "Capital Costs," *Economist,* July 9, 1994, p. 13.

13. Mayer, p. 188.

14. *Ibid.*

15. *Japanese Corporate Governance: A Comparative Study of Systems in Japan and the United States,* summarized and edited by David H. Kaufman for The Pacific Institute/The Asia Institute (New York: Pacific Institute/Asia Institute, 1994), pp. 6–7.

16. Roberta S. Karmel, "Living With U.S. Regulations: Complying with the Rules and Avoiding Litigation," *Fordham International Law Journal* 17 (1994), pp. 153–154.

17. Pat McConnell, "Practical Company Experience in Entering U.S. Markets: Significant Issues and Hurdles from the Advisor's Perspective," *Fordham International Law Journal* 17 (1994), pp. 121–122.

18. *Ibid.*

19. A number of financial reporting statements have been streamlined. For example, a "landmark step" allows foreign companies to submit, without supplement, modification, or reconciliations, a cash flow statement prepared in accordance with International Accounting Standard IAS No. 7. This is a step back from the SEC's previous hard stance, which required five-year reconciliation statements under generally accepted accounting principles (U.S. GAAP).

20. The SEC reduced the public float threshold from $300 million to $75 million and cut the required reporting history from 36 months to 12. This should reduce both the paper work required to be filed with the SEC and the time taken by the agency to review it.

21. Kevin D. Cramer and Catherine M. Stavrakis, "SEC Simplifies Foreign Companies' Access to U.S. Markets," *International Securities Regulation Report,* Buraff Publications, May 3, 1994, pp. 50–54.

22. Karmel, p. 153.

23. Breeden, p. 85.

24. McConnell, p. 126.

II

HOW TO ENTER US MARKETS

Chapter 3

Legal Requirements for Entering US Securities Markets

Foreign issuers of securities[1] have traditionally been reluctant to enter the US securities markets, primarily because of the extensive disclosure requirements imposed by US federal securities laws and the issuers' own widespread perception of the litigiousness of US shareholders who, in addition to the demands discussed later in Chapter 6, often go to court to challenge the accuracy of the disclosures they do receive. With the globalization of the financial and securities markets, however, multinational companies based in Europe, Asia, and other parts of the world are finding it increasingly difficult to compete without seeking equity or debt capital from investors in the United States. Indeed, as Chapters 1 and 2 demonstrated, the growing demand by American investors for foreign equity has prompted companies from such diverse nations as Argentina, China, and Germany to bring their securities to the United States, often in the form of American Depositary Receipts (ADRs) representing ownership interests in the underlying shares.[2] The previous chapters also discussed the advantages to foreign issuers of entering US markets, including affording them access to the US markets' consistent depth, liquidity, and transparency, which in turn, foster investor confidence, reduce issuer capital-raising costs, and may produce broader name recognition acquired in the United States—which might later help them market products or services to US consumers.[3]

A foreign company considering entry into the US securities markets will be faced with a number of possible alternatives, all of which were described, at least briefly, in Chapter 2. The first is a private placement, which will be discussed at length later in this chapter. The second is a listing of securities on the New York Stock Exchange (NYSE), the American Stock Exchange (AMEX), or one of the interdealer markets within the National Association of Securities Dealers Automated Quotation System (NASDAQ), all of which are subject to the supervisory authority of the US Securities and Exchange Commission (SEC) and all of which we will refer to as self-regulatory organizations, or SROs. The third method is a registered public offering. A fourth alternative is trading in the informal over-the-counter (OTC) secondary markets, which generally does not require listing the securities on a stock exchange or procuring their quotation in a NASDAQ market, or registering them with the SEC until a certain minimum level of US share ownership (300 holders of record) is reached. Regardless of which of these alternatives they may pursue, most foreign companies to date have used ADRs to create a market for their securities in the United States.

Foreign issuers considering a public offering in the United States must weigh a variety of factors, the most important of which is the perceived burden of complying with the SEC's requirement for filing of financial statements either prepared in accordance with or reconciled to US generally accepted accounting principles (US GAAP) and audited by an independent certified public accountant.[4] Requirements for reconciliation of differing accounting principles, which many foreign companies believe erect a significant barrier to entry into the US securities markets, will be discussed in Chapter 4.

This chapter focuses on the federal securities laws with which foreign issuers must comply in order to raise equity or debt capital in the United States through a primary offering, whether in the public or private securities markets. Federal securities regulation, which applies concurrently with the various laws of the country's 50 states and is supplemented by the rules of the various SROs, is centralized in two key statutes administered and enforced by the SEC: the Securities Act of 1933 (referred to in this book as the Securities Act)[5] and the Securities Exchange Act of 1934 (referred to as the Exchange Act).[6] The Securities Act governs primary and secondary offerings of securities, mandating (1) the registration of securities offered or sold to the public by issuers, their affiliates, and certain other persons, including underwriters, and (2) the disclosure—in a prospectus delivered to each offeree or purchaser of the securities—of detailed, material business and financial information relating to the issuer and its securities as well as the material terms of the particular offering.

Stringent antifraud provisions of the Securities Act prohibit fraud in connection with the offer or sale of securities, to ensure that issuers and other participants in a primary offering or sale furnish all information necessary to an informed investment decision.

A total of 51 American state and territorial jurisdictions (except the nation's capital, the District of Columbia) also require registration under "blue-sky" statutes of securities offered or sold to residents.[7] Like the federal Securities Act, these state laws bar fraud in the offer or sale of securities, with most permitting defrauded purchasers to sue the issuer and underwriters.[8]

The Exchange Act extends the Securities Act's disclosure-based approach to the US secondary, or trading, markets. Through detailed registration and periodic reporting requirements that will be outlined in Chapter 4, the Exchange Act and the SEC's rules derived from this statute together ensure that issuers of publicly traded securities provide a continuous flow of current financial and other material information to investors. In addition, the Exchange Act empowers the SEC to regulate the securities markets in the United States, both directly and through close oversight of the SROs. All national securities exchanges and all associations of securities dealers and broker-dealers as well as all nonexempt investment companies and investment advisers must register with the SEC and are subject to a panoply of SEC rules.

As implemented through SEC regulations, the Exchange Act further prescribes certain disclosure and procedural rules applicable to third-party tender offers, issuer repurchases, going-private transactions, and solicitations of shareholder votes directly or by proxy, and it requires officers, directors, and 10 percent shareholders of any public company to return to the company profits realized on any "short-swing" trading transaction in the company's stock (i.e., a purchase and sale, or sale and purchase, of such stock within six months). Most foreign issuers are exempt from the act's proxy and short-swing profit recovery provisions except to the extent, as discussed in the next chapter, that SRO rules require the solicitation of proxies from, and the delivery by mail of proxy materials to, holders of listed securities. Finally, and perhaps most importantly, foreign issuers should remain mindful of the expansive antifraud remedies made available under the Exchange Act to the SEC and private litigants to deter fraud in connection with the purchase or sale of securities in the US primary and secondary markets.

USE OF ADRS BY FOREIGN PRIVATE ISSUERS TO ACCESS US CAPITAL MARKETS

ADRs are currently the preferred mechanism for foreign issuers seeking entry into US securities markets. In simplest terms, an ADR is a negotiable certificate that represents a proportionate ownership interest in securities of a non-US company held by a depositary in a custodial account. The depositary is typically a US bank or trust company, which in turn appoints a custodian to hold the deposited securities in the foreign issuer's country of incorporation while the ADRs remain outstanding.[9] ADR holders may demand delivery of the underlying foreign security at any time or may sell that security in the foreign markets.[10]

An ADR involves three separate securities: (1) the underlying foreign security; (2) an American Depositary Share (ADS) representing one security or a fraction or multiple of the underlying security, which may be debt but is more commonly equity; and (3) the ADR itself, which is a receipt for the ADS.[11]

Participation in an ADR program provides US investors with several benefits not available through direct ownership of foreign securities. First, the ADR mechanism interposes the depositary (or its foreign branch or correspondent) between the foreign issuer and the US security holder. Depositaries generally monitor the issuer's declaration of dividends in the home country and collect the dividends and convert them to US dollars for distribution to US holders.[12] Second, the clearance and settlement process for ADRs is typically the same as for other domestic securities traded in US markets. American investors can thus own an interest in securities of foreign issuers while holding securities that trade, clear, and settle within automated US systems and US time periods.[13] Third, the ADR mechanism allows US investors greater access to information regarding the foreign issuer than they might otherwise have without the intermediation of the depositary. By agreement, the depositary usually receives and forwards annual reports and other disclosure documents furnished by the foreign issuer to the ADR holders. Also, the depositary will exercise any voting rights attaching to the underlying securities on behalf of the ADR holders, according to their instructions.

ADRs have been utilized by foreign companies in connection with mergers and acquisitions, restructurings, and employee benefit plans, as well as private offerings structured to permit institutional resales in the United States under Rule 144A of the Securities Act (to be discussed in a later section of this chapter).[14] Foreign issuers frequently raise capital in the United States through privately placed ADRs, which are exempt from registration under the Securities Act because they do not involve a public offering. Private placements can generally be accomplished more quickly and often at far lower cost than public offerings and do not give rise to periodic reporting requirements under the Exchange Act unless and until the number of US equity holders exceeds 300 (and the issuer has 500 such holders worldwide and more than $5 million in assets).[15]

Types of ADR Programs

ADR programs are either sponsored or unsponsored. Unsponsored ADR programs, which have become exceedingly rare as a result of a 1983 change in SEC rules, are typically created without active participation by the foreign private issuer and often in response to interest in that issuer's securities on the part of American investors, broker-dealers, and the depositary bank.[16] A depositary may request a letter of nonobjection from the foreign issuer in order to promote good relations with the issuer and to obtain access to the issuer's disclosure documents. Once a registration statement on Form F-6[17] for the ADRs (and, in the case of a public offering, a Form F-1, F-2, F-3, or F-4 registering the deposited shares, as discussed below[18]) has been filed with the SEC and has become effective, the depositary can accept deposits of the foreign issuer's securities and issue ADRs against those deposits.

An overwhelming majority of the ADR programs established since 1983, as noted, have been sponsored by the issuer of the underlying security. A sponsored ADR program is created jointly by a foreign private issuer and a depositary. The issuer of the deposited securities enters into a deposit agreement with the depositary that also binds all ADR holders and signs the Form F-6 registration statement.[19]

The deposit agreement sets forth the rights and responsibilities of all parties. Generally, the issuer of the deposited securities agrees to bear some of the costs relating to the facility (such as dividend payment fees of the depositary), although ADR holders continue to pay such costs as deposit and withdrawal fees.[20] Depositaries usually agree to distribute notices of shareholder meetings and voting instructions ensuring that ADR holders will be able to exercise voting rights through these intermediaries. Moreover, the depositaries often contract to furnish corporate communications and other relevant information to the ADR holders at the request of the foreign issuer.[21]

ADR programs fall within three general categories, according to the degree to which the issuer of the deposited securities has penetrated the US securities markets. A level 1 ADR trades in the OTC pink sheets or NASD-administered Electronic Bulletin Board Service and, if owned by more than 300 US holders of record as of the last day of its most recent fiscal year (and as of that date, more than 500 holders worldwide and more than $5 million in total assets), must be eligible for an exemption from Exchange Act registration and reporting, as discussed in Chapter 4. To qualify for this registration exemption, the issuer must supply the SEC with any material information it produces and distributes in the home country. Although a level 1 program cannot be used to raise capital, it offers foreign issuers an easy and low-cost method for establishing a presence in US markets and creating an interest in their securities among US investors.[22]

Level 2 ADRs are quoted in the NASDAQ system or listed on a national securities exchange but have not been offered to the public in the United States through a registered public offering. To list ADRs or any other security on one of the exchanges or to procure their quotation in a NASDAQ market, a Form 20-F must be filed with the SEC to fulfill the registration requirement imposed by Section 12 of the Exchange Act. Exchange Act registration and periodic reporting requirements, as described in greater detail in the next chapter, hold the issuer to the stringent US accounting and disclosure standards. Because it must comply with the rigorous Exchange Act registration provisions, which include the mandatory filing with the SEC of financial statements that have been reconciled to US GAAP, a level 2 issuer is well-positioned to make a public offering in the US marketplace. Indeed, the issuer may be qualified to use a short-form registration statement (as described later in this chapter) for such an offering if it has been filing timely periodic reports with the SEC for a specified period.[23]

A level 3 ADR is one that is offered to the public after a Securities Act registration statement has been filed with the SEC. In many cases, the security may also be simultaneously approved for quotation in NASDAQ or for listing on a national securities exchange. As in the case of a level 2 program, the prospectus filed under the Securities Act must comply with US accounting and disclosure standards.[24]

Securities Act Registration

Under Section 5 of the Securities Act, it is illegal, in the absence of an exemption, for any person directly or indirectly to offer or sell securities[25] to the public without first filing a registration statement with the SEC.[26] A registered offering provides a number of clear benefits to the issuer, most prominently the ability to solicit a wide variety of investors beyond the members of the institutional investor community to which private placements are ordinarily directed.

Balanced against these benefits are the delay and other costs typically associated with the formal registration process. Not only must a registration statement, consisting mainly of a prospectus, be filed with and in many instances reviewed by the staff of the SEC's Division of Corporation Finance (which review may span anywhere from four to six weeks and may result in several amendments to the document), but a substantial registration fee tied to the aggregate offering price must also be paid.[27] Additional and often large sums must be expended for underwriters, lawyers, and accountants. The costs of reconciling foreign financial statements to US GAAP alone may be significant but, as discussed, would have to be incurred in any event to obtain a listing on a stock exchange or a quotation in NASDAQ. Periodic disclosure obligations arising from a public offering—even where a concurrent SRO listing is not sought—may likewise be viewed as burdensome.

General SEC registration procedures. Registered public offerings must be structured to comply with the Securities Act and SEC rules adopted under this statute, applicable state blue-sky laws, and NASD requirements applicable to underwriters and securities firms participating in the selling group. Before the registration statement is filed with the SEC at its headquarters in Washington, D.C., activities to "condition" the market for the proposed offering are prohibited.[28] Specifically, offers or sales of the securities to be issued prior to the filing of the registration statement are illegal and may result in the SEC's refusal to declare the registration statement effective if the staff concludes that the illegal offering activities artificially stimulated the market for the securities or misled potential investors. An issuer is permitted by SEC rules, however, to announce its intent to make a public offering, so long as the announcement is confined to identifying the issuer, disclosing the title, amount, and basic terms of the securities to be offered, and briefly stating the purpose and manner of the offering.[29] This announcement must also declare that the actual offering will be conducted only by means of a statutory prospectus, and it may not reveal the identities of the proposed underwriters and selling group members.

Negotiations between the issuer and prospective underwriter and among members of the underwriting group normally occur during the prefiling period. Preparation of the SEC registration statement—consisting mainly of the prospectus—is also typically coordinated at this time by management and counsel for the issuer and managing underwriter, together with the independent accounting firm responsible for auditing the requisite financial statements.[30]

Once the registration statement is filed with the SEC, the securities may be offered to, and indications of interest solicited from, potential investors. No sales may be made, however, until the registration statement is declared effective by the SEC. Throughout the period between the filing date and the effective date of the registration statement—a minimum of 20 days and often up to six weeks or longer in the case of an initial public offering to allow for SEC staff review and comment—solicitations of offers to buy and indications of interest may be made both orally and through certain limited written communications in the preliminary prospectus. Such communications are subject to antifraud liability under both the Securities Act and the Exchange Act.[31]

The preliminary prospectus, an important means of disseminating information on the issuer and the offering terms during the period between the filing and effective date, is generally known as the "red herring" because of the red legend on the cover page cautioning that the document is preliminary in nature. In most instances the preliminary prospectus does not contain pricing, and it lacks certain other information unavailable until the offering closes, but it otherwise approximates in content the final or definitive prospectus that must be delivered to each purchaser when a sale is consummated. Acceptance of buy orders from investors and actual sales of the offered securities are not allowed, as discussed, until after the registration statement becomes effective.

An issuer, along with the underwriters and any other person involved in the distribution process, must take particular care during this intermediate period (as well as the period prior to the filing of the registration statement) to avoid undue publicity regarding either the securities subject to the offering or the issuer itself. Such activities could be regarded by the SEC as an improper effort to selectively precondition the market for these securities with information not contained in the prospectus. Some sound advice in this regard for foreign issuers, in the common setting of a global offering with a US component, has been outlined in an important treatise:

> Publicity can be a significant issue in a global offering with a US tranche, primarily because other jurisdictions do not impose such strict limitations. Steps must be taken to ensure that publicity permitted in another jurisdiction does not leak into the United States.[32]

Despite its restrictions on solicitations apart from the prospectus, the SEC has recognized that some information on the issuer and its business must continue to flow into the markets. Accordingly, the SEC expressly permits the publication of a limited advertisement regarding the offering—known as a "tombstone" ad—after the registration statement is filed.[33] Tombstone ads—which in practice often are not used until the day after the effective date of the registration statement[34]—may disclose only the title, the amount, and certain terms of the securities being offered; the manner and expected date of sale of those securities; and, finally, some basic information with respect to the issuer, the identities of the managing underwriters, and the names and addresses of persons from whom a copy of the preliminary prospectus may be obtained. Cautionary language must be included, stating that the securities may not be sold before the registration statement is declared effective, that the ad itself is not an offer to sell, and that sales may be impermissible in some states, depending on whether the offering complies with state law. Along with the foregoing, the SEC will likely not challenge, as impermissible publicity, routine or ordinary-course corporate communications—such as periodic SEC filings or quarterly earnings releases—that are disseminated for rea sons other than soliciting offers to buy the securities. Companies should be careful, however, to avoid incorporating statements in these public communications that could be regarded by the SEC's staff as a solicitation.

The SEC's Division of Corporation Finance (the SEC staff) has adopted a policy of facilitating registration procedures for foreign issuers to the maximum extent possible. For example, the SEC itself, as well as the staff, has been open to prefiling conferences with foreign issuers contemplating US entry through the public markets. If requested, division staff will conduct a confidential, prefiling review of a foreign issuer's draft registration statement to permit early compliance with staff comments, thereby making it easier for the issuer to coordinate commencement of US and non-US tranches of an international offering. Within the limitations imposed by the SEC's requirements of reconciliation to US GAAP—and, where not inconsistent with protecting investors—the staff has exhibited considerable flexibility during the review and comment process by relaxing some disclosure standards. Unlike securities regulators in some other countries, and indeed in the 50 states of the United States, the SEC staff's review focuses on the adequacy of the disclosures made in the registration statement (of which the prospectus is an integral part) rather than the merits of the offering itself.

Following the SEC's declaration that a registration statement has become effective, both offers and sales may be made to the investing public. Confirmations of sales must be accompanied or preceded by a copy of the final version of the prospectus. Additional written sales literature may be used now, so long as the purchaser receives a copy of the final prospectus. Registrants should bear in mind, again, that restrictive antifraud provisions mandate that no written or oral solicitation may contain any material misstatement or omit information necessary to render the statements actually made not misleading. Fraud in an effective registration statement (that is, the final prospectus) can expose the issuer, directors, underwriters, and persons signing the prospectus, and experts (such as independent accountants) whose reports are used in connection with the prospectus, to a form of "strict" liability for damages.[35]

SEC-mandated registration documents. Because most foreign issuers tapping the US securities markets elect to do so through the establishment of an ADR program, our discussion of the required registration documents will concentrate on ADRs. Except for the requirement of separate registration forms for the ADRs and the deposited securities, respectively, the same principles of registering public offerings as already discussed apply to an offering of any foreign security, whether or not it involves an ADR. For purposes of the Securities Act registration provisions, ADRs and the underlying securities are considered separate securities, with each class of security subject to the registration requirements unless an exemption is available.[36] The ADRs must be registered on a Form F-6, while the deposited securities—if offered to the public—must be registered on one of the several appropriate forms *other* than Form F-6—that is, either Form F-1, F-2, F-3, or F-4.

Form F-6 for ADRs. Form F-6, which can be used by foreign issuers solely to register ADRs under the Securities Act, provides that the issuer of the ADRs is the "legal entity created by the agreement for the issuance of ADRs" for purposes of the act. Even though the depositary signs the registration statement on behalf of that entity, it is not deemed to be an issuer, a person signing the registration statement, or a person controlling the issuer for Securities Act liability purposes.[37] If the ADR program is sponsored—which as discussed is currently the norm in the United States—the foreign issuer of the deposited securities, its principal officers, a majority of the board of directors, and its authorized representative in the United States must also sign the registration statement.[38]

Where ADRs are offered to the public in the United States, the underlying securities themselves must be either registered or exempt from registration under the Securities Act.[39] An ADR holder must also be able to withdraw the deposited securities represented by its ADRs at any time, subject only to: (1) temporary delays caused by closing the transfer books or the deposit of shares in connection with voting at a shareholders' meeting or the payment of dividends; (2) payment of fees, taxes, or similar charges; or (3) compliance with laws relating to ADRs or the withdrawal of deposited securities.[40] Moreover, Form F-6 can be used only if, as of its filing date, the issuer of the deposited securities either is, or is concurrently becoming, a reporting issuer under the Exchange Act or is exempt from the registration and reporting requirements of the Exchange Act by virtue of Rule 12g3-2(b) (discussed in Chapter 4).[41]

The registrant must provide, in the prospectus portion of the Form F-6 registration statement, a description of the ADRs being registered. Notice must also be furnished therein of the availability of information about the issuer of the deposited securities at the SEC.[42] In addition, all fees and charges imposed on the ADR holder must be described.

Registration of deposited securities, ordinary shares, or any other non-ADR security. The four SEC registration forms used to register non-ADR securities of foreign issuers for a public offering in the United States—F-1, F-2, F-3, and F-4—parallel the registration forms used by US issuers for that purpose. Each "F" series form requires disclosure of the basic information regarding the issuer that is prescribed by Form 20-F under the Exchange Act—which, as discussed in the next chapter, is the core document that serves as both the Exchange Act registration statement and the annual report for foreign companies—as well as a detailed description of the terms of the particular offering and the securities being offered. The four forms differ primarily with respect to the amount of information that an issuer need not include in full if the issuer has or is providing it through (commonly referred to under SEC rules as "incorporated by reference from") Form 20-F and any other Exchange Act filings.

To be eligible to use the more streamlined Form F-2 or Form F-3 ("short-forms") to register securities, the issuer must already have been filing Exchange Act periodic reports with the SEC. Eligibility to use either of these two forms is also tied to the size of the issuer, as discussed below. Form F-1 is used by issuers that have never filed reports with the SEC or are otherwise unqualified to register securities on one of the two short forms.

The most streamlined vehicle for Securities Act registration is Form F-3. The SEC recently adopted new rules that lower that form's eligibility thresholds.[43] A foreign issuer that wishes to use this form for a primary or secondary offering for cash need have only a minimum global public float of US $75 million (reduced from $300 million)[44] and a reporting history of 12 months that includes the filing of at least one annual report on Form 20-F (reduced from 36 months). There is no public float condition for using this form to register investment-grade nonconvertible securities, qualified secondary distributions, rights offers, dividend or interest reinvestment plans, conversion of outstanding securities or exercise of outstanding transferable warrants.

Another significant rule change allows foreign issuers registering securities on Form F-3 to use unallocated "shelf" registration to the same extent as US issuers. Accordingly, qualified foreign issuers now have the financing flexibility to register debt, equity, and other securities on a single registration statement without having to specify the amount of each class of securities to be "taken down from the shelf," or offered, in the future. Like US issuers, however, non-US issuers using this mechanism must disclose both the specified types and the aggregate dollar amount of securities that may be offered.

Form F-3 calls for information concerning: (1) the offering, including the plan of distribution, use of proceeds, description of securities, and risk factors; (2) the issuer, through reference to the information set forth in its latest and future Exchange Act annual reports on Form 20-F and, if appropriate, Form 6-K under the Exchange Act; (3) material changes in the issuer's affairs since the latest annual report; and (4) financial statements of any business acquired or to be acquired by the issuer.

Form F-2 may be used to register securities to be offered in transactions other than an exchange of securities with another issuer (which must proceed under Form F-4[45]). This form's eligibility requirements are similar to those of Form F-3, except that the issuer must have been filing Exchange Act reports for 36 months, and all periodic reports referred to in the form must be delivered with the prospectus. A three-year reporting history is unnecessary if the issuer has a worldwide public float of US $75 million, is a reporting company, and has filed at least one annual report with the SEC. Nor is a three-year reporting history required if the issuer intends to offer only investment-grade, nonconvertible debt securities.

Form F-1 is available to register all securities of foreign private issuers except those used as consideration for an exchange offer (which as noted must be registered on Form F-4) and has the same informational requirements as Forms F-2 and F-3. There is one critical difference: All information must be included in the F-1 prospectus to be delivered to each prospective buyer, since reference to information disclosed in SEC periodic reports is not allowed. For this reason, Form F-1 is typically used for initial public offerings into the United States.

Forms F-1, F-2, and F-3 each include requirements for the filing of certified financial statements that either comply with or are reconciled to US GAAP. As explained in full in the next chapter, two reconciliation standards are defined in Exchange Act Form 20-F: Item 17, which is the least restrictive method since reconciliation is limited to certain measurable items, and Item 18, which compels full reconciliation of all primary and supplemental financial statement disclosures. While registrants filing annual reports on Form 20-F may choose between the two methods, registrants that lack a US reporting history, and thus are consigned to Form F-1, must furnish Item 18 financial statements. Form F-2 registrants likewise must reconcile their financial statements to US GAAP in accordance with Item 18, except in connection with an offering of investment-grade securities. Given their ability to rely on information reported in their Forms 20-F, Form F-3 registrants need only provide Item 17 financial statements unless they voluntarily elect to comply with Item 18. SEC restrictions on the age of financial statements included in foreign issuers' Securities Act registration statements, whether or not incorporated through Form 20-F, were recently relaxed substantially, as noted in Chapter 4.

The multijurisdictional disclosure system (MJDS) adopted for Canadian issuers allows eligible Canadian companies to register securities under the Securities Act and to register securities and report under the Exchange Act by filing with the SEC documents prepared in accordance with Canadian requirements.[46]   Special registration forms, to which a Canadian prospectus is attached for filing as a single registration statement with the SEC, are available to specified Canadian issuers for registering offerings of equity, debt, and other securities, as well as rights offers, exchange offers, and mergers or other business combinations. Reconciliation of Canadian financial statements to US GAAP is nonetheless required. Canadian registrants using MJDS forms may not invoke the unallocated shelf procedures now available to foreign issuers eligible to use Form F-3.

Exchange Act Reporting

As discussed in greater detail in the following chapter, a foreign issuer that makes a public offering of ADRs or any other class of securities in the United States and/or lists those securities on a national securities exchange or procures their quotation in NASDAQ becomes subject to the periodic reporting requirements of the Exchange Act.[47]   A foreign issuer whose equity securities have not been offered to the US public or listed but which are traded in the OTC market may either: (1) comply with the periodic reporting requirements under the Exchange Act; (2) if the issuer has *more* than 300 shareholders in the United States (and more than 500 worldwide and more than $5 million in total assets), establish and maintain a reporting exemption by furnishing information to the SEC under Rule 12g3-2(b); or (3) if the issuer has fewer than 300 shareholders in the United States, rely on an automatic exemption from reporting.[48]

PRIVATE PLACEMENTS IN THE UNITED STATES

Section 4(2) of the Securities Act provides the principal alternative to registration of securities by exempting private placements from the Securities Act's registration requirements.[49] Regulation D, adopted by the SEC to provide guidance in the form of a "safe harbor" for private placements,[50] sets forth a specific set of conditions under which an offering will not be deemed a public offering subject to registration under the act.[51]

Rule 144A also provides a nonexclusive safe harbor from the registration requirements of the Securities Act for specified resales of restricted securities to and among qualified institutional buyers (QIBs). Based on the theory that sophisticated institutional investors do not require the protection of the Securities Act registration requirements, the rule was adopted in 1990 chiefly to encourage foreign issuers to add a US tranche to multinational securities offerings without incurring the substantial costs of SEC registration. By making a private placement in the United States in order to render the securities eligible for institutional resales under Rule 144A, issuers are able to ensure the liquidity demanded by many institutional buyers without bearing the expense, delay, and other burdens typically associated with public offerings.

Securities sold in a private placement are regarded as restricted, and thus may not be resold immediately in the public secondary markets in the United States unless an exemption is available.[52] Rule 144A under the Securities Act provides a safe harbor that permits limited resales into the public market after a two-year holding period and unlimited resales after a three-year holding period.[53] Resales of restricted securities to and among institutions are also permitted under the provisions of Rule 144A, which will be discussed later in this chapter. In contrast, securities sold outside the United States in accordance with the SEC's Regulation S safe harbors for distributions and resale transactions, respectively, are *not* deemed restricted for US resale purposes so long as they have been held offshore for a prescribed period following the initial, non-US distribution. The Regulation S safe harbors, which are available to foreign and US issuers as well as to persons reselling their securities outside the territorial boundaries of the United States, are addressed in a later section of this chapter.

Section 4(2) of the Securities Act: The "Traditional" Private Placement

Section 4(2) of the Securities Act generally exempts from registration under the act "transactions by an issuer not involving any public offering." As first articulated by the US Supreme Court, this exemption rests on the general principle that the disclosure prescribed by the act is unnecessary for those prospective purchasers with sufficient financial sophistication and access to relevant information to enable them to "fend for themselves."[54]

Subsequent judicial and administrative interpretations of Section 4(2) have given rise to an analysis based on numerous factors for determination of whether an issuer may rely on the private placement exemption. Since they ultimately bear the burden of proving that they qualify for the exemption, issuers planning a private offering in the United States must consider the following: the nature and sophistication of the offerees; their relationship to the issuer (e.g., employment or familial); their access to information about the issuer and the securities that would otherwise have been delineated in a Securities Act registration statement; the absence of any general advertising or solicitation of offers; and the presence of certain representations, covenants, and procedures designed to prevent resale of the unregistered securities by the initial purchasers to persons who lack the requisite sophistication and/or superior informational access prescribed by Section 4(2).

The issuer's private placement exemption could be lost if the original purchaser subsequently sold the privately placed securities to the public without registration or an exemption from registration. In this case, the original purchaser could be found—either by the court or by the SEC in an administrative proceeding—to be a statutory "underwriter," a person who took the securities from the issuer with a view toward distribution,[55] causing the resale of the securities and possibly the original sale of securities by the issuer, in violation of Sections 5 and 12(1) of the Securities Act.

To protect its Section 4(2) exemption, the issuer of securities in a Section 4(2) private placement will require all initial purchasers to represent that they are acquiring the securities for investment purposes only and not with a view toward distributing the securities to the public. Such purchasers must also represent that they are sophisticated investors capable of evaluating the merits and demerits of the transaction and of bearing the economic risks of investment. Given the specter of strict liability for a Section 5 violation should a private placement fail to qualify for the 4(2) exemption,[56] issuers normally impose a combination of the following: (1) restrictions on resales unless the securities are registered under the Securities Act or covered by an exemption; (2) "stop transfer" provisions that bar transfers without evidence of compliance with the Securities Act; (3) legends on the certificates representing the securities that spell out the transfer restrictions; and (4) a prominent description of resale restrictions in the accompanying offering materials.

Even where the Section 4(2) exemption applies, the issuer and other participants could be held liable for fraud in connection with the offer or sale of unregistered securities in the original issuance (and perhaps in the secondary markets) under the Securities Act. Yet another possible source of liability for fraud in the issuer's sale of unregistered securities, as well as their resale by a purchaser in the private placement, is the potent combination of Section 10(b) of the Exchange Act and its implementing regulation, SEC Rule 10b-5. Both the SEC and investors may sue under these provisions, as discussed in greater depth in the next chapter. Since early 1995, however, issuers and other sellers no longer face the specter of negligence liability for material misstatements or omissions[57] made in a private placement-offering circular or prospectus.

Regulation D

Although years of actual practice have led to the development of detailed standard procedures and documentation to reduce much of the uncertainty for those issuers wishing to rely on the Section 4(2) exemption, the SEC adopted Regulation D in 1982 to give additional guidance to issuers using this exemption. Regulation D provides three limited safe harbors, with the one most commonly invoked codified in Rule 506 under Section 4(2). Failure to comply with the requirements of Regulation D, as discussed, will not preclude the issuer from being deemed to have made a valid private placement under Section 4(2).[58] In practice, many issuers making a private placement comply with the Regulation D requirements without attempting formally to qualify for any of the three available safe harbors.

Rule 506 of Regulation D forms the basis for most private placements by issuers attempting to qualify for the Section 4(2) exemption. Offers and sales may be made under this safe harbor to an unlimited number of "accredited investors"—defined as most institutions and certain individual purchasers who meet specified net worth or income tests—along with 35 other purchasers who, either alone or in combination with their representatives, must be "reasonably" believed by the issuer to have "such knowledge and experience in financial and business matters that each is capable of evaluating the merits and risks of his prospective investment."

Foreign issuers should be aware that purchasers of securities offered and sold outside the United States in accordance with Regulation S will not affect the count of coincident offers and sales of the same securities made in the United States in accordance with Regulation D. That is, persons who purchased securities sold abroad under Regulation S would not be included in the number of purchasers calculated for Regulation D purposes.[59]

Other conditions that must be met to qualify for the Rule 506 safe harbor are as follows:

1. Limitation on the Manner of Offering. Neither the issuer nor any person acting on its behalf may offer or sell the securities using any form of general solicitation or general advertising, including (but not limited to) the following:

   a. Any advertisement, article, notice, or other communication published in any newspaper, magazine, or similar media or broadcast over television or radio.

   b. Any seminar or meeting whose attendees have been invited by any general solicitation or general advertising.[60]

   As a well-known commentator has observed, an issuer engaged in the private placement of equity securities, or securities convertible into equity, may find itself with two conflicting responsibilities: a duty to inform its existing shareholders of the dilutive effect of the offering and the need to comply with the Regulation D prohibition against general solicitation or advertising activities that might destroy the safe harbor and, ultimately, even the underlying Section 4(2) exemption.[61] Although the SEC has offered some guidance with respect to announcements in the United States of offshore offerings under Regulation S,[62] there is little comfort on this question in the context of US private offerings.

2. Information Requirements. Regulation D does not require the delivery of any information to accredited investors[63] although there are informational delivery requirements applicable to nonaccredited purchasers. The type of disclosure to be furnished to nonaccredited purchasers prior to the sale of the unregistered securities is dependent on whether the issuer is subject to the reporting requirements of the Exchange Act. For securities offerings in excess of $7,500,000, issuers must provide nonaccredited investors with financial statements that would be required in a registration statement filed under the Securities Act.[64] A foreign issuer eligible to use Form 20-F must disclose the same information required in a registration statement filed under the Securities Act.[65]

   Information provided to any offeree, whether accredited or nonaccredited, must comply with the general antifraud provisions of the Securities Act and the Exchange Act. Accordingly, information given to any investor may not be materially false or misleading.

3. SEC Filing. Any issuer offering securities in reliance upon Regulation D must file a Form D with the SEC within 15 days of the first sale of securities. Form D requires disclosure of information about the issuer, including the names of its executive officers and directors and beneficial owners of 10 percent or more of any class of its equity securities. Certain offering information is also mandated, most notably the offering price, the minimum investment permitted, jurisdictions in which purchasers have been or will be solicited, identities of persons receiving compensation for soliciting purchasers, the number of accredited and nonaccredited investors participating and the size of their respective purchases, and the proposed use of the offering proceeds.

Because the form is a public document, the necessity of disclosing price and volume information may discourage some issuers from using Regulation D. Failure to file a Form D will not technically disqualify an otherwise valid Regulation D offering but may preclude subsequent reliance on any of its three safe harbors.

4. Limitations on Resale. Any securities acquired under Rule 506 of Regulation D are restricted and thus cannot be resold in the United States without registration under the Securities Act or an exemption from registration.[66] An issuer must "exercise reasonable care to assure that the purchasers of the securities are not [statutory] underwriters" whose resale of the securities could cause the issuer to lose the benefits of both the Section 4(2) exemption and the Rule 506 safe harbor thereunder.[67]

Rule 144A—Private Placement

Rule 144A provides a nonexclusive safe harbor from the registration requirements of the Securities Act for specified resales of restricted securities to and among qualified institutional buyers.[68] Available for institutional resales of securities of both US and foreign issuers, the rule has enabled US institutions to participate in primary offerings of foreign securities made directly in the United States, rather than pursue investment opportunities offshore at presumably higher transactional costs, by affording issuers greater assurance that their Section 4(2) exemption will not be destroyed by subsequent public resales of the unregistered securities. Or, as explained in a well-known treatise, "Rule 144A affects the entire US private placement process because it clarifies and codifies the theory behind permissible resales and permits the simplification of procedures applicable both to original placements and resales, and thus can increase the marketability of the securities on original issuance."[69]

Generally, securities eligible for resale under Rule 144A are initially sold by issuers to dealers and other QIBs in private placements in reliance upon Section 4(2) or Regulation D of the Securities Act.[70] Rule 144A may also be used by a foreign issuer that wishes to offer, through a dealer, a private US tranche of ADRs as part of a public offering being made offshore under the terms of Regulation S.[71] Once the private placement is completed, the QIBs can resell Rule 144A securities immediately to other QIBs in the United States without waiting the two to three years that normally must elapse before they can legally resell restricted securities acquired in a private placement into the US public markets.[72]

Cautionary statements by the SEC's staff suggest that securities purchased offshore under Regulation S cannot be resold to QIBs in the United States in reliance upon Rule 144A. Instead, US resales of the Regulation S securities would either have to be registered or covered by another exemption from registration.[73]

From a practical standpoint, a Rule 144A offering is usually the preferred method of raising capital in the United States for a foreign issuer that is not in a position to register with the SEC or that is making a worldwide global offering and wishes to sell a relatively small amount in the United States (generally valued at between $30 million and $50 million).[74] Some foreign issuers employ a Rule 144A offering as a means of entering US capital markets with the intent of subsequently seeking an SRO listing of a *different* class of securities (as explained below, Rule 144A precludes the creation of a "side-by-side" public market for securities offered under that Rule through an SRO listing) or of conducting an SEC-registered exchange offer using the privately placed securities as consideration.

Key advantages of a private placement tailored to permit QIBs resales under Rule 144A are the relative speed and efficiency with which the resale can be cleared. In most circumstances, the process consumes no more than two to three months, and the cost is lower than that typically incurred in connection with a registered public offering.[75] Conversely, the major disadvantages of a Rule 144A offering are the expected risks that the issuer could lose the original offering exemption because some noncomplying resale transactions have taken place and the constraints on resale to non-QIBs that in some instances may compel a substantial discount of the offering price.

Trends in the Rule 144A placement market.   Since its adoption in April 1990, Rule 144A has attracted significant numbers of foreign companies to the US securities markets. During the period from adoption through December 31, 1993, $25.631 billion worth of securities of (or relating to) 300 foreign issuers (including securities of US issuers that are guaranteed by foreign entities) have been sold in 330 Rule 144A placements.[76] This accounts for approximately 28 percent of the gross dollar amount of securities sold in the United States through Rule 144A placements and about 48 percent of all companies whose securities have been sold in Rule 144A placements.[77]

Rule 144A placements have consistently been used to offer and sell foreign common equity securities on a private basis in the United States.[78] As of the close of 1993, there had been 157 Rule 144A placements totaling $6.863 billion involving the common equity securities of 168 foreign issuers. By comparison, only one US issuer sold common equity securities ($250,000 worth) through a Rule 144A placement during the same period.[79] Finally, the volume of Rule 144A placements by foreign issuers increased substantially in 1993 after remaining stagnant in 1992 and 1991. There were 181 Rule 144A placements for $14.8 billion of securities of foreign issuers, as compared with 60 Rule 144A placements for $4.3 billion of securities in 1992.[80]

Rule 144A has frequently been used by both US and foreign issuers of investment-grade debt securities. However, Rule 144A placements are being increasingly used for offerings of noninvestment-grade debt securities of US companies and, to a lesser extent, foreign companies. There have been 138 Rule 144A placements of noninvestment-grade debt securities, with 116 placements for $18.287 billion of securities of US issuers and 22 placements involving $3.168 billion of securities of foreign issuers.[81]

Insurance companies and investment companies are the major overall purchasers of securities offered in Rule 144A placements. Investment companies are the principal purchasers of Rule 144A-eligible common equity securities, preferred equity securities, and convertible or exchangeable debt securities. Insurance companies are the principal purchasers of asset-backed securities and, along with investment companies, buy most of the nonconvertible debt securities offered in Rule 144A placements.[82]

To put these data in perspective, the private placement market comprises a fairly small portion of total US securities financing activity. For example, even though the dollar volume of Rule 144A placements in-

creased more than 200 percent from almost $18 billion in 1992 to almost
$60 billion in 1993,[83] the total number of Rule 144A offerings consum-
mated since 1990 still constituted less than 5 percent of all registered offerings over the same period.[84] According to the SEC, despite the attractiveness to foreign issuers of Rule 144A as an alternative method of
offering equity securities in the United States,

> registered offerings are overwhelmingly the favorite means to raise equity
> capital [in the United States]. Registered equity offerings by foreign issuers
> increased by more than 50 percent last year [1993] to more than 12 1/2 times
> the amount of Rule 144A equity placements by foreign issuers.[85]

Requirements of Rule 144A. Central to an understanding of
Rule 144A are its Preliminary Notes, which supplement the formal conditions to be met for reliance on this safe harbor, allowing resales among
qualified institutions. These notes follow, in full below, with bracketed
commentary from the author:

1. This rule relates solely to the application of Section 5 of the [Se-
   curities] Act and not to antifraud or other provisions of the federal
   securities laws.

   [In other words, the antifraud provisions of the federal securities
   laws still apply to all Rule 144A transactions.]

2. Attempted compliance with this section does not act as an exclusive election; any seller hereunder may also claim the availability
   of any other applicable exemption from the registration requirements of the Act.

   [Thus, an institutional seller may also rely on the statutory exemptions available for sales by persons other than the issuer or a
   dealer (Section 4(1) of the Securities Act), or sales by a dealer
   (Section 4(3) of the Securities Act).]

3. In view of the objective of this section and the policies underlying the Act, this section is not available with respect to any transaction or series of transactions that, although in technical compliance with this section, is part of a plan or scheme to evade the
   registration provisions of the Act. In such cases, registration under the Act is required.

4. Nothing in this section obviates the need for any issuer or any
   other person to comply with the securities registration or broker-
   dealer registration requirements of the Securities Exchange Act of
   1934 (Exchange Act), whenever such requirements are applicable.

[In the case of an issuer, once the number of holders of Rule 144A equity securities reaches or exceeds 300 and the issuer has more than 500 holders of such securities worldwide and more than $5 million in total assets, the issuer must register those securities with the SEC under Section 12 of the Exchange Act. Exchange Act registration requirements are discussed in the next chapter.]

5. Nothing in this section obviates the need for any person to comply with any applicable state law relating to the offer or sale of securities.

   [Issuers, underwriters, and other persons selling the Rule 144A securities must ensure that the offering and subsequent resales comply with, or qualify for an exemption from, applicable state "blue-sky" laws.]

6. Securities acquired in a transaction made pursuant to the provisions of this section are deemed to be 'restricted securities' within the meaning of Rule 144(a)(3)."[86]

   [Accordingly, resales of these securities in the United States must conform to Rule 144 or otherwise qualify for an exemption from registration, or may be effected offshore in compliance with the conditions of Regulation S.]

7. The fact that purchasers of securities from the issuer thereof may purchase such securities with a view to reselling such securities pursuant to this section will not affect the availability to such issuer of an exemption under section 4(2) of the Act, or Regulation D under the Act, from the registration requirements of the Act.[87]

There are four basic requirements for compliance with Rule 144A. First, the seller or any person acting on behalf of the seller must reasonably believe that offerees and purchasers of the securities are QIBs.[88] Rule 144A(d) provides that the seller or person acting on the seller's behalf may rely on the following methods of determining whether the prospective purchaser is a QIB: (1) a certification by the chief financial officer or other executive officer of the purchaser stating that QIB qualification standards have been met; (2) the most recent publicly available financial statements; (3) the most recent publicly available information appearing in a recognized securities manual; and (4) the most recent publicly available information appearing in documents filed with the SEC, another US governmental agency, a foreign governmental agency, or an SRO.

The second condition for qualification for the Rule 144A resale exemption requires the seller and any person acting on its behalf to take "reasonable steps" to notify purchasers that the seller may be relying on Rule 144A.[89] This condition can be satisfied by placing a legend on the confirmation of sale or by including statements in the private placement memorandum reflecting reliance on Rule 144A.

Third, to prevent the development of a "side-by-side" private market for securities traded in the US public markets, thereby siphoning trading volume away from the public markets to the potential detriment of non-QIB investors, any Rule 144A security to be offered or sold must be "non-fungible." In other words, the Rule 144A safe harbor is not available for the offer or sale of securities that, when issued, would be of the same class as securities listed on a national securities exchange or quoted in an automated US interdealer quotation system (which includes NASDAQ but excludes the NASD's OTC Electronic Bulletin Board Service and the pink sheet market).[90] ADRs that are traded on a US exchange or NASDAQ are considered fungible with the underlying securities on deposit and therefore cannot be offered or sold under Rule 144A if the underlying securities are listed on the US stock exchanges or quoted in the NASDAQ non-OTC markets. One commentator points out that foreign securities traded on a non-US exchange or other offshore market can qualify as Rule 144A securities provided, again, that securities of the same class are *not* traded on the facilities of a US stock exchange or quoted in NASDAQ.[91]

Common equity securities will be considered to be of the same class as equity securities offered under Rule 144A if they are of substantially similar character with regard to dividends, voting rights, and liquidation, thus giving the holders substantially similar rights and privileges. Convertible securities and warrants will be treated as part of the same class as the underlying security unless the effective conversion or exercise premium, respectively, is 10 percent or more or (in the case of warrants) unless the warrants are nonexercisable for three years.[92] Debt securities offered under Rule 144A will be deemed part of the same class as other debt securities of the issuer if terms relating to interest rate, maturity, subordination, security, convertibility call, and redemption are substantially identical. However, nonconvertible preferred and debt securities viewed as different series will generally be treated as nonfungible classes of securities for Rule 144A purposes.[93]

The fourth, or informational, requirement of Rule 144A applies primarily where an issuer is neither filing periodic reports with the SEC nor supplying home-country disclosures to the SEC under the Exchange Act exemption from registration and reporting secured by Rule 12g3-2(b) (discussed in next chapter).[94] In either circumstance, the issuer must promise to provide, upon request, certain basic financial information to the holder of a Rule 144A security or any prospective purchaser of that security designated by the holder.[95] Such information must be "reasonably current"[96] and must encompass the following: (1) a very brief statement of the nature of the issuer's business and the products and services offered; (2) the most recent balance sheet and profit and loss and retained earnings statements; and (3) similar financial statements for such part of the two preceding fiscal years during which the issuer has been in operation.[97]

Typically, the issuer of Rule 144A-eligible securities will disseminate an offering circular to prospective buyers that describes the company and factors relevant to the offering and presents certain financial information.[98] Subject to the standards set forth in the Rule, the nature and scope of financial data supplied in a Rule 144A offering are negotiated by the investment banker and the offeror and are usually prepared in accordance with the home country's accounting principles.[99] It has become standard practice, however, to include in a circular a narrative description of the differences between the home-country accounting principles and US GAAP. Additionally, the offering circular will often include the same management's discussion and analysis (MD&A) that would normally be part of a prospectus.

A Rule 144A offering may expose the issuer, as well as the broker-dealer or other seller furnishing the information, to liability for fraud under Exchange Act Section 10(b) and Rule 10b-5 thereunder. A recent decision by the US Supreme Court indicates, however, that Securities Act liability for negligent misrepresentations or omissions will no longer attach to such offerings.[100]

The Application of the SEC's Trading Practices Rules

The SEC has issued a series of antimanipulation rules under the Exchange Act that apply to both public and private offerings made in the United States, as well as to those made abroad; for example, in the case of a multinational offering with a US tranche. Known as the "trading practices rules," Rules 10b-6, 10b-7, and 10b-8 under the Exchange Act are intended to protect investors from purchasing securities at a price that has been artificially raised or supported by persons having a significant interest in the success of the offering.

Rule 10b-6 is designed to prevent persons participating in a securities *distribution*[101] from artificially conditioning the market to stimulate demand for the securities and to protect the integrity of the securities trading market as an independent pricing mechanism.[102] These twin goals are accomplished by prohibiting persons participating in a distribution from bidding on or purchasing—or inducing others to purchase—the securities being distributed (or any security of the same class and series as the security being distributed or any right to purchase that security) until their involvement in the distribution has ceased.[103] Certain exceptions to this general prohibition may be invoked by the issuer or other participant to permit an orderly distribution to occur or to limit disruption of the trading market for the securities being distributed. Two of these exceptions to Rule 10b-6's general ban are the specified stabilizing practices allowed by Rule 10b-7 and the rights transactions specifically permitted by Rule 10b-8.

First, Rule 10b-7 renders illegal any stabilizing bid made to facilitate an offering of a security *except* for the purpose of preventing or retarding a decline in the open market price of the security.[104] The rule establishes the price level at which a permissible stabilizing bid may be entered and sets the priority for execution of independent bids at times when a stabilizing bid has been entered.[105] In addition, it regulates the number of stabilizing bids that an underwriting syndicate may enter into within any single market and the entry of stabilizing bids on markets other than the principal market for the security being stabilized. Rule 10b-7 also requires that notice be given that the market is being or will be stabilized.[106]

Second, Rule 10b-8 applies to any person participating in a distribution of securities being offered through rights on a *pro rata* basis to existing shareholders. This rule permits rights offerings to proceed subject to specified restrictions on the price at which the securities being distributed (or securities of the same class and series), may be offered or sold.[107]

Private placements by foreign issuers under Rule 144A are clearly subject to the trading practices rules. In prior years, when foreign securities were offered in the United States as part of a multinational distribution, the resultant applicability of Rules 10b-6, 10b-7, and 10b-8 often compelled the issuer and other distribution participants to cease marketing activities in the securities in their principal trading markets outside the

United States pending completion of the US distribution.[108] Some market participants therefore believed that the developing Rule 144A securities market could not achieve its full potential because foreign issuers were reluctant to add a US tranche to multinational offerings and thereby trigger the extraterritorial application of the trading practices rules.[109] SEC efforts to accommodate foreign trading practices by granting exemptions on both an individual transaction basis and a class basis did not suffice to ameliorate these concerns.

Accordingly, the SEC adopted new exceptions to the trading practices rules in 1993 to facilitate Rule 144A distributions of foreign securities to QIBs. Market-making activities could thereby proceed in all jurisdictions, including the United States, without compliance with the trading practices rules during distributions of foreign securities eligible for Rule 144A resales if the securities were offered and sold in the United States to QIBs (or persons reasonably believed to be QIBs) in transactions exempt from registration under Securities Act Section 4(2), Rule 144A, or Regulation D.[110] However, the SEC warned that these new exceptions could not be invoked to insulate distribution participants from liability for violations of the general antifraud and antimanipulation provisions of the federal securities laws, including Sections 9(a) and 10(b) and Rule 10b-5 of the Exchange Act, and Section 17(a) of the Securities Act.[111]

In adopting the 1993 exceptions to the trading practices rules for Rule 144A offerings, the SEC stated that the potential applicability of the exceptions to a multitranche offering would not affect the determination of whether that offering in the aggregate was of sufficient magnitude to be deemed a distribution for purposes of Rule 10b-6. For an offering made simultaneously in the United States to QIBs (under Rule 144A) and to institutional accredited investors (under Regulation D), for example, all of the securities sold in the United States must be added together for purposes of determining whether there is a Rule 10b-6 distribution, even though the portion involving a Rule 144A distribution may be excepted from the rule.[112] But, under the reasoning outlined in the latest rule changes, securities offered and sold by the issuer to QIBs in the United States under Rule 144A, and abroad in a concurrent Regulation S offering, must be aggregated to determine whether a distribution exists for purposes of Rule 10b-6. Critics thus complained that the utility of the new Rule 144A exceptions would be greatly diminished by applying the trading practices rules to transactions of this type.

Again proving itself responsive to legitimate issuer concerns in this area, the SEC's staff in early 1994 extended the availability of the new exceptions to:

> permit bids, purchases, and inducements to purchase the Rule 144A-eligible foreign security being distributed, any security of the same class and series, or any right to purchase such security (collectively, "related securities") by distribution participants and their affiliated purchasers when such Rule 144A-eligible foreign security or related security is offered or sold in transactions in compliance with Regulation S to Specified Non-US Persons during a concurrent Rule 144A QIB Distribution of the Rule 144A-eligible foreign security.[113]

Significant developments in the securities markets and in distribution practices that have transformed the US capital-raising process—including the expanded role of institutional investors, new trading instruments and strategies, enhanced transparency of securities transactions, expanded surveillance capabilities, and globalization of the markets—recently prompted the SEC to publish a concept release announcing that it was beginning a comprehensive review of the trading practices rules.[114] Although numerous questions are posed in the release, no changes have yet been proposed. The SEC indicated in the release that it intends to study comments submitted by members of the public in response to these questions to determine whether additional modifications of existing regulations are necessary.

REGULATION S: SAFE HARBOR FOR PRIMARY AND SECONDARY OFFSHORE TRANSACTIONS

Regulation S, which was adopted in 1990 concurrently with Rule 144A, clarifies the SEC's position on the extraterritorial scope of the registration requirements of the Securities Act and creates primary and resale safe harbors for issuers, distributors, and other persons wishing to offer or sell securities outside the United States.[115] By thus codifying a territorial approach to enforcement of the act, the set of rules that make up the new regulation establishes the principle that "registration of securities is intended to protect the US capital markets and investors purchasing in the US market, whether US or foreign nationals,"[116] but does not extend to US citizens who reside and buy securities in another country. This approach thus reflects the SEC's realization that well-established principles of comity and the reasonable expectations of participants in the global markets justify reliance on the laws of the jurisdiction where a securities transaction takes place.[117]   Although the General Statement portion of Regulation S says that the registration requirements of the Securities Act do not apply to offers or sales of securities that occur beyond the boundaries of the United States, the SEC explicitly declined to circumscribe the extraterritorial reach of either the antifraud provisions of the federal securities laws or state laws relating to the offer and sale of securities. Nor does Regulation S protect offshore transactions that, while in technical compliance with its terms and conditions, in reality are part of a plan or scheme to avoid registration.[118]

Conditions for Eligibility Under Regulation S

At least in theory, issuers of securities offshore could rely solely on the SEC's position in the Regulation S General Statement that non-US offerings are outside the scope of Section 5 of the Securities Act and therefore need not be registered. Because few issuers and other sellers are willing to risk violating Section 5, however, most structure their transactions to qualify for one of the two safe harbors embodied in Regulation S. The "issuer" safe harbor applies to offshore offers and sales by issuers, distributors, their respective affiliates (other than certain affiliated officers and directors), and persons acting on behalf of any of the foregoing. The "resale" safe harbor covers resales abroad by persons other than those eligible to rely upon the issuer safe harbor.

Two general conditions must be fulfilled to take advantage of either the issuer and resale safe harbors. First, any offer or sale must be made in an "offshore transaction." No offers or resales made in the United States, of course, can be considered offshore transactions. The buyer must be (or the seller must reasonably believe that the buyer is) offshore at the origination of the buy order. This particular requirement can be met for purposes of the issuer safe harbor if the sale is made in, on, or through a physical trading floor of an established foreign securities exchange or, for purposes of the resale safe harbor, if the sale is made in, on, or through the facilities of a designated organized foreign securities market and the transaction is not prearranged with a buyer in the United States.

The second general condition is that no *directed selling efforts* may be made in the United States in connection with an offer or sale of securities. Directed selling efforts are defined as activities undertaken for the purpose of, or that could reasonably be expected to have the effect of, conditioning the market in the United States for any of the securities being offered, sold (issuer safe harbor), or resold (resale safe harbor) in reliance on Regulation S.[119]

An important concept under Regulation S is that of a "US person." For purposes of this regulation, the term *US person* refers to any person resident in the United States.[120] Residence, rather than citizenship, primarily determines such status: a US citizen who resides in China is not a US person, whereas a Chinese citizen who is a resident of the United States will be deemed a US person. Certain refinements of this concept for institutions and other purchasers that are not natural persons enable offers and sales to be made to US broker-dealers or investment advisers managing discretionary accounts for the benefit of non-US persons without themselves being deemed a US person.[121] Similarly, a corporation or partnership owned by US persons but organized under the laws of a foreign country itself will not be a US person, so long as the entity has not been created principally to invest in unregistered securities.[122]

Issuer safe harbor. The issuer safe harbor is divided into three categories of securities offerings, based upon factors such as the issuer's reporting status and nationality and the risk that the issuer's securities will flow back into the United States. Category 1 is the least restrictive of the three, since it encompasses securities for which there is a minimal prospect of flowback because there is not much interest among US investors in the class of securities to be offered or sold abroad. If the issuer meets one of several detailed, objective tests for ascertaining that US market interest is unlikely to exist, the offering will qualify for the safe harbor as long as the two general conditions previously outlined are met. The offering must be an offshore transaction, and it must be unaccompanied by any directed selling efforts in the United States. Securities falling within category 1 may be resold immediately in the United States and will not be deemed restricted securities.

Category 2 covers offerings of securities of both foreign and US reporting issuers, offerings of debt securities, asset-backed securities, and specified preferred stock of nonreporting foreign issuers *with a substantial US market interest*. In addition to the two basic Regulation S conditions (an offshore transaction and no US directed selling efforts), category 2 offerings must satisfy transactional restrictions intended to ensure that the securities come to rest offshore: The securities may not be offered or sold to or for the benefit or account of a US person for a period of 40 days from the later of the date of closing or the date the first offer of securities is made to persons other than a distributor participating in the offering.[123] Issuers and distributors relying on the category 2 safe harbor further must "ensure (by whatever means they choose) that any nondistributor to whom they sell securities is a non-US person and is not purchasing for the account or benefit of a US person."[124] To this end, an issuer must incorporate cautionary legends regarding the restrictions in its offering documents, obtain written assurances from participants in the offering that they will comply with all category 2 restrictions, and provide confirmation notices specified to securities professionals that the restrictions are being complied with.

Category 3, the most restrictive of the issuer safe harbors because of a heightened potential for US flowback, includes any offers or sales of securities not encompassed within the first two categories. Among the types of offerings in this category are distributions of equity securities by nonreporting issuers in which there is a substantial US market interest. Additional restrictions superimposed on those prescribed by category 2, which also apply here, are a one-year foreign holding period for equity securities, the use of a temporary global security for debt offerings, certain stop-transfer procedures for equity offerings, purchaser undertakings to resell equity securities in compliance with Regulation S or otherwise in compliance with the Securities Act, and certifications by the purchaser that the securities are not being purchased by or for the account of a US person.

Despite the numerous constraints on securities offerings falling within the second and third categories, securities that have been acquired by a purchaser in such offerings could arguably be resold in the United States prior to expiration of the specified offshore holding period if the purchaser is unaffiliated with the issuer or any other participant in the foreign distribution. Since these securities will be deemed restricted until the particular offshore holding period expires, however, their US resale would have to be registered under the Securities Act or qualify for exemptive treatment under Section 4(2), Rule 144A, or Regulation D. Assuming an otherwise valid Regulation S primary offering under either category 2 or category 3, private, nonaffiliate resales into the United States of such securities are not prudent at least until the pertinent restricted period (40 days or one year, respectively) expires.

Securities that flow back into the United States will not be regarded as restricted if acquired in a category 1 offering, or if they have previously been held abroad for the requisite period following their acquisition in an offering made under category 2 or category 3. Even assuming the validity of the issuer's Regulation S exemption and the unrestricted status of the securities purchased in the issuance, any offshore purchaser contemplating resale into the United States must have his or her own exemption from Securities Act registration for this transaction—usually the statutory exemption available for secondary trading activities.[125] Caution should also be exercised in reselling these securities in the United States if there is any doubt as to whether the securities were part of an issuance that, while technically in compliance with the applicable Regulation S issuer safe harbor, nevertheless may have been the product of a wrongful scheme or plan to avoid Securities Act registration. In such instances, there is a risk that the SEC later may sue any participant in the issuance for violations of Section 5 and possibly the antifraud provisions of the federal securities laws.

Resale safe harbor. A separate safe harbor is available to persons other than issuers and distributors (but including certain officers and directors of either) who wish to resell unregistered securities outside the United States.[126] As noted, such secondary market transactions need only comply with the two general conditions described above. The resale safe harbor may also be invoked by dealers and persons receiving selling concessions subject to additional conditions.

Interplay of Regulation S and Rule 144A

The close interrelationship of Regulation S and Rule 144A has been the subject of considerable commentary.[127] The SEC stated in the release announcing the adoption of Regulation S that "legitimate selling activities . . . in connection with the sale of securities in compliance with Rule 144A . . . generally will not result in [disqualifying Regulation S] directed selling efforts."[128] Accordingly, issuers may undertake private placements in the United States at the same time that they are making an offshore Regulation S offering without violating that Regulation's prohibition against US directed selling efforts. Substantial care must nevertheless be taken to avoid spillover of such securities into the US public markets, thereby resulting in a Section 5 violation.

Commentators likewise have argued that securities acquired offshore in a Regulation S issuer offering may be resold under Rule 144A to QIBs in the United States—regardless of whether the original offshore holding period has expired—without the delay and other restrictions characteristic of the "traditional" Section 4(2) private placement. However, as previously discussed in this section (pages 75–77), public statements by the SEC's staff suggest that use of this approach by either a foreign or US issuer could violate Section 5 of the Securities Act. Pending clarification by the SEC or its staff, such use of the two regulations is therefore not advisable.

The ability of QIBs to rely on the Regulation S resale safe harbor to sell abroad Rule 144A securities issued by foreign companies in the United States significantly enhances the liquidity of those securities, making them far more attractive to the American institutional investor. To illustrate, common equity securities sold under Rule 144A by a European company in ADR form to US QIBs in conjunction with a broader European offering may be resold by such QIBs in the same secondary markets in which the securities sold in Europe will trade.[129]

Potential Problems Arising under Regulation S

Regulation S has brought a necessary level of certainty to foreign and domestic issuers selling securities offshore by reducing the chilling effect of the potential extraterritorial application of the registration requirements of the Securities Act.[130] However, the SEC and its staff have expressed increasingly strong concern that Regulation S is being used "in sham transactions that are nominally offshore but in fact are transacted simply to evade registration."[131] A former commissioner announced that the staff is giving serious consideration to recommending that the SEC amend Regulation S to foreclose further abuse and has suggested in this regard that Regulation S securities be deemed restricted for US resale purposes.[132]

Based on such concerns, the SEC is carefully examining certain types of Regulation S offerings, primarily offerings of equity securities made by US reporting issuers under category 2, to determine whether they have been designed to evade registration.[133] Some of these transactions have reportedly involved deep discounts from US market prices for the securities, coupled with immediate flowback of the securities into the United States upon expiration of the 40-day restricted period.[134] Other practices subject to close SEC scrutiny are the use of offshore entities formed by US persons to purchase securities; and purchaser hedging transactions, such as short sales or option trades, apparently intended to minimize investment risk during the offshore "holding" period.[135] Such transactions seem to invoke the principle, articulated in Regulation S, that a transaction that may be in technical compliance with all safe harbor conditions nevertheless will not be insulated against Section 5 liability if the transaction was intended to subvert US registration requirements.[136]

New Safe Harbor for Announcements of Regulation S and Other Offerings

Early in 1994 the SEC adopted a rule, Rule 135c under the Securities Act, that affords some liability protection for issuer announcements of offerings not registered or required to be registered under the Securities Act. This regulatory safe harbor should assist issuers in balancing the need to keep investors informed of material developments, including securities offerings, with Securities Act limitations that an issuer must observe when offering securities in private placements (including Rule 144A offerings), as well as in offshore offerings under Regulation S that by definition may not involve US directed selling efforts.

Rule 135c's new safe harbor is available to domestic and foreign companies reporting under the Exchange Act, and to foreign issuers that are exempt from reporting under Rule 12g3-2(b). Reporting companies must file the permitted announcement with the SEC under cover of Form 8-K or Form 6-K, whichever is applicable, while a nonreporting issuer with a Rule 12g3-2(b) exemption must submit the announcement to the SEC like any home-country document in accordance with that rule. The announcement may not be used for the purpose of conditioning the market in the United States for the securities being offered through the private placement.

In addition, the announcement must state that the securities offered have not been and will not be registered under the Securities Act and may not be offered or sold in the United States without registration or an exemption from registration. Other information that may be contained in the announcement is limited to the following: (1) the name of the issuer; (2) the title, amount, and basic terms of the securities being offered; (3) a brief statement of the manner and purpose of the offering, without naming the underwriters or placement agents; (4) statements or legends required by a state or foreign law or administrative authority; and (5) in the case of certain rights offerings, exchange offers, or offers to employees, specified additional information.

NOTES

1. All references in this chapter, as in the rest of the book, to foreign companies or foreign nongovernmental or private issuers mean companies that meet the US Securities and Exchange Commission's regulatory definition of "foreign private issuer" set forth, in Rule 405 of the Securities Act of 1933 and Rule 3b-4 of the Securities Exchange Act of 1934. Companies that meet this definition are eligible for reporting under a separate disclosure system that is designed specifically to accommodate the practices and policies of their respective home countries. Under this definition, a nongovernmental corporation that is organized or incorporated under the laws of a foreign country is deemed a "foreign private issuer" *unless* more than 50 percent of its outstanding voting securities are held of record (either directly or through voting trust certificates or depositary receipts) by residents of the United States, *and* (1) the majority of its executive officers or directors are US citizens or residents, (2) more than 50 percent of its assets are located in the United States, or (3) its business is administered primarily in the United States. A foreign-chartered corporation that does not meet these criteria is subject to all provisions of the US federal securities laws that apply to US issuers.

2. See data and discussion in Chapter 2 of this book.

3. See M. Saunders, "American Depositary Receipts: An Introduction to US Capital Markets for Foreign Securities," *Fordham International Law Journal* 50 (1993), pp. 48, 50–54. Daimler-Benz, the first and as yet the only German company to list securities on a US stock exchange, was prompted to take this step by a recognition that, as a global enterprise, it could no longer afford to limit its equityholder base to home-country investors. According to the company's CEO:

   > Our basic industrial business is becoming more and more global. We cannot continue the tradition of designing and producing everything here in Germany and then exporting it. We are producing more and more outside Europe—indeed in the US. As a result, we will become industrial citizens in most countries, and therefore we cannot continue with just a German shareholding in our company.

   "CEO Interview: Daimler-Benz's Edzard Reuter, A Visionary's Legacy," *Institutional Investor,* September 1994, pp. 31–32.

4. S. Rothwell, "When Companies Over There Want to Sell Securities Over Here," *Business Law Today* (July–August 1993), p. 34.

5. 15 U.S.C. §§ 77a-77aa. Where debt securities are issued through the instrumentalities of interstate commerce, which means that they are offered and sold in more than one state, the issuer must comply with both the Securities Act and the Trust Indenture Act of 1939, 15 U.S.C. §§ 77aaa-77bbbb. Except when an exemption is available, debt securities must be issued under a qualified indenture under which one or more eligible trustees will serve. At least one of the trustees must be a US corporate

or institutional trustee authorized by law to exercise corporate trust powers and subject to supervision by federal, state, territorial, or District of Columbia authority.

6. 15 U.S.C. §§ 78a-78ii.

7. Some of the states exempt offerings of securities that will be listed for trading on one or more of the principal national securities exchanges, such as the NYSE or the AMEX. See *Blue Sky Law Reporter,* Commerce Clearing House (CCH), Chicago, Illinois, p. 851.

8. Blue-sky laws of all US state and other jurisdictions are collected in the Commerce Clearing House's *Blue Sky Law Reporter.*

9. See "American Depositary Receipts," SEC Release No. 33-6894 (May 23, 1991) (hereinafter cited at "ADR Release").

10. Once the ADR holder sells the underlying security in a foreign market, it must return the ADR to the depositary, which then releases that security for delivery against the sale. See Harold Schimkat, "The SEC's Proposed Regulations of Foreign Securities Issued in the United States," *Fordham Law Review* 60 (1992), p. 203.

11. Nancy Young, "Using American Depositary Receipts to Access the US Capital Markets," *Insights* 8 (March 1994), p. 15.

12. Saunders, p. 52.

13. See memorandum of the SEC's Division of Corporation Finance, "American Depositary Receipts," February 12, 1993.

14. See "ADR Release"; Saunders, pp. 50–51.

15. The registration and reporting requirements of the Exchange Act are discussed in greater detail in Chapter 4.

16. See "ADR Release." Unsponsored ADRs have become virtually obsolete because of hidden costs and other problems associated with this type of ADR facility, including SEC rules that provide strong disincentives to their creation. Only three new unsponsored ADR programs have been established since 1983. See J. Velli, "American Depositary Receipts: An Overview," *Fordham International Law Journal* 17 (1994), pp. 38 and 43.

17. 17 C.F.R. § 239.36.

18. 17 C.F.R. §§ 239.31, 239.32, 239.33 or 239.34, respectively.

19. See "ADR Release."

20. *Ibid.*

21. *Ibid.*

22. See Velli, p. 44.

23. *Ibid.*

24. *Ibid.* Where the securities being offered to the public will be listed on a national securities exchange or quoted in NASDAQ, the issuer must register the securities under the Exchange Act (for the listing or quotation) as well as the Securities Act (for the public offering); see Chapter 4. A simplified Exchange Act registration statement on Form 8-A generally is used in this context; the form incorporates material information from the Securities Act registration statement. Except in the case of an initial public offering, the Securities Act registration statement in turn incorporates information from the issuer's Form 20-F which, as discussed in Chapter 4, serves as both an Exchange Act registration statement and an annual report for foreign issuers.

25. The term *security* is defined broadly in the Securities Act to include not only the more familiar equity or debt securities, but also various hybrid or derivative instruments. Section 2 of the Securities Act expressly defines "security" as "[a]ny note, stock, treasury stock, bond, debenture, evidence of indebtedness . . . or in general, any interest or instrument commonly known as a 'security,' or any certificate of interest or participation in, temporary or interim certificate for, receipt for, guarantee of, or warrant or right to subscribe or to purchase, any of the foregoing." 15 U.S.C. § 77b(1). A registrable security also may be deemed to exist in the form of an "investment contract," which has been described by the US Supreme Court as an arrangement whereby one invests money in a common enterprise with the expectation of deriving a return through the efforts of others. See *SEC v. W. J. Howey Co.,* 328 US 293, 298-99 (1946). Under this analysis, investments in an orange grove, golf courses, a franchise, a condominium, beavers, and diamonds have been held to be securities subject to the registration requirements of Section 5 of the Securities Act.

26. 15 U.S.C. § 77e; see Section 12(1) of the Securities Act [15 U.S.C. § 77l(2)].

27. The fee is currently 1/29 of 1 percent of the aggregate maximum offering price.

28. See Section 5(c) of the Securities Act [15 U.S.C. § 77e(c)].

29. Rule 135 under the Securities Act [17 C.F.R. § 230.135].

30. The basic rules governing the registration process are set forth in the SEC's Regulation C under the Securities Act, beginning with Rule 400 (17 C.F.R. §§ 230.400–.497). See also Chapter 4 (discussion of US accounting and auditing requirements).

31. See Section 12(2) of the Securities Act [15 U.S.C. § 77l(2)], Section 10(b) of the Exchange Act [15 U.S.C. § 78m(b)], and Rule 10b-5 thereunder [17 C.F.R. § 240.10b-5] (proscribing offers or sales of securities by means of misleading statements or omissions of material facts).

32. E. Greene, A. Beller, G. Cohen, M. Hudson, and E. Rosen. *U.S. Regulation of the International Securities Markets* 1, 2d ed. Englewood Cliffs, New Jersey: Prentice Hall Law & Business, 1993), p. 61 (hereinafter cited as Greene et. al.).

33. See Rule 134 under the Securities Act [17 C.F.R. § 230.134].

34. See Greene et. al., pp. 61–62.

35. See Section 11 of the Securities Act [15 U.S.C. § 77k]. A series of affirmative defenses are available to the issuer or other defendant, including expiration of a one-year statute of limitations and, for persons *other than the issuer,* the exercise of due diligence. See also Section 17(a) of the Securities Act [15 U.S.C. § 77q(a)].

36. See "ADR Release."

37. *Ibid.*

38. *Ibid.*

39. See Form F-6, General Instruction I.A.2.

40. See "ADR Release."

41. Rule 12g3-2(b) provides an exemption from the reporting requirements under the Exchange Act for foreign issuers that furnish to the SEC material information that they publicly file or publish in their home countries under law or according to stock exchange requirements or that they otherwise distribute to their security holders; see Chapter 4.

42. See Form F-6, Item 1.

43. See SEC Release No. 33-7053 (April 19, 1994).

44. The term *public float* refers to the "aggregate market value worldwide of voting stock held by non-affiliates of the registrant. . . ." General Instruction I.B. of Form F-3.

45. Form F-4 is available for business combinations and similar transactions involving the issuance of a foreign private issuer's securities. This form requires information concerning the transaction (including *pro forma* financial information), the issuer, the company being acquired, and shareholder voting conditions, dissenters' rights, and certain management information.

46. See SEC Release No. 33-6902A (March 23, 1992) and SEC Release No. 33-6902 (June 21, 1991). The Canadian version of MJDS is largely parallel in scope to the SEC's MJDS. Effective in 1991, the Canadian MJDS was implemented through National Policy Statement No. 95 in conjunction with orders and rulings by Canada's provinces and territories.

47. See Rule 12g3-2(a) [17 C.F.R. §240.12g3-2(a)]; see also "ADR Release."

48. *Ibid.*

49. 15 U.S.C. § 77d.

50. See SEC Release No. 33-6389 (March 8, 1982). The term *non-exclusive* as used by the Commission in this context means that reliance on the safe harbor does not preclude invocation of other Securities Act exemptions or safe harbors thereunder; for example, Section 4(2).

51. See Greene et al. (note 33), at § 4.02[1].

52. "Restricted securities" means one of the following:

    (i) Securities that are acquired directly or indirectly from the issuer, or from an affiliate of the issuer, in a transaction or chain of transactions not involving any public offering.

    (ii) Securities acquired from the issuer that are subject to the resale limitations of Regulation D or Rule 701(c) under the Act.

    (iii) Securities that are subject to the resale limitations of Regulation D and acquired in a transaction or chain of transactions not involving any public offering.

    (iv) Securities that are acquired in a transaction or chain of transactions meeting the requirements of Rule 144A.

53. The purpose of the rule is to prohibit the creation of public markets in issuer's securities where adequate public information is not available while permitting the public sale of limited amounts of securities owned by affiliates where adequate information about the issuer is available to the public. 17 C.F.R. § 230.144.

54. See *SEC v. Ralston Purina Co.,* 346 U.S. 119 (1953).

55. See Section 2(11) of the Securities Act [15 U.S.C. § 77b(11)].

56. See Section 12(1) of the Securities Act. Even if the Section 4(2) exemption is available, an issuer and certain other persons also may be held liable for any materially false or misleading statements or omissions (oral or written) in connection with the offer or sale of the securities. See Section 12(2) of the Securities Act, Section 10(b) of the Exchange Act, and Rule 10b-5 thereunder.

57. See *Gustafson v. Alloyd Co., Inc., U.S. Law Week* 63 (U.S. Sup. Ct., February 28, 1995).

58. Rule 504 of Regulation D provides a safe harbor for offerings under $1 million, and is intended to implement the small-offering exemption set forth in Section 3(b) of the Securities Act. Also based on Section 3(b), Rule 505 makes available a safe harbor for certain limited offerings not exceeding $5 million.

59. See Preliminary Notes to Regulation D.

60. Rule 502(c) of Regulation D.

61. See Greene et. al.

62. See Rule 135c under the Securities Act (safe harbor for announcements of offshore offerings, discussed at the conclusion of this chapter).

63. See Rule 502(b) of Regulation D.

64. Rule 502(b)(3) of Regulation D.

65. Rule 502(b)(i)(C) of Regulation D.

66. Rule 502(d) of Regulation D.

67. Reasonable care may be shown by the following:
    (1) Reasonable inquiry to determine if the purchaser is acquiring the securities for himself or for other persons.
    (2) Written disclosure to each purchaser prior to sale that the securities have not been registered under the Act and therefore cannot be resold unless they are registered under the Act or unless an exemption from registration is available.
    (3) Placement of a legend on the certificate or other document that evidences the securities, stating that the securities have not been registered under the Act and setting forth or referring to the restrictions on transferability and sale of the securities. *Ibid.*

68. Rule 144A under the Securities Act [17 C.F.R. § 230.144A]. In general, the term "QIB" is defined to encompass a broad variety of institutions that in the aggregate own and invest on a discretionary basis at least $100 million in securities of unaffiliated issuers. Banks (whether foreign or domestic) and savings and loan associations must have a net worth of at least $25 million, in addition to meeting the requirement of $100 million in securities. Registered broker-dealers need not meet the $100 million test but instead may qualify at QIBs if they have $10 million in securities, whether purchased for intermediation or investment purposes, or limit their participation to agency and riskless principal transactions.

69. See Greene et. al., p. 154.

70. See *SEC Staff Report on Rule 144A* (July 20, 1994), (hereinafter cited as *SEC Staff Report*).

71. See H. Bloomenthal, *Securities Law Handbook* (Webster, New York: Clark Boardman, 1995), p. 411.

72. See Velli, p. 53.

73. See M. Steinberg and D. Lansdale, Jr., "Regulation S and Rule 144A: Creating a Workable Fiction in an Expanding Global Securities Market," *International Lawyer* 29 (Spring 1995), pp. 59–60.

74. *Ibid.*

75. Steinberg and Lansdale, p. 54.

76. See *SEC Staff Report,* p. 3.

77. *SEC Staff Report,* p. 3.

78. *SEC Staff Report,* p. 5.

79. *Ibid.*

80. *Ibid.*

81. *SEC Staff Report,* p. 7.

82. See *SEC Staff Report,* p.14–21.

83. Letter from Arthur Levitt, Chairman of the SEC, to Representatives John D. Dingell and Edward J. Markey, July 20, 1994, discussing recent developments in the Rule 144A market (available through the SEC's Public Reference Room).

84. *Ibid.*

85. *Ibid.*

86. See note 52.

87. Rule 144A under the Securities Act.

88. See Rule 144A(d)(1).

89. See Rule 144A(d)(2).

90. See Rule 144A(d)(3)(i).

91. See Bloomenthal (note 72), p. 405.

92. See Rules 144A(d)(3)(i), 144A(a)(6), and 144A(a)(7).

93. See SEC Release No. 33-6862 (April 23, 1990).

94. The issuer itself may not be an investment company subject to the registration and other requirements of the Investment Company Act of 1940.

95. See Rule 144A(d)(4). The requisite information is deemed available if the issuer is a reporting company and takes reasonable steps to ensure that the buyer is aware that the seller may rely on Rule 144A. See Rule 144A(d)(2).

96. Rule 144A(d)(4)(ii) provides:

    The requirement that the information be "reasonably current" will be presumed to be satisfied where:

    (1) the balance sheet is as of a date less than 16 months before the date of resale, the statements of profit and loss and retained earnings are for the 12 months preceding the date of such balance sheet, and if such balance sheet is not as of a date less than 6 months before the date of resale, it shall be accompanied by additional statements of profit and loss and retained earnings for the period from the date of such balance sheet to a date less than 6 months before the date of resale; and

    (2) the statement of the nature of the issuer's business and its products and services offered is as of a date within 12 months prior to the date of resale; or

    (3) with regard to foreign . . . issuers, the required information meets the timing requirements of the issuer's home country or principal trading markets.

97. See Rule 144A(d)(4)(i) (requiring that where reasonably available, the financial information must be audited). With respect to foreign private issuers, the audited financial statements need not conform to SEC accounting requirements.

98. See Velli, p. 53.

99. W. Decker, "The Attractions of the US Securities Markets to Foreign Issuers and the Alternative Methods of Accessing the US Markets: From the Issuer's Perspective," *Fordham International Law Journal* 17 (1994), pp. 14–15.

100. See note 57.

101. The term *distribution* is defined for Rule 10b-6 purposes to mean:

[A]n offering of securities, whether or not subject to registration under the Securities Act of 1933, that is distinguished from ordinary trading transactions by the magnitude of the offering and the presence of special selling efforts and selling methods.

Rule 10b-6(c)(5).

102. 17 C.F.R. § 240.10b-6 (1994).

103. See *Review of Antimanipulation Regulations of Securities Offerings,* SEC Release No. 34-33924 (April 26, 1994).

104. 17 C.F.R. § 240.10b-07 (1994). As defined in Rule 10b-7(b)(3), the term *stabilizing* means:

[T]he placing of any bid, or the effecting of any purchase, for the purpose of pegging, fixing or stabilizing the price of any security: *Provided, however,* that a bid shall not constitute a stabilizing bid unless or until it is shown in the market.

105. *Ibid.*

106. *Ibid.*

107. Rule 10b-8.

108. See Greene et. al., at § 4.06[3].

109. See SEC Release No. 33-7028 (November 3, 1993).

110. *Ibid.*

111. *Ibid.*

112. See *Ibid.*

113. The no-action request indicated that the usefulness of the recently adopted exceptions would be limited if the trading practices rules were applied to offers and sales to specified non-US persons under Regulation S that are made concurrently with a Rule 144A distribution. Specified non-US persons include (1) discretionary or similar accounts (other than an estate or trust) held for the benefit or account of a non-US person by a US fiduciary, as described in Rule 902(o)(2) of the Securities Act; and (2) international organizations and their agencies, affiliates, or pension plans, as described in Rule 902(o)(7). See *Sullivan & Cromwell* (SEC staff no-action letter available to the public on February 22, 1994).

114. See SEC Release No. 34–33924 (April 26, 1994).

115. See Rules 901-904 of Regulation S and Preliminary Notes; SEC Release No. 33-6863 (April 24, 1990) (adopting Regulation S).

116. See SEC Release No. 33-6863 (April 24, 1990).

117. *Ibid.*

118. See Preliminary Note 5 to Regulation S.

119. Rule 903(b). Such efforts encompass advertising and publications with a general circulation in the United States but exclude tombstone ads in a publication of predominantly non-US circulation or ads required to be published by foreign law and containing no more information than legally mandated. Preliminary Note 7 to Regulation S states in this regard that:

Nothing in these rules precludes access by journalists for publication with a general circulation in the United States to offshore press conferences, press releases and meetings with company press spokespersons in which an offshore offering . . . is discussed, provided that the information is made available to the foreign and United

States press generally and is not intended to induce purchases of securities by persons in the United States. . . .

120. See Rule 902(o)(1)(i).

121. See Rule 902(o)(2).

122. See Rule 902(o)(1)(viii). Even if the foreign entity was formed by US persons for the purpose of investing in unregistered securities (e.g., a hedge fund), it nevertheless will not be a US person if it is owned exclusively by certain "accredited investors" within the meaning of Rule 501(a) of Regulation D.

123. SEC Release No. 33-6863 (April 24, 1990).

124. *Ibid.*

125. Section 4(1) of the Securities Act [15 U.S.C. § 77d(1)].

126. See Rule 904 of Regulation S.

127. See, for example, Greene et. al., pp. 166–169.

128. SEC Release No. 6863 (April 19, 1990), at n. 64.

129. See Greene et. al., pp. 167–168.

130. Remarks of Commissioner Richard Y. Roberts, Northwest State Federal Provincial Securities Conference, February 26, 1993, discussing SEC initiatives in international finance.

131. *Ibid.* See also Remarks of Commissioner Richard Y. Roberts, "Securities Public Policy Issues of Interest," delivered before the Twenty-Seventh Annual Rocky Mountain State-Federal-Provincial Securities Conference, Denver, Colorado (October 14, 1994).

132. *Ibid.*

133. *Ibid.* See also quoted remarks of SEC Division of Corporation Finance officials Linda C. Quinn and Meredith Cross, delivered at the 1994 SEC Speaks conference, in *The SEC Today* (March 15, 1994), p. 2.

134. See Outline of the SEC's Division of Corporation Finance, *The SEC Speaks in 1995* 3, Practicing Law Institute, New York (March 1995), pp. 327–328; See also Greene and Schneck, "Recent Problems Arising Under Regulation S," *Insights* 8, August 1994, pp. 2 and 3.

135. *Ibid.*

136. See Greene & Schneck, p. 4.

Chapter 4

Legal Requirements for Trading in US Secondary Markets

The preceding chapter examined the relative benefits and drawbacks associated with a foreign issuer's decision to raise capital in the United States through private or public securities offerings. This chapter will describe additional mechanisms for accessing US markets, through listing or quotation of securities, respectively, on a national securities exchange or in the National Association of Securities Dealers Automated Quotation System (NASDAQ). (The US national securities exchanges and NASDAQ are collectively referred to as self-regulatory organizations, or SROs). Also described are the periodic reporting requirements of the SEC that are applicable to a foreign issuer deemed to have voluntarily entered the US securities markets, whether by means of a public offering, listing or quotation of its securities on a national securities exchange or in NASDAQ, or the widespread trading of its securities in the over-the-counter (OTC) secondary markets in the United States.

Any foreign private issuer that offers its securities to the public in the United States or that seeks to create a secondary trading market here either by listing a class of its securities on a US securities exchange or arranging for their quotation in NASDAQ necessarily triggers the registration requirements of Section 12 of the Securities Exchange Act of 1934 (again, as in Chapter 3, referred to as the *Exchange Act*). Registration under Section 12 obligates the registrant to file periodic reports with the US Securities and Exchange Commission (SEC). Even a foreign company that neither sells nor lists its securities in the United States may be subject to the Exchange Act registration and reporting requirements if it has 300 or more US shareholders and assets of more than minimal value anywhere in the world. Whether foreign or domestic, an issuer must remain mindful that the Exchange Act registration requirement that it must satisfy if its securities are traded on a national securities exchange or NASDAQ or are held by at least 300 US shareholders is separate from and entirely independent of the registration requirement that arises under the Securities Act of 1933 when the issuer makes a public offering in the United States.

In addition to creating a continuous disclosure obligation for all Exchange Act registrants that must be met by making prescribed filings with the SEC, the Exchange Act imposes other substantive duties on foreign and US reporting companies alike, such as the maintenance of accurate books and records and an adequate system of internal accounting controls;[1] and compliance with special SEC filing requirements in connection with self-tenders,[2] third-party tender offers,[3] and other transactions involving the securities of those companies. The act also mandates the filing of reports of beneficial ownership of more than five percent of a reporting company's equity securities by any person other than the company itself, which must be filed when that person crosses this ownership threshold.[4] Because these various Exchange Act requirements generally apply regardless of how they may conflict with the laws or practices of the issuer's home country—which may impose their own requirements on a particular transaction, such as a tender offer for a foreign issuer that includes that issuer's US shareholders—the issuer may under some circumstances be relieved of mandatory compliance with the act under an express statutory exemption or a grant of a waiver or exemption by the SEC.[5]

As was discussed in Chapter 2, significant numbers of non-US companies have been willing to bear the costs of full compliance with the periodic disclosure rules of the Exchange Act, whether by listing debt, equity, or American Depositary Receipts (ADRs) on a national securities exchange or NASDAQ market, or by offering securities to the investing public. All foreign private issuers with less than 50 percent of their outstanding common stock in the hands of US record holders[6] that offer, list, or procure the quotation of their securities in the US public markets are eligible to use a series of specialized disclosure forms and schedules designed by the SEC to accommodate the unique needs of issuers subject primarily to another country's regulatory regime. The separate disclosure system for foreign issuers will be described later in this chapter. Many other companies have chosen such alternative means of entering the US securities markets as Rule 144A-style private placements or the creation of unlisted ADR programs, which allows these companies to bypass the US reporting scheme entirely so long as the number of equity holders in the United States remains below 300.

Regardless of the public or private nature of the markets they enter, many foreign companies have chosen to sponsor ADR programs for the issuance and trading of their securities in this country to permit US settlement of transactions and the payment of dividends in dollar denominations. Indeed, issuer sponsorship of a US program is a prerequisite both to listing ADRs on a national securities exchange such as the NYSE and to use of the SEC's streamlined Form F-6 for registering the ADRs under the Securities Act.

EXCHANGE ACT REGISTRATION AND REPORTING

What Triggers a Foreign Issuer's Exchange Act Registration and Periodic Reporting Duties?

Foreign companies that have made a public securities offering in the United States need not register those securities under Section 12 of the Exchange Act, but must comply with the periodic reporting requirements of the Exchange Act.[7] A reporting obligation incurred by a foreign company solely by virtue of having made a public offering may be suspended when the number of its US resident shareholders drops below 300 by the beginning of any fiscal year *except* the year in which that offering is completed (or when the number of US shareholders is less than 500 and the value of the total assets of the issuer has not exceeded $5 million on the last day of each of its three most recent fiscal years) *and* the company files a certification of this event with the SEC on Exchange Act Form 15. As explained in the next paragraph, however, companies meeting this test may still be obligated to register the same class of securities under the Exchange Act and continue to file SEC reports in subsequent years if the securities are equity rather than debt, and the number of US holders reaches or exceeds 300. Although those foreign issuers that offer unregistered securities in the United States in a private placement of securities eligible for Rule 144A-exempt resale must provide a minimal level of information to their institutional purchasers (as discussed in Chapter 3), these issuers will generally not become subject to the Exchange Act's registration and ongoing disclosure requirements unless, again, the securities are equity and are held of record by at least 300 persons resident in the United States.

Even without a public offering or an exchange or NASDAQ listing, a relatively large volume of trading of a foreign company's equity securities in the US OTC markets alone may give rise to registration and periodic reporting obligations under the Exchange Act if that company has $5 million or more in assets and 500 or more holders of record of its equity worldwide, with at least 300 of such holders in the United States.[8] An Exchange Act registration statement must be filed with the SEC within 120 days after the end of the fiscal year in which a foreign issuer exceeds these asset and number-of-shareholder thresholds, to be followed by the filing of periodic reports prescribed by the SEC's disclosure scheme for non-US companies. This obligation will arise even if a foreign company takes no affirmative step to enter the US securities markets but nonetheless, through global trading of its equity securities, accumulates 300 or more holders of record in the United States. The SEC has created a key exemption, codified in Exchange Act Rule 12g3-2(b) and discussed in more detail later in this chapter, that permits non-US companies to meet otherwise applicable Exchange Act reporting requirements by supplying home-country disclosure documents to the SEC.

A prudent foreign issuer will therefore monitor the level of US ownership of its equity securities regularly to determine whether cross-border trading and perhaps even the creation of an unauthorized ADR program in the United States by a bank or broker-dealer may have caused it inadvertently to cross the Section 12 jurisdictional threshold of 300 US equity holders (assuming, again, that the issuer has 500 or more equity holders around the globe and more than $5 million in total assets). In this event, the issuer should take immediate steps either to register the class of equity securities in question with the SEC or to comply with the conditions for a Rule 12g3-2(b) exemption. While the SEC to date has not sued or otherwise sanctioned foreign issuers for failure to comply with involuntarily incurred Exchange Act registration and reporting obligations, the preferred course is to minimize this risk through preemptive action. Commentators have suggested that there may also be exposure to private suits brought to force Section 12 registration, which would provide added impetus for compliance.[9]

Another means of triggering continuous Exchange Act disclosure obligations is by listing a class of securities—whether newly issued or already outstanding; or in the form of ordinary shares, ADRs on those shares, or debt—on a US stock exchange,[10] or by procuring the quotation of such securities in NASDAQ's automated interdealer markets.[11] Both foreign and US companies in these circumstances must register the class of listed or quoted securities with the SEC under Section 12 of the Exchange Act and file specified annual and certain other periodic disclosure documents with the SEC.

Many institutional investors in this country, according to one observer, "prefer the security of an immediate pricing mechanism that comes with a listed ADR."[12] Where ADRs are listed on a national securities exchange, both the ADRs and the deposited securities must be registered under Section 12 of the Exchange Act because of the immediate conversion feature of this class of derivative securities. For ADRs quoted in NASDAQ, however, only the deposited securities must be so registered. In either case, as noted, Section 12 registration gives rise to a periodic reporting obligation on the part of the foreign issuer.

To underscore its concern that US investors receive sufficient information regarding an issuer of foreign securities trading in the US markets, whether that issuer is filing SEC-mandated reports or supplying home-country documents under Rule 12g3-2(b), the SEC has imposed a specific obligation on US broker-dealers to consider whether current information is available in the United States when trading or quoting foreign securities.[13] For purposes of this obligation, Rule 12g3-2(b) disclosures are deemed sufficient to protect US broker-dealers from liability for recommending a security without the required informational basis.[14]

The SEC's Section 12 Registration Process

Registration statement on Form 20-F. Under the SEC's special disclosure system for foreign issuers, Form 20-F may be used both to register a class of securities under Section 12 of the Exchange Act and to comply with the Act's annual report requirement. This form is divided into four basic parts, including specified financial statements.

Part I of Form 20-F requires a detailed description of the foreign registrant's business by category of activity, its major properties, and the nature of the markets in which its securities trade both within and beyond the borders of the United States. As part of the business description, foreign registrants must disclose revenues by segments and geographical areas and include a narrative discussion of any segment or geographic area whose contribution to total operating profit (loss) is materially disproportionate to its relative contribution to revenues. Operating profits or losses by segment and/or geographic area must be shown only insofar as mandated by applicable foreign law, rule, or stock exchange requirement or otherwise provided to the public.

To the extent disclosed to its shareholders or otherwise made public, the registrant must furnish information on management's material transactions with the registrant over the last three fiscal years, the total amount of outstanding options held by directors and officers as a group, and remuneration of all managers and directors on an aggregate basis for the last fiscal year. Holders of 10 percent or more of any class of the registrant's securities must be identified if known.

Additional items in Part I require discussion of foreign exchange controls on the import or export of capital or other limitations affecting nonresident holders' receipt of dividends or interest payments or exercise of voting rights. Part I also mandates disclosure of all pending legal proceedings or governmental investigations.

Selected financial data for the last five years—including net sales or operating revenues, income (loss) from continuing operations, income (loss) from continuing operations per common share, total assets, long-term obligations and redeemable preferred stock, and cash dividends declared per common share—must be provided in Part I to highlight for investors certain significant trends in the registrant's financial condition and results of operations. These data must be reconciled to US generally accepted accounting principles (US GAAP) under one of the two standards discussed below. All taxes, including withholding provisions to which US holders may be subject under home-country laws, must likewise be reported.

At the core of the Part I disclosure is Management's Discussion and Analysis of Financial Condition and Results of Operations (MD&A) for the periods covered by the financial statements called for by Part IV of the form. Essentially a narrative explanation designed to interpret important aspects of the financial statements for shareholders, the MD&A affords a view of the registrant's business from the perspective of its management. As such, the MD&A compels a detailed discussion of liquidity, capital resources, results of operations, and other specified historical and prospective financial information the SEC deems necessary to investors' understanding of the registrant's financial condition, material changes in that condition, and operating results.

A statement contained in the MD&A or elsewhere in Form 20-F that projects a registrant's revenues, earnings, or other financial items, outlines management's plans and objectives for future operations, discusses the registrant's prospective economic performance, or reveals an assumption underlying any of the foregoing is protected by a so-called safe harbor from both SEC and private plaintiff fraud claims if it has a reasonable basis and was disclosed in good faith. Safe-harbor coverage extends to such projections only when they are included in an SEC document, whether voluntarily or because mandated by the MD&A.[15] Except where dictated specifically by the MD&A or by filing requirements relating to mergers or acquisitions, however, registrants seldom provide contingent information due to the heightened risk of shareholder litigation associated with such disclosures.

The SEC's Division of Corporation Finance, which through its Office of International Corporate Finance (OICF) generally reviews and comments on foreign issuers' registration statements, places great emphasis on the adequacy of the MD&A disclosure and may require extensive and time-consuming revisions if not satisfied that a particular MD&A is in compliance. Accordingly, working familiarity with SEC and staff interpretations of this disclosure item is critical to expediting the staff review process.[16]

Part II of Form 20-F mandates a detailed description of the securities subject to registration. According to prominent practitioners in this area:

> While not required by the form, the practice has developed in the case of registration of equity securities of describing the principal features of the foreign corporate law applicable to the issuer [in Part II]. Particular attention is given to the process by which directors are elected and the matters that must be submitted to a vote of shareholders, as well as the rules applicable to the conduct of shareholder meetings.[17]

Indebtedness of the registrant and certain subsidiaries is the focus of Part III of Form 20-F. Specifically, the issuer must identify any of its indebtedness or that of a significant subsidiary in connection with which there has been, during the year, a default in the payment of principal, interest, or sinking fund obligation or in the performance of any other material term that has not been remedied within 30 days. This disclosure is required, however, only if the total amount of indebtedness exceeds five percent of the total assets of the issuer and its consolidated subsidiaries. Part III also calls for disclosure of any material modification, such as the imposition of working capital restrictions and other limitations on dividend payments, of constituent instruments defining the rights of holders of registered securities.

Perhaps the most controversial and burdensome of all SEC disclosure regulations, from the perspective of many foreign issuers, are those rules mandating the filing, in connection with Part IV of Form 20-F, of audited financial statements with much of the same content as those required of US reporting issuers.[18] Specifically, foreign issuers must include audited balance sheets for the two most recent fiscal year-ends, statements of income and cash flows for the three most recent fiscal years preceding the date of the most recent audited balance sheet being filed, and changes in shareholders' equity.[19] Financial statements prescribed by Part IV may, but need not, be prepared in accordance with US GAAP. If an issuer chooses not to comply directly with US GAAP, its financial statements must be presented in conformity with accounting principles generally accepted in its home country and accompanied by an audited quantitative reconciliation to US GAAP and a narrative description of any material differences.

There are two types of reconciliation to US GAAP contemplated by Form 20-F, each of which dictates the form and content of the requisite financial statements: (1) Item 17, requiring reconciliation only of the differences in measurement items—primarily for income statement and balance sheet amounts—and (2) Item 18, mandating full reconciliation, including the provision of all supplemental data prescribed by US GAAP, such as full industry and geographical segment data. Thus, Item 17 calls for footnote disclosure primarily conforming to home-country rules, while Item 18 compels inclusion of almost all US GAAP disclosures, many of which, like tax and industry segment information, are not required by non-US GAAP. If a US GAAP disclosure not expressly required by Item 17 is particularly significant to an issuer relying on this item, however, the substance of that disclosure must be explained in the issuer's MD&A.

Compliance with the more limited Item 17 reconciliation standard is permissible for registration statements and annual reports on Form 20-F, although a foreign issuer may elect to reconcile under Item 18.[20] Recall, however, that Item 18-reconciled financial statements are mandatory for public offerings registered on Securities Act Form F-2 (except for investment-grade securities) or Form F-1. Accordingly, it would clearly be more cost-efficient for an issuer contemplating a public offering while simultaneously obtaining an SRO listing (or shortly after doing so) to reconcile its Form 20-F financial statements in accordance with Item 18.

Foreign issuers often complain that it is difficult to identify and measure all significant variations between US and home-country accounting principles in connection with reconciliation, even under the less burdensome standards of Item 17.[21] For example, many issuers describe as excessive the requirement of both Item 17 and Item 18 to reconcile net income and shareholders' equity, as measured under home-country accounting principles, with equivalent US GAAP amounts.[22] Where relevant, reconciliation of balance sheet accounts and discussion of other classification differences on the balance sheet and income statement also cause difficulties for issuers attempting to conform to either item.

In April 1994, the SEC adopted substantial amendments to Form 20-F and certain other disclosure documents intended to streamline the reporting system for foreign issuers.[23] Of potentially greatest significance was the SEC's amendment of Form 20-F to permit a foreign issuer's inclusion in that form, without reconciliation, of a cash flow statement prepared in accordance with International Accounting Standards No. 7, "Cash Flow Statements," as amended (IAS 7). This is the first time the SEC agreed to accept as authoritative an international accounting standard, suggesting an enhanced receptivity to the international harmonization and mutual recognition initiatives that the SEC is exploring with securities regulators of other nations. In announcing this initiative, however, the SEC cautioned that such reconciliation accommodations would continue to be made only where the quality of disclosure furnished to US investors is not compromised.

Another 1994 amendment to Form 20-F enables first-time registrants with the SEC to reconcile the required financial statements and selected financial data for only the two most recently completed fiscal years and any required interim period. Each subsequent year, another year of reconciliation would be added. However, this amendment does not change the requirements with respect to the primary financial statements to be included in SEC filings: audited balance sheets for the two most recently completed fiscal years; audited income and cash flow statements for the three most recently completed fiscal years; and separate financial statements of significant acquirees or investees.

Eight of the previously required financial statement schedules calling for supplemental details of accounts such as marketable securities, reserves, and property, plant, and equipment were eliminated under the 1994 revisions.[24] However, the loss of this supplemental information should not diminish the overall quality of a foreign issuer's financial disclosure, since even those companies reconciling to US GAAP under the less burdensome Item 17 must discuss such information in the MD&A section of Form 20-F if that information would be particularly significant to investors.

Also rescinded by the SEC in 1994 was the requirement to reconcile separate financial statements of acquired businesses and equity investees under the 30 percent significance level.[25] Item 17 reconciliation is now permissible for businesses that exceed the 30 percent threshold. Another revision permits a foreign issuer that uses *pro rata* consolidation (as opposed to the equity method) for a joint venture to provide summarized condensed financial information regarding its joint venture interest, including cash-flow information.

In late 1994, the SEC formally accepted another two international accounting standards. Thus, the SEC no longer mandates reconciliation to US GAAP for the effects of use of a translation methodology with respect to a company's operations in a hyperinflationary economy. Foreign issuers now have the choice of using the methodology prescribed by International Accounting Standard No. 21, "The Effects of Changes in Foreign Exchange Rates." This standard requires that amounts in the financial statements of the hyperinflationary operation be restated for the effects of changing prices in accordance with International Accounting Standard No. 29, "Financial Reporting in Hyperinflationary Economics," and then translated to the reporting currency.

Reconciliation requirements likewise were eliminated for those foreign issuers that have consistently applied International Accounting Standard No. 22, "Business Combinations." This reform alleviates a foreign issuer's record-keeping burden by allowing it to forgo reconciliation of differences that arise from the issuer's method of accounting for business combinations—pooling or purchase—if the method used conforms with International Accounting Standard No. 22. Nor is a foreign issuer obligated any longer to reconcile differences that arise from the divergent amortization periods for goodwill and negative goodwill under US GAAP and International Accounting Standard No. 22.

Recently, the SEC liberalized its rule limiting the age of financial statements included in foreign private issuers' registration statements. Even though foreign issuers for many years have been under no obligation to file quarterly reports with the SEC, they previously could not make public offerings in the United States during certain periods of the year (termed *blackout periods*), because a prior version of Rule 3-19 of Regulation S-X provided that a foreign issuer's audited financial statements could not be older than six months at the time of a registered offering. In amending Rule 3-19 in late 1993, the SEC raised the maximum age of audited financial statements in a Securities Act registration statement to 10 months and also extended financial statement updating requirements for non-US companies by one month for annual audited financial statements and by four months for semiannual unaudited financial statements.[26] The effect of the amendment is thus to accept for purposes of both the Securities Act and the Exchange Act the semiannual reporting standards of Japan, members of the European Union, and various other countries.

Another amendment to Rule 3-19 adopted in late 1993 eliminated the former US GAAP reconciliation requirement for interim reports under certain circumstances if adequate narrative disclosures are furnished. Where, for example, a registration statement includes interim financial data more current than the data contained in the latest reconciled annual or semiannual financial statements, the later financial data need not be reconciled so long as any material variation in accounting that was not previously disclosed and quantified in the reconciliation for an annual or semiannual period is described, and the quantified impact of the material variation is reported. A companion amendment to Rule 15d-2 under the Securities Act (periodic reporting obligation incurred by issuers making a registered securities offering) was adopted to give foreign issuers an additional three-month period in which to file their audited year-end financial statements, consistent with the laws of many European countries and Japan that allow six months after the close of the fiscal year for filing the annual report and accompanying audited year-end financial statements.

In another change,[27] foreign issuers now have more latitude in choosing the reporting currency to be used for presentation of financial statements in SEC filings. Such amounts can be stated in primary financial statements using the currency in which information is reported to a majority of shareholders. Previously, a foreign issuer was required to present its financial statements in the currency of either its country of incorporation or of its primary economic environment.

Daimler-Benz's experience in adapting to US GAAP financial statements prepared under German accounting standards, as an SEC-mandated prerequisite to listing its ADRs on the NYSE, provides an ideal example of what foreign issuers can expect when entering the US capital markets via an exchange listing. As widely reported in the financial press, the SEC refused to declare effective the company's required Section 12 registration statement on Form 20-F until key financial statement items stated in accordance with German GAAP were reconciled to US GAAP. Most commentators have noted the impact on the company's reported financial condition of differences in the measurement of earnings, which in effect transformed a small profit under German GAAP to a significant loss under US GAAP.[28] An important difference between German and US GAAP lies in application of the prudence concept inherent in German GAAP, which can lead to substantial overstatement of income in bad business years, as losses are charged directly to existing provisions and reserves, and old provisions are released to income. Such a distortion, coupled with poor disclosure of provisions and reserves, had previously concealed Daimler's declining financial condition from equity investors.[29]

SEC staff review and comment process: SEC declaration of effectiveness. The SEC has developed a nonpublic procedure for the filing and staff review of the financial statements and remaining portions of a foreign issuer's registration statement under either the Securities Act or the Exchange Act or both. In early 1994, the SEC announced that such documents could be reviewed by the staff in draft form on a confidential basis specifically to facilitate stock market listings and cross-border offerings. To avail itself of these procedures in connection with the Section 12 registration statement, the issuer must request nonpublic treatment specifically from the attorney in the operating branch of the Division of Corporation Finance responsible for reviewing the registration statement or from the separate division unit—the OICF—that oversees and ultimately approves the branch attorney's review of and comment upon all foreign issuer filings. Foreign issuers are well-advised to document and address their requests to the appropriate personnel in both parts of the Division and to contact the OICF immediately to ensure prompt disposition of such requests.

Before a Section 12 registration statement covering securities to be listed on a national securities exchange can become effective, the particular SRO must certify to the SEC its approval of the issuer's application for listing.[30] Barring delays caused by SEC staff review and comment—which may extend to as long as a year, depending on whether disputes arise over such issues as US GAAP reconciliation—the registration statement will be declared effective 30 days after the SEC receives the SRO's certification, or such shorter time as the SEC may determine at the request of either the SRO or the issuer.[31] A somewhat different process governs SEC registration of an equity security for which quotation is sought in the NASDAQ system.[32]

Where a prospective registrant declines to address the SEC staff's comments on a pending Exchange Act registration statement, or the staff concludes that its refusal to declare that registration statement effective (in the case of a national securities exchange) is not a sufficient deterrent to an imminent violation, the SEC may deny, suspend for up to 12 months, or revoke after a hearing any Section 12 registration of an issuer that has violated any provision of the Exchange Act or the SEC's rules thereunder. These sanctions may be applied not only to an already registered security but also to a security for which registration has been sought from the SEC if the registration statement contains material misrepresentations or omissions that are not corrected during the staff review and comment process. The effect of such an order, of course, would be to foreclose listing or trading of any such security on the facilities of a US SRO.

The SRO Listing/Quotation Process

Secondary-market trading of securities in the US public markets is generally conducted on either the national securities exchanges—the NYSE, the American Stock Exchange (AMEX), and another six active regional registered exchanges—or NASDAQ's National Market Service (NASDAQ/NMS) for companies with larger market capitalizations and other NASDAQ automated interdealer quotation systems. Both the NYSE and AMEX are "auction" markets, or markets in which the pricing of transactions is determined in direct contacts on an exchange floor between brokers acting on behalf of buyers and sellers, with member firms or "specialists" charged with maintaining a fair and orderly market in particular securities. By contrast, the NASDAQ markets are "dealer" markets, or markets in which electronically linked market makers quote bid and offered prices for transactions in specific securities and execute trades at those prices.

There is a separate OTC market for which price and volume information is disclosed in the so-called pink sheets distributed by a commercial publisher to broker-dealer firms or in the NASD-operated Electronic Bulletin Board Service established in 1990.[33] Spreads (between bid prices and asking prices) and transaction costs tend to be higher for securities traded in the pink sheets than for those traded in the listed markets since this market is far less transparent. Foreign securities traded in the OTC markets to date have not been subject to mandatory Section 12 registration, provided that the issuer of those securities has fewer than 300 shareholders in the United States or, if it has more than 300 such holders, the Rule 12g3-2(b) exemption is available.[34]

Foreign issuers are increasingly finding that, in order to gain the broadest possible investor base in the United States for their ADRs or other securities, they must seek an SRO listing. As of the end of 1994, the NYSE had listed the ADRs of 210 foreign issuers, NASDAQ's NMS and NASDAQ's other market listing carried interdealer quotations for the ADRs of 104 foreign companies, and the AMEX had a total of 8 foreign ADR listings, primarily from Canada.[35] Though reliable data on the scope of OTC trading of foreign securities do not exist, one commentator estimates that unlisted ADRs of such major non-US companies as Nestlé, Deutsche Bank, and Cifra may account for as much as $50 billion worth of trading in the United States.[36]

To list its securities on a national securities exchange or procure their quotation in NASDAQ, a foreign issuer must submit an SRO listing application, pay a fee, and meet certain SRO eligibility criteria. Concurrently, the issuer must have filed with the SEC a Section 12 registration statement which, in turn, must become effective before the SRO will approve the application. For this reason, foreign issuers that wish to have their securities traded on the facilities of a particular SRO first must satisfy any SEC staff comments on the registration statement and related documentation.

Because of the interrelationship of the SRO listing and SEC registration processes, staffs of the SROs and the SEC have developed various informal mechanisms for exchanging relevant information on a prospective registrant. The coordination process developed by the NYSE provides a useful illustration of the efficient interaction of the SEC and the national stock exchanges in the foreign listing area. Like the SEC, the NYSE will generally undertake a preliminary, confidential review of a foreign issuer's eligibility for listing that can be preapproved in anticipation of the SEC's declaration of the effectiveness of the Section 12 registration statement.[37] There is no fee for this review, which has been invaluable to foreign issuers engaged in nonpublic negotiations with the SEC to resolve the often complex accounting and disclosure questions raised in connection with the SEC's staff review and comment process.

Once a foreign issuer is advised orally and in writing by the responsible NYSE staff that a confidential review of its submission indicates that the SRO's foreign eligibility standards have been met, which generally occurs within two or three weeks after the review application has been received by the staff, the issuer must file an original listing application no more than six months later. Substantially the same information and supporting documentation must be furnished in connection with the formal application along with an opinion of counsel bearing on such matters as the legality of the issuer's organization and the validity of its securities. The same NYSE staff members who conducted the confidential eligibility review normally evaluate the formal listing application and recommend a disposition to the NYSE Listing Committee, which meets weekly to consider and act upon pending applications. For those applications that are approved, a NYSE certification to this effect is sent to the SEC to expedite the agency's registration process.

Even when an application is approved on eligibility grounds by the NYSE Listing Committee, final approval for trading will not be given unless the Section 12 registration statement on file with the SEC becomes effective. After the NYSE certification is received by the SEC, there is an additional SEC-imposed waiting period of up to 30 days (unless accelerated at the request of the NYSE and/or the issuer) before the SEC registration statement becomes effective. Moreover, the issuer must pay a one-time preset listing charge of $36,800 and initial fees calculated according to a schedule based on the number of shares or ADRs originally listed.[38] The minimum fee for examination of a formal application is $1,500. With respect to ADR listings, the fees are determined according to the number of outstanding ADRs rather than the number of underlying shares. Where shares or ADRs are issued subsequent to the original listing, whether of the same or another class, they must also be listed and a fee paid for the additional or new securities. A continuing fee that can total up to $500,000 is payable annually thereafter for each class of security, which is also calculated under a prescribed schedule.[39]

SRO listing eligibility standards. Of the three major SROs, the NYSE and AMEX have developed special standards and procedures for listing ordinary shares, ADRs, and other securities of foreign issuers. At least to date, the NASD applies essentially the same standards to foreign and domestic issuers. Listing standards of each of these SROs are outlined below.

NYSE. To qualify for listing on the NYSE, a foreign issuer must fulfill four key criteria. First, the issuer must have, worldwide, a minimum of 5,000 holders of 100 or more shares—to be determined on the basis of beneficial ownership, if known, rather than record ownership.[40] Second, the issuer must have a minimum of 2.5 million shares publicly held throughout the world with a market value of at least $100 million. Third, the issuer must have $100 million of aggregate consolidated net tangible assets and cumulative pretax income of $100 million for the last three years, with a minimum of $25 million in pretax income for each of these years. Fourth, and perhaps most important, the issuer will be eligible for listing under the less burdensome standards applicable to nondomestic companies "only where there is a broad, liquid market for the company's shares in its country of origin."[41]

If a foreign issuer so elects, or does not meet the home-country market liquidity criterion just noted, it may seek to qualify under the share distribution and value, earnings, and asset standards fixed by the NYSE for domestic issuers. NYSE domestic issuer standards impose lower asset and earnings tests but mandate a minimum of 2,000 holders and average monthly US trading volume of 100,000 shares during the most recent six months. The issuer also must have a minimum of 1.1 million shares publicly held in the United States with a market value of $18 million (excluding designated insider holdings). Although the domestic issuer standards generally require that the issuer's consolidated net tangible assets be worth at least $18 million, this measure of the issuer's size is less important than others, such as the value of the US public float. Finally, the domestic standards prescribe pretax income of $2.5 million for the issuer's most recent fiscal year and $2 million for each of the two preceding years or, alternatively, cumulative pretax income of $6.5 million for the last year, with a minimum of $4.5 million, and a profit in each of the last three years.[42]

AMEX. Unlike the NYSE, the AMEX does not rely strictly on numerical tests to determine a foreign issuer's eligibility for listing. Instead, this SRO will "consider the laws, customs and practices of the applicant's country of domicile" on such matters as the independence of the board of directors, the provision of financial statements, and the quorum necessary for shareholders' meetings. Under nonbinding guidelines, however, the AMEX has essentially established a baseline with its suggestion that foreign companies that wish to list should have a minimum of 800 holders of 100 or more shares and one million shares held publicly with a market value of at least $3 million.[43] A foreign issuer has the option of meeting domestic listing standards, which establish less onerous size and earnings tests but require a more extensive US share distribution.[44]

NASDAQ. Eligibility standards for NASDAQ and NASDAQ/NMS quotations of new issues of common shares or ADRs are, for the most part, identical for domestic and foreign issuers. To be traded on NASDAQ, an issuer must have a minimum of 100,000 publicly held shares of common stock worldwide or, in the case of ADRs, 100,000 ADRs registered with the SEC, 300 holders of record of the common shares, and two registered market makers for the shares or ADRs for which listing is sought.[45] The minimum bid price for a listed security is $3.00, and a class of listed securities must have an aggregate market value of $1 million. An issuer also must have total assets of at least $ 4 million and total capital and surplus of at least $2 million. Somewhat more stringent versions of these asset, market value, and volume tests govern acceptance for quotation in the NASDAQ/NMS.[46]

Continuing SRO listing obligations. To maintain a listing on a US securities exchange or NASDAQ, a foreign (or US) issuer must agree to comply prospectively with disclosure standards and various corporate governance requirements specified by the SRO's rules and policies. Neither the NYSE, the AMEX, nor the NASD has adopted separate provisions for foreign issuers but instead may modify or waive at a foreign issuer's request certain obligations relating to financial reporting and corporate governance.

Foreign companies typically seek waivers where the US SRO's rules differ from or conflict with home-country laws or practices. As of 1987, waiver requests submitted to the NYSE need only be accompanied by an opinion of independent counsel licensed to practice in the issuer's country of origin confirming that the noncomplying standards the issuer proposes to obey in lieu of meeting NYSE standards are not prohibited by the laws of that country.

Financial reporting and other SRO-mandated disclosures. Rules of the NYSE, AMEX, and NASDAQ/NMS mandate, as a condition of continued listing, an issuer's provision to shareholders of annual reports including audited financial statements.[47] An issuer must also file with the SRO and publish quarterly earnings reports,[48] a requirement that is typically waived for foreign issuers to the extent of permitting such publication on a semiannual basis where consistent (or not inconsistent) with controlling law or common practice in the issuer's home country.[49] As discussed, the SEC is the final arbiter on substantive financial reporting issues relating to these documents, including most prominently the nature and extent of reconciliation of financial data to US GAAP and conformity with independence standards for auditors. Finally, specified information that can reasonably be expected to have a material effect on the market for the issuer's securities must be disclosed.[50]

Corporate governance standards. All listed companies, whether foreign or domestic, must meet certain standards of corporate governance. Depending on the SRO—with NASDAQ rules generally tending to be somewhat less restrictive than those of the NYSE and AMEX—listed companies must have at least two outside directors on their boards and must establish and maintain an audit committee composed of varying numbers of independent directors.[51] Directors who are affiliates, officers or employees of the issuer or any subsidiary are normally not deemed to possess the requisite independence.[52] Staff of the NYSE and the AMEX, respectively, are willing to waive board structure and composition criteria at the request of a foreign issuer where it appears that the requestor has proposed alternatives that are consistent with home-country laws or practices.[53] One such criterion that will not be relaxed by the NYSE, however, is the requirement that the audit committee or its equivalent monitor transactions between the issuer and its management with the goal of protecting the issuer's best interests.[54]

A listed company, further, must hold an annual shareholders' meeting, for which proxies must be solicited and proxy material disseminated. An appropriate quorum must be established, ranging from at least a majority of the outstanding voting securities for the NYSE,[55] to a 33 1/3 percent threshold for the AMEX and the NASDAQ/NMS.[56] Given the mandatory language of its rule, the NYSE refuses to waive the annual meeting requirement.[57] Quorum and proxy solicitation requirements may nevertheless be waived by the NYSE for a foreign issuer if not applicable under or barred by home-country laws.[58] None of the three major SROs extends to foreign issuers its version of the controversial "one-share/one-vote" rule, according to which each share of listed common stock is entitled to one vote.

Shareholder approval must be sought by NYSE-listed companies for any issue of common or convertible common stock that has or will have voting power equal to 10 percent or more of the outstanding voting power prior to issuance or that will result in the issuance of an amount of common shares that will equal or exceed 20 percent of the preissuance number of outstanding shares.[59] A shareholder vote is also mandated in connection with issuer equity or equity-based grants to corporate insiders,[60] certain related-party transactions,[61] and change-in-control transactions.[62] While there is no express indication in the three SROs' rules that any shareholder approval requirement is subject to waiver, the NYSE has suggested that such a requirement may be waived if it is inconsistent with home-country laws and an adequate substitute protection is available under such laws.[63] A well-respected commentator warns, however, that NYSE provisions relating to insider purchases and sales of issuer stock by insiders or receipt of stock options from the issuer may not be waived.[64] Holders of foreign securities listed on the NYSE also retain nonwaivable protections against certain issuer antitakeover measures and redemptions of such securities, as well as any issuer tender offer for its own or another listed company's securities.[65]

The SEC periodic report system. Since its adoption in 1982, the SEC's special disclosure system for foreign issuers has required each such issuer to file an annual report on Form 20-F—the same form that may be used, as discussed, by issuers seeking Section 12 registration of a class of securities—within six months of the end of the issuer's fiscal year. Also required to be filed, together with SEC Form 6-K, are those interim reports of the issuer made public by law or practice. Financial statements contained in these interim reports need not be reconciled to US GAAP.

Finally, foreign issuers must file promptly with the SEC—and supply to each US SRO on which its securities are traded—the Form 6–K as well as significant information regarding the issuer or its subsidiaries either mandated by home-country law or stock exchange requirements or otherwise distributed to shareholders. As set forth in General Instruction B to the form, this information could relate to changes in management or control, acquisitions or dispositions of material assets, dismissal of certifying accountants, changes in financial condition or results of operations, material legal proceedings, material increases or decreases in the number of outstanding securities or indebtedness, modifications of the company's charter or other constituent documents governing the terms of any class of securities registered with the SEC, the outcome of a shareholder vote, or any other information that the issuer considers to be of material importance. Unless already disseminated in English, information made available to the public through a press release or materials transmitted directly to shareholders must be translated or summarized in English and attached to the original document and the Form 6-K for filing with the SEC. A brief description of the published documents accompanying the form is sufficient in all other situations, although any English summary or translation that the issuer has prepared for any other reason must also be filed.

The SEC's disclosure system for foreign issuers makes several significant accommodations to home-country practices and policies. The following are summaries of some of the more significant accommodations:

1. Interim reporting need only be consistent with home-country regulatory and stock exchange practices, permitting foreign issuers to forgo entirely the filing of quarterly reports with the SEC required of domestic issuers. Indeed, as noted above, even a semiannual report need not be filed here unless made public by the foreign issuer in the home country. As a practical matter, however, the rules of the NYSE, AMEX, and NASD (for NMS quotation) compel submission of interim reports on at least a semiannual basis, and these reports must therefore be filed with the SEC.

2. Broad exemptions for foreign issuers have been carved out of the SEC's proxy rules and the Section 16 short-swing profit recovery provisions applicable to officers and directors. Accordingly, a foreign issuer need not file an SEC-mandated proxy statement or otherwise solicit proxies from its shareholders in the United States in conformity with the federal proxy rules. (In the absence of a waiver, however, the SROs require provision of proxy materials to US holders of listed securities as a condition to obtaining and maintaining a listing.) Nor need a foreign issuer's officers and directors reasonably fear shareholder suits demanding that they surrender profits from matched sales and purchases within a six-month period, though such officials should remain aware of the risk of incurring insider trading liability under the general antifraud provisions of the federal securities laws (discussed in the final section of this chapter) should they buy or sell the issuer's securities on the basis of material, confidential information prior to its disclosure to the public.

3. Disclosure requirements regarding compensation of senior executives and directors of foreign issuers allow aggregate reporting, if

consistent with home-country rules, by contrast with the individual disclosure US issuers must supply for each of their five most senior executive officers.

4. Financial statements contained in offering documents need only be updated principally on a semiannual rather than a quarterly basis, as discussed.

HOME-COUNTRY DISCLOSURE: THE 12g3–2(b) REGIME

Securities of a foreign private issuer traded in the United States that would ordinarily trigger the Exchange Act's registration and periodic reporting requirements may be exempt from those requirements if the issuer furnishes to the SEC certain information distributed to its shareholders or made public under requirements in its home country or by a non-US exchange on which its securities are listed. The SEC in turn makes this information available to the investing public in the United States. Access to such information supplied by foreign issuers facilitates trading by allowing US broker-dealers to rely on this information in initiating quotations for securities of such issuers, rather than incur the additional costs that would otherwise be necessary for obtaining sufficient information to demonstrate the requisite "reasonable basis" for recommending these securities to their customers.[66]

Codified in SEC Rule 12g3-2(b), this Exchange Act registration exemption cannot properly be invoked if the foreign issuer has or previously has had, within the past 18 months, securities listed on a national securities exchange or quoted in NASDAQ[67] or has assumed an independent reporting obligation by virtue of having made a public offering in the United States. Nor can a foreign issuer rely on the 12g3-2(b) exemption if it acquires another issuer that is registered with or reports to the SEC. However, companies may rely on this exemption to establish an ADR program enabling their securities to be traded in the US OTC market or to satisfy the information requirements for a Rule 144A private placement in this country.

The Rule 12g3-2(b) exemption is not automatically available, but instead must be secured through the submission of an application to the Office of International Corporate Finance of the SEC's Division of Corporation Finance. As part of this application, a foreign issuer must furnish to the SEC any information that is "material to an investment decision" *and,* since the beginning of the issuer's last fiscal year, has been made public under home-country laws, filed with any stock exchange on which its securities are traded, or distributed to its shareholders. Such information may relate to the issuer's financial condition or results; changes in its business, asset acquisitions, or dispositions; or changes in management, management remuneration, and related-party transactions—as well as events that a US company would have to report with a filing of Form 8-K as a material development, such as a change in control or auditors.[69]

An issuer is also required to include in its Rule 12g3-2(b) application a summary of information that the issuer is now or may be compelled in the future to disclose in its home country; for example, in public offering or tender offer documents, even if neither transaction is contemplated at the time of the application. This summary must state when or by whom each document will be made public or filed. Another mandatory summary must detail, to the extent known to or obtainable by the issuer "without reasonable expense or effort," data on: (1) the number of holders of each class of equity securities resident in the United States; (2) the amount and percentage of each such class held by US residents; (3) a description of the circumstances in which these securities were acquired; and (4) the date and circumstances of the most recent distribution of securities by the issuer or an affiliate. The SEC proposed in 1991, but has not yet adopted, a requirement that information on US shareholders be provided annually by exempt issuers under Rule 12g3-2(b).[70]

There is no prescribed form for the Rule 12g3-2(b) application, nor is there a fee. While OICF staff does not subject a Rule 12g3-2(b) application to the same review and comment process accorded "filed" documents,[71] it does examine the initial application materials and advise the issuer whether it will be added to the SEC's periodic list of foreign private issuers claiming the exemption. In some instances, the staff may request additional information to ensure that all prerequisites to the exemption have been met. If the staff discovers no impediment to the issuer's claim of exempt status (e.g., an indication that the issuer is a non-US investment company with more than 100 beneficial owners resident in the United States[72]), a file number will be assigned to the issuer to allow the public to identify and secure access to information supplied to the SEC. As a former head of the OICF points out, an issuer should not assume that the exemption has been perfected before the assignment of an SEC filing number, which may not occur until several weeks after the application is made.[73]

To preserve the exemption, the issuer thereafter must promptly submit to the SEC any material information when filed, disclosed, or distributed in the issuer's home country or other place of listing. Any change in the applicable home-country reporting requirements in the last fiscal year must be reflected in an amendment to the initial list of such requirements accompanying the application. The assigned SEC filing number should be used to identify all submissions.

Rather than make case-by-case determinations of materiality, many foreign issuers simply send all press releases and other corporate communications to the SEC, whereas others send only those documents filed with home-country regulatory authorities. Unless the issuer's home country has a fairly well-developed system of securities regulation, however, the latter approach is not advisable.

Home-country documents transcribed in English are generally required for both the initial and subsequent Rule 12g3-2(b) information submissions. In addition, press releases and other materials disseminated directly to shareholders must be translated or adequately summarized in English and furnished to the SEC. With respect to other issuer materials, an English version or summary will be required only if it has been prepared for some other purpose. Where an English-language version or summary of a document falling in this second category is unavailable, the issuer need only submit a brief description of that document.

Except in the extraordinary case, the sole notice a foreign private issuer will have that it may continue to rely on the exemption is its inclusion in the list of Rule 12g3-2(b)-eligible issuers published periodically by the SEC. As the agency has cautioned, however, such inclusion does not signal that agency's affirmation that the issuer has complied or is complying with all conditions of the exemption.

LIABILITY CONSIDERATIONS

A former SEC commissioner recently observed that "excessive, frivolous litigation is rapidly becoming the No. 1 concern of (foreign) companies that are eligible to list but choose not to—overtaking concern about US GAAP."[74] Another former commissioner points out that "many foreign issuers find dealing with US security analysts much more troublesome than staying out of the courts and avoiding litigation under Section 10(b) and Rule 10b-5 of the Exchange Act."[75] These two apparently divergent perspectives are not necessarily inconsistent since issuer statements to analysts who in turn communicate these statements to the public securities markets frequently generate shareholder antifraud suits against the issuer.

An inevitable concomitant of the transparency and liquidity of the US equity markets is the intense inquisitiveness of analysts and institutional investors, who often bombard public companies, US and foreign alike, with demands for more information—particularly in the form of earnings projections and other forward-looking or "soft" financial data—than would otherwise be mandated by the SEC's disclosure requirements. Though the responsive and relatively constant flow of corporate information to the investment community does enhance the efficiency of this country's capital markets, issuers may be exposed to greater litigation risk should predictive statements not be realized. Whether perceived or real, a consensus has thus emerged among reporting companies that provision of the future-oriented information demanded by the US marketplace is unwise and should be avoided despite the availability of some regulatory protection in this context.[76]

Perhaps the most potent of the antifraud provisions of the US securities laws is SEC Rule 10b-5, which implements Section 10(b) of the Exchange Act and is the primary vehicle for both SEC enforcement actions and private shareholder suits in cases of suspected fraud. Rule 10b-5 renders it unlawful for any person using channels of commerce within the jurisdiction of the United States (e.g., the mails or the telephone) to make a material misstatement or omission in connection with the purchase or sale of a security. As amplified by the courts, the rule requires the SEC or the private plaintiff to prove that the defendant acted or failed to act with the requisite state of mind—or "scienter"—a requirement that can be satisfied with evidence of reckless disregard of the truth as well as a knowing or willful violation.[77] The US Supreme Court has held that information is "material" if "there is a substantial likelihood that a reasonable shareholder would consider it important" in making an investment or voting decision.[78]

Of particular concern to foreign and domestic issuers alike is the difficulty of ascertaining precisely when and how much disclosure must be made to the investing public of material corporate information. As defined primarily by the federal courts, a company has an affirmative duty to disclose material information only when: (1) a statute or rule, such as the rules prescribing the content of Form 20-F, so mandates; (2) disclosure is necessary to prevent other statements made by the company from being materially false, incomplete, or misleading; (3) the company is issuing or purchasing its securities; or (4) company insiders are trading in the company's own securities. SRO rules, as discussed, also impose on listed companies certain disclosure duties with respect to material events.

Engaging in conduct known virtually around the world as "insider trading" is outlawed by several provisions of the federal securities laws: Section 10(b) of the Exchange Act and SEC Rule 10b-5 adopted thereunder and, if the trading occurs in connection with a tender offer for securities registered under the Exchange Act, SEC Rule 14e-3. The term *insider trading* generally is understood to refer to the unlawful trading of an issuer's securities while in possession of confidential material information. Since neither the SEC nor the Congress has codified a definition of *insider trading,* however, the law in this area has been fashioned by the federal courts in actions brought by the SEC and private parties. As one well-known treatise points out, "as a result, the penalties are severe, but the conduct prohibited is uncertain."[79]

Congress has given the SEC a formidable arsenal of enforcement weapons to combat fraud in connection with securities transactions within the agency's jurisdiction. Not only does the SEC possess extensive investigatory powers, but it may also sue for injunctive and other relief in the federal courts or initiate its own administrative proceeding against a suspected wrongdoer. Since 1990, the SEC has been empowered to request civil monetary penalties in the courts that, depending on the gravity of the offense, may range from a few thousand dollars to $500,000 per violation perpetrated by a corporate defendant. With respect to administrative proceedings, the SEC has the authority to order any person found to have violated or to be violating any provision of the Exchange Act to cease and desist from such violation. Failure to comply with such a cease-and-desist order subjects the violator to an SEC-imposed fine. Cases involving serious fraud, such as insider trading, also may be referred to the US Department of Justice for criminal prosecution.

CONCLUSION

Foreign companies seeking to raise capital in the US securities markets should bear in mind that the SEC's regulatory perspective is evolving contemporaneously with the rapid internationalization of corporate operations and securities transactions. As this chapter has shown, the agency has carefully balanced its overriding concern that US investors receive full and fair disclosure regarding the issuer of any security—whether that issuer is domestic or foreign—with the need to attract new entrants to the US securities markets, given the harsh economic realities of today's competitive global environment. With the notable exception of the Canadian Multijurisdictional Disclosure System (MJDS),[80] however, the SEC has thus far resisted calls for adoption of a reciprocal approach whereby the home-country filings of foreign issuers would be deemed to satisfy US disclosure requirements if the home country accords the same treatment to eligible US issuers. Moreover, compliance with US independence standards for auditors (except for certain rights offerings) and reconciliation of financial statements to US accounting principles remain mandatory even for Canadian companies participating in the MJDS.

At the same time, the SEC has accepted, without significant inquiry into their fundamental adequacy, home-country disclosures submitted under Rule 12g3-2(b) by companies whose securities are traded in the less efficient and more poorly regulated OTC markets. Some critics have suggested that the time has come for the SEC to undertake a dramatic reassessment of its current policies to limit the availability of the Rule 12g3-2(b) exemption, while concomitantly accepting as sufficient the home-country disclosures of companies that must comply with regulatory schemes of sovereign nations that, like Canada or the United Kingdom, have investor protections substantially equivalent to those in the United States.[81] Others, perhaps most notably officials of the NYSE, have urged the SEC simply to accept without reconciliation to US GAAP the financial reports of "world-class" foreign companies.[82]

Despite these criticisms, the SEC has moved substantially toward modifying its rules and regulations in recognition of the increasing interdependency of the US and other world securities markets. As discussed, the SEC has made a variety of accommodations for foreign issuers including, most notably, the acceptance of three international accounting standards (the presentation of cash flow statements, hyperinflation adjustments, and business combinations). Still pending on the SEC's rulemaking agenda are proposals to facilitate cross-border rights offerings[83] and tender and exchange offers[84] by non-US issuers. Exemptions and waivers are now granted on a case-by-case basis to permit multinational tender and exchange offers to proceed in the United States.[85] In sum, the SEC shows every sign of maintaining its current, flexible approach toward reducing compliance burdens for foreign issuers where consistent with the interests of US shareholders.

NOTES

1. See Section 13(b)(2) of the Exchange Act [15 U.S.C. § 78m(b)(2)].

2. See Rule 13e-4 under the Exchange Act [17 C.F.R. § 240.13e-4].

3. See Section 14(d) of the Exchange Act [15 U.S.C. § 78n(d)] and Regulation 14D [17 C.F.R. §§ 240.14d-1–240.15a-6] thereunder (setting forth disclosure and procedural requirements applicable to both bidder and target companies; jurisdiction is triggered by an offer for a class of equity securities registered under Section 12 of the Exchange Act); and Section 14(e) of the Exchange Act and Regulation 14E thereunder (antifraud prohibitions applicable to tender offers, including those for securities not covered by section 14(d) and Regulation 14D thereunder).

4. See Sections 13(d) and 13(g) of the Exchange Act [15 U.S.C. §§ 78m(d) and (g)] and Regulation 13D/G [17 C.F.R. §§ 240.13d-1–13d-102 thereunder. A "beneficial owner" of a security is defined to mean "any person who, directly or indirectly, through any contract, arrangement, understanding, relationship, or otherwise has or shares: (1) voting power . . . and/or (2) investment power. . . ."

5. Unlike the laws of many other countries, the US tender offer rules are triggered by the residence of the investor rather than the nationality of the target. Accordingly, there is a significant potential for conflict between the rules of the SEC and the target issuer's home country. Recognizing that the perceived overbreadth of the US tender offer rules may prompt foreign bidders to exclude US shareholders from multinational tender or exchange offers, however, the SEC has granted relief from compliance with specific tender-offer rules to alleviate or prevent such conflict. See, for example, *In re Enterprise Oil plc, SEC Release No. 34-33967 (April 28, 1994); In the Matter of the Procordia Aktiebolag and Aktiebolaget Volvo Offers for Pharmacia Aktiebolag,* SEC Release No. 34-27671 (February 2, 1990); *In the Matter of the Ford Motor Co. Ltd.,* 5. SEC Release No. 34-27425 (November 7, 1989). Still pending is a 1991 SEC proposal to permit tender offers for a foreign issuer's securities to proceed in the United States on the basis of the applicable regulation of the target company's home jurisdiction, where a small percentage—10 percent or less—of the securities subject to the offer are held in this country. See SEC Release No. 33-6897 (June 5, 1991).

6. Rule 12g5-1 under the Exchange Act provides that "securities shall be deemed to be 'held of record' by each person who is identified as the owner of such securities on records of security holders maintained by or on behalf of the issuer." There are several exceptions; for example, securities identified as held of record by a corporation, partnership, or trust will be treated as being held by one person, even if trustees or other coholders are named. See Rule 12g5-1(a)(2) [17 C.F.R. § 240.12g5-1(a)(2)].

7. See Section 15(d) of the Exchange Act [15 U.S.C. § 78l(b)].

8. See Section 12(g) of the Exchange Act [15 U.S.C. § 78l(g)] and Rules 12g-1 and 12g3-2(a) thereunder [17 C.F.R. §§ 2240.12g-1 and .12g3-2(a)]. According to SEC Rules 12g3-2 and 12g5-1 (see note 7), a security is deemed to be held of record by each person identified as a security holder in records maintained by or on behalf of the issuer. Issuers generally have no duty to inquire into the extent of US ownership of their securities and thus may rely on their own records except where securities are held of record by a US broker, dealer, or bank or a nominee for any of the foregoing. In the latter case, the issuer must inquire of these financial intermediaries regarding the US ownership of the securities, which will be counted as held in the US by the number of separate US resident customer accounts. Moreover, if the issuer is aware

of the existence of an ADR program for its equity securities, whether sponsored or unsponsored, the issuer must contact the depositary, request the number of US holders on depositary records, and include this figure in its calculation of the total number of US security holders. The issuer is entitled to rely in good faith on information provided by financial intermediaries regarding the residence of beneficial owners of its securities and by the ADR depositary regarding the record holders of ADRs evidencing equity securities. See Rules 12g3-2(a) and 12g5-1(b)(1). Issuers supplying home-country information to the SEC under the 12g3-2(b) exemption must report information annually as to the number of holders and percentages of shares (and ADRs) held in the United States.

9. See W. Stahr and J. Palenberg, "Rule 12g3-2(b) under the Securities Exchange Act: A Primer for Foreign Companies," *International Lawyer* 27 (1993), pp. 963 and 975.

10. See Section 12(b) of the Exchange Act [15 U.S.C. § 78l(b)].

11. See Section 12(g)(1) of the Exchange Act and Rule 12g-1 thereunder; see also NASD Manual (CCH), Schedule D, Para. 1804.

12. An investment manager at Alliance Capital Management who keeps approximately 30 percent of his $500 million portfolio invested in ADRs is quoted as stating that, "as a buyer the only thing that adds any real value to us is a listing" (p. 112). Retail investors in the United States also derive comfort from the ability to track prices of exchange-listed ADRs through a variety of print and electronic media. S. Davis, "The Allure of ADRs," *Institutional Investor* (September 1994), pp. 109 and 112.

13. See Rule 15c2-11 [17 C.F.R. § 240.15c2-11].

14. Rule 15c2-11(a)(4) requires a broker-dealer initiating a quotation for securities of a foreign issuer to maintain in its files and to make reasonably available upon request the home-country information furnished to the SEC in compliance with Rule 12g3-2(b) since the beginning of the issuer's last fiscal year.

15. The SEC is considering changes to the existing safe harbors (Rule 175 under the Securities Act and Rule 3b-6 under the Exchange Act) in response to widespread issuer criticisms that these provisions do not afford adequate protection against litigation based on forward-looking disclosures. See SEC Release No. 33-7101 (October 13, 1994).

16. Except where the SEC has expressly delegated authority to act on its behalf to the staff, the actions of the staff do not bind the SEC in any way. Thus, most interpretations and positions of the staff may be appealed to or challenged before the SEC. At the same time, the recommendations of the staff carry substantial weight with the SEC and should not be disregarded by issuers or other persons subject to the US federal securities laws.

17. E. Greene, A. Beller, G. Cohen, M. Hudson, and E. Rosen, *U.S. Regulation of the International Securities Markets: A Guide for Domestic and Foreign Issuers Intermediaries* 2d ed. vol. 1 (Englewood Cliffs, New Jersey: Prentice Hall Law & Business 1994), p. 46.

18. One commentator observed:

> When we talk and hear about [foreign issuers'] "burden of disclosure," what people are most often talking about is that they don't like the information that needs to be included in [the] . . . reconciliation. It may be a case where there has been an aggressive revenue recognition approach followed in the home country that would have to be reconciled with US GAAP and thus highlighted; it may be the hidden reserves, or secret reserves in countries like Switzerland and Germany; it may be

the pension information in cases where a company may have a massive[ly] under-funded pension plan, and the pension information under US GAAP would show a huge reconciling item of increased pension expense and/or a large pension liability. It's these sorts of disclosure that non-US companies are very cautious about.

W. Decker, "The Attractions of the US Securities Markets to Foreign Issuers and the Alternative Methods of Accessing the US Markets: From the Issuer's Perspective," *Fordham International Law Journal* 17 (1994), pp. 10 and 13.

19. See Rule 3-19 of Regulation S-X. The audit of the mandated financial statements must have been conducted by independent accountants under auditing standards and practices substantially similar to US generally accepted auditing standards (GAAS). See Rules 3-19, 2-01 and 2-02 of Regulation S-X. To satisfy the SEC's staff that the accountants who examined the financial statements and signed the accompanying auditors' report are independent and likely applied GAAS, a foreign issuer is well advised to retain an international accounting firm with a US presence. In this connection, the SEC has stated that Canadian issuers meeting US disclosure requirements through the filing of Canadian documents under the auspices of the Multijurisdictional Disclosure System implemented by the SEC and Canadian regulatory authorities in 1991 may provide financial statements audited in conformity with Canadian GAAS. See SEC Release No. 33-6902 (June 21, 1991).

20. A foreign private issuer's election of Item 17 reconciliation for Form 20-F will not affect its ability to use the streamlined Securities Act registration statements on Forms F-2 and F-3. See H. Bloomenthal, *Securities Law Handbook* (Clark Boardman 1995) §§ 31.02 and 31.03[1].

21. For a country-by-country discussion of the types of reconciliations observed by the SEC's Division of Corporation Finance in foreign issuer filings, see Securities and Exchange Commission, Division of Corporation Finance, *Survey of Financial Statement Reconciliations by Foreign Registrants* (May 1, 1993) (available from the SEC's Public Reference Room).

22. See E. Rader, "Accounting Issues in Cross-Border Securities Offerings," *Fordham International Law Journal* 17 (1994), p. 129.

23. See SEC Release No. 33-7053 (April 19, 1994).

24. In April 1994, the SEC eliminated the following financial statement schedules previously mandated by rules under Regulation S-X: Rule 12-02—Marketable Securities—Other Investments; Rule 12-03—Amounts Receivable from Related Parties and Underwriters, Promoters, and Employees Other Than Related Parties; Rule 12-05—Indebtedness of and to Related Parties—Note Current; Rule 12-06—Property, Plant and Equipment; Rule 12-07—Accumulated Depreciation, Depletion and Amortization of Property, Plant and Equipment; and Rule 12-08—Guarantees of Securities of Other Issuers. Two more were eliminated in late 1994: Short-Term Borrowings and Supplementary Income Statement Information. See SEC Release No. 33-7118 (December 13, 1994).

25. See SEC Release No. 33-7055 (April 19, 1994). Issuers must include audited financial statements of significant acquired businesses in SEC documents, with significance measured according to tests based on the size of the issuer's investment in the acquired business and that business's pretax income relative to the amounts reported in the issuer's most recent audited financial statements. The number of years of audited financial statements of the acquired business that must be filed varies with the level of its significance. The total asset comparison previously required was eliminated in late 1994. See SEC Release No. 33-7118 (December 13, 1994).

26. See SEC Release No. 33-7026 (November 3, 1993).

27. See SEC Release No. 33-7117 (December 13, 1994).

28. R. Breeden, "Foreign Companies and U.S. Securities Markets in a Time of Economic Transformation," *Fordham International Law Journal* 17 (1994), p. 77 (Mr. Breeden was SEC Chairman during the period in which Daimler's Section 12 registration statement was reviewed and approved by the SEC.) According to Breeden, Daimler's first half 1993 profits were reported under German GAAP at almost DM200 million and when reconciled to US GAAP, that amount was reduced to a loss of just under DM1 billion. Another report estimated the company"s profit of 168 million DM ($97 million) under German GAAP for the first half of 1993 to be a loss of 949 million DM ($548 million) after conforming to US GAAP and eliminating the impact of hidden reserves. See D. Duffy and L. Murray, "The Wooing of American Investors," *The Wall Street Journal,* February 25, 1994, p. A14.

29. See, for example, "Daimler-Benz: A US GAAP Based Stock," *Merrill Lynch Accounting Bulletin No. 19,* October 20, 1993.

30. Such SRO certification is a pre-condition to the effectiveness of a Section 12 registration statement only in connection with a class of securities to be listed on a national securities exchange. See Section 12(d) of the Exchange Act and Rule 12d1-3 thereunder. Compare with note 33, below (registration statement for NASDAQ-quoted securities becomes effective through lapse of time in the absence of SEC action to bar registration).

31. If the SEC's staff is unable to complete its review and comment within 30 days after receipt of the national securities exchange's certification, it must ask the exchange to cooperate by deferring approval for trading or ask the aspiring registrant to persuade the SRO to delay the certification.

32. A registration statement pertaining to securities that are the subject of a NASDAQ listing application ordinarily becomes effective automatically 60 days after the SEC filing or within such shorter period as the SEC may direct. See Section 12(g)(1) of the Exchange Act. Unlike the national securities exchanges, NASD certification thus is not a prerequisite to SEC effectiveness. It is important to emphasize, however, that the NASD will not approve an application for inclusion of a security in the NASDAQ system unless any required SEC registration statement has become effective (filed under Section 12(g) of the Exchange Act and, in the case of a new issue of foreign securities, under Section 5 of the Securities Act. See NASD Manual (CCH) Para. 1804. Accordingly, it is not unreasonable to conclude that there may be dialogue between the SEC and NASD staffs if either perceives a legal or other impediment to obtaining a valid Exchange Act registration for securities that are the subject of a pending NASDAQ application.

33. The pink sheets are a daily listing of market-maker quotations or indications of interest operated by the Commerce Clearing House/National Quotation Bureau. The Electronic Bulletin Board Service is an electronic service operated by the National Association of Securities Dealers, Inc., which also administers the NASDAQ inter-dealer market system. ADR quotations are displayed on the Bulletin Board in static form and may be updated only twice daily. Generally, brokers trading in either of these OTC markets contact one of the listed market makers in the securities. See SEC Release No. 33-6894 (May 23, 1994), at footnote 33 and accompanying text.

34. The NASD's OTC Electronic Bulletin Board Service has operated under continuous grants of interim SEC approval, the most recent of which expired October 3, 1994. See SEC Release No. 34-34613 (August 30, 1994). Still pending is the NASD's re-

quest for permanent approval of the Service, filed in 1992. See SEC Release No. 34-30766 (June 1, 1992). The NASD has sought an interim extension of the service through December 31, 1994, under a proposed rule that would reaffirm the SEC's preliminary determination that foreign securities, including ADRs, would not lose their eligibility for an exemption from Exchange Act Section 12(g) registration requirements by virtue of market makers' quotations in the Service. See the Wall Street Letter 26, pp. 1 and 5.

35. See Table 2–1, chapter 2 above.

36. See W. Glassgall, "The Global Investor," *Business Week,* September 19, 1994, p. 99. See also E. Greene, D. Braverman, and S. Sperber, "Hegemony or Deference: US Disclosure Requirements in the International Capital Markets," *The Business Lawyer* 50 (1995). Citing data reported by the Bank of New York.

37. Certain information must be furnished by a foreign applicant for listing in support of a request for confidential eligibility review. As set forth in Section 104.02 of the NYSE Listed Company Manual, this information includes the following:

   a. Certified copy of charter and by-laws, translated into English.
   b. Specimens of certificates of other securities traded or to be traded in the US market.
   c. If any securities to be listed are ADRs, a copy of the depositary agreement with the institutional depositary. With regard to item (c) it is important to reemphasize that only issuer-sponsored ADRs can be listed. A copy of the depositary agreement is also a mandatory supplement to the basic listing agreement.
   d. Annual reports to shareholders for the last three years, either in the English version, if available, or accompanied by translations of each such report.
   e. The latest proxy statement or equivalent material made available to shareholders for the most recent annual or general meeting, translated into English.
   f. Worldwide and US stock distribution schedules.
   g. Supplementary data to assist the NYSE in determining the character of the share distribution and the number of publicly held shares—for both US and global holdings, including:
      i. Names of 10 largest holders.
      ii. NYSE member firms holding 1000 or more shares or other units.
      iii. List of stock exchanges or other markets on which the issuer's securities currently are traded as well as the price range and volume of those securities over the preceding five years.
      iv. Stock owned or known to be controlled by directors, officers, and their immediate families and other holders of 10 percent or more.
      v. Any type of restriction, and the details thereof, relating to the issuer's shares.
      vi. Estimate of non-officer employee ownership.
      vii. Issuer shares held in profit sharing, pension, or similar employee benefit plans.
   h. If the issuer has any partially owned subsidiaries, detailed information on the public and private ownership of the remainder, as well as any director or officer ownership.
   i. List of the issuer's principal bankers and a statement of the holdings of its stock by any one of these bankers in excess of 5 percent.
   j. The identity of any regulatory agency with jurisdiction over the issuer or any portion of its operations and the extent and impact of regulation by such agency on taxation, accounting, foreign exchange control, and similar matters.

    k. Identification of the issuer's directors and principal officers by name, title, and primary occupations.

    l. Total number of employees and general status of labor relations.

    m. Description of pending material litigation and opinion as to the potential impact thereof on the issuer's operations.

38. See NYSE Listed Company Manual, § 902.02. The pertinent initial fees per million shares or ADRs are: (a) for the first and second million shares or ADRs, $14,750; (b) for the third and fourth million shares or ADRs, $7,400; (c) for the fifth million up to 300 million shares or ADRs, $3,500; and (d) for shares or ADRs in excess of 300 million, $1,900.

39. See NYSE Listed Company Manual, § 902.02. The annual fee schedule effective January 1, 1992, the most recent available, is the greater of the minimum fee of $1,500 or the fee calculated on a per-share or per-ADR basis, as follows: either (a) on a per-share or per-ADR basis, (i) first and second million shares or ADRs, $1,600 per million; (ii) in excess of 2 million shares or ADRs, $805 per million of shares or ADRs; *or* (b) on a minimum-fee basis, (i) up to 10 million shares or ADRs, $15,700; (ii) over 10 million to 20 million shares or ADRs, $23,550; (iii) over 20 million to 50 million shares or ADRs, $31,400; (iv) over 50 million to 100 million shares or ADRs, $47,000; (v) over 100 million to 200 million shares or ADRs, $62,700; and (vi) over 200 million shares or ADRs, $78,100.

40. See NYSE Listed Company Manual, § 103.01. Recognizing that the widespread use of bearer shares outside the United States might render it difficult for foreign issuers to establish that they have the requisite number of shareholders on a global basis, the NYSE permits as a substitute for documentation for the number of holders a "sponsorship," or attestation, by a member firm as to the liquidity and depth of the market for the applicant issuer's shares in its primary trading market outside the United States. NYSE Listed Company Manual, § 103.03. However, this provision makes clear that the NYSE staff must be satisfied that a broad and independent market for the subject securities exists. Accordingly, "for companies listing with minimal US distribution, the primary non-US market must provide the liquidity against which US arbitrage transactions must be effected." NYSE Listed Company Manual § 103.03.

41. *Ibid.*

42. *Ibid.* at § 102.00.

43. AMEX Company Guide § 110.

44. To meet domestic listing standards, an issuer must have a minimum of: (a) 500,000 shares held in the United States by 800 holders or, in the alternative, by 400 holders if the average daily US trading volume of the shares equals or exceeds 2000 shares during the most recent six months, or one million shares held in the United States by 400 holders; and (b) an aggregate market value of $3 million and a per-share price of $3.00. An issuer must also have $4 million of stockholders' equity and pre-tax income of $750,000 for the last fiscal year or two of its prior three fiscal years. See AMEX Company Guide, §§ 101, 102.

45. See NASD Manual (CCH), Schedule D, Paras. 1803-04.

46. See NASD Manual (CCH), Schedule D, Paras. 1807-13.

47. See NYSE Listed Company Manual § 203.1; AMEX Company Guide §§ 610-11; NASD Manual (CCH), Schedule D, Para. 1812(b)(NMS quotation).

48. See NYSE Listed Company Manual § 203.2; AMEX Company Guide § 623; NASD Manual (CCH), Schedule D, Para. 1812.

49. See NYSE Listed Company Manual § 103.00; AMEX Company Guide § 110; see also Greene (note 18), pp. 50–57.

50. See NYSE Listed Company Manual § 202.5; AMEX Company Guide §§ 401-05; NASD Manual (CCH), Schedule D, Para. 1806A.

51. See NYSE Listed Company Manual § 303; AMEX Company Guide § 121; NASD Manual (CCH), Schedule D, Paras. 1812(c), (d) (NMS).

52. See NYSE Listed Company Manual § 303; AMEX Company Guide § 121; NASD Manual (CCH), Schedule D, Para. 1812(c).

53. See NYSE Listed Company Manual § 103; AMEX Company Guide § 110.

54. See NYSE Listed Company Manual § 307.

55. See NYSE Listed Company Manual §§ 303.00 and 310.00(A).

56. See AMEX Company Guide § 123; NASD Manual (CCH), Schedule D, Para. 1812(f).

57. See NYSE Listed Company Manual § 302.

58. See NYSE Listed Company Manual § 104; AMEX Company Guide § 110.

59. See NYSE Listed Company Manual § 312.03(c); NASD Manual (CCH), Schedule D, Para. 1812(i)(NMS).

60. See NYSE Listed Company Manual § 312.03; AMEX Company Guide § 711; NASD Manual (CCH), Schedule D, Para. 1812(i)(NMS).

61. See NYSE Listed Company Manual § 312.03(d); AMEX Company Guide § 713.

62. See NYSE Listed Company Manual § 312.03(d); AMEX Company Guide § 712; NASD Manual (CCH), Schedule D, Para. 1812(c)(NMS).

63. See NYSE Listed Company Manual § 103.

64. Greene, Branerman and Sperber, p. 52.

65. See *Ibid.*, citing NYSE Listed Company Manual §§ 308.00, 311.00-311.01, and 311.03, respectively.

66. See Rules 15c2-11(a)(4) and 15c2-11(a)(5) under the Exchange Act.

67. See Rules 12g3-2(d)(1), 12g3-2(d)(3). There is an exception for certain "grandfathered" companies quoted in NASDAQ that have supplied Rule 12g3-2(b) information continuously since 1983. See Rules 12g3-2(i)-(iii).

68. See Rule 12g3-2(d)(1).

69. Greene, Branerman and Sperber, p. 119.

70. See SEC Release No. 34-29277 (June 14, 1991). As part of a broader rule initiative proposed in 1991 to facilitate cross-border tender and exchange offers (see SEC Release No. 33-6897 (June 5, 1991)), the Commission proposed to require that all submissions under Rule 12g3-2(b) be made under cover of one of two proposed new forms: proposed Form 12-F for initial submission under Rule 12g3-2(b) and proposed Form 12F-A for all subsequent submissions. The fundamental purpose of this disclosure in the 12g3-2(b) context would be to make US holder information more readily accessible to investors and other third parties. To date, none of these proposals has been adopted.

71. Because the information provided by a Rule 12g3-2(b)-exempt issuer is not deemed to be filed with the SEC, it will not expose the issuer to liability for fraud under Section 18 of the Exchange Act. However, the issuer could be sued by the SEC or a private plaintiff for fraudulent statements or omissions in submitted documents under other antifraud provisions, such as Section 12(2) of the Securities Act (misstatements

in connection with the offer or sale of a security) or Section 10(b) of the Exchange Act and Rule 10b-5 thereunder (general antifraud provisions barring fraud in connection with the purchase or sale of a security).

72. Foreign investment companies legally cannot have more than 100 US beneficial holders unless they create a US affiliate that registers with the SEC.

73. See S. Hanks, "Rule 12g3-2(b): Backdoor or Trapdoor?," *International Finance Law Review* (April 1991), pp. 36 and 37.

74. Davis, p. 112 (quoting former Commissioner Carter Beese).

75. R. Karmel, Living With U.S. Regulations: Complying With the Rules and Avoiding Litigation, *Fordham International Law Journal* 17 (1994), p. 152.

76. See Rule 175 under the Securities Act and Rule 3b-6 under the Exchange Act. Both rules provide issuers some protection from SEC and private litigation arising from disclosure of a forward-looking statement if that statement was contained in an SEC filing, was made in good faith, and had a reasonable basis when made. In light of complaints from issuers and other critics, the SEC issued a release seeking public comment on whether some change in the present safe harbor is warranted. See SEC Release No. 33-7101 (October 13, 1994).

77. See *Central Bank of Denver v. First Interstate Bank of Denver, N.S.,* 114 S.Ct. 1439 (1994); *Aaron v. SEC,* 446 U.S. 680 (1980); *Rolf v. Blyth, Eastman, Dillon & Co.,* 570 F.2d 38 (2d Cir.), *cert. denied,* 439 US 970 (1978). In the US Supreme Court held that there was no private cause of action for aiding and abetting a Rule 10b-5 violation. Many believe, including those Justices dissenting from the *Central Bank* majority opinion, that the holding of this case extends to the SEC. See *Central Bank,* 114 S.Ct. at 1460 (Stevens, J., dissenting).

78. *Basic Inc. v. Levinson,* 485 US 224, 231-232 (1988) (citing *TSC Indus., Inc. v. Northway, Inc.,* 426 US 438, 449 (1976)).

79. Greene, Branerman and Sperber, p. 8.

80. The MJDS framework covers U.S.-Canadian securities offerings, including rights and exchange offers and cash tender offers, as well as Exchange Act registration and periodic reporting and trust indenture requirements for debt offerings. See SEC Release No. 33-6902 (June 21, 1991) (adopting the MJDS system with Canada). See also SEC Release No. 33-6902A (March 23, 1992). Subsequent amendments were made in accordance with the following SEC releases: No. 33-7004 (June 28, 1993), No. 33-7025 (November 3, 1993), and No. 7040 (December 27, 1993). The Canadian MJDS for US issuers is substantially similar in scope to the US version. Effective July 1, 1991, the Canadian MJDS was implemented through a combination of National Policy Statement No. 45 and blanket orders and rulings by the securities authorities of each Canadian province and territory.

81. See Greene, Branerman and Sperber.

82. See J. Cochrane, "Are U.S. Regulatory Requirements for Foreign Firms Appropriate?" *Fordham International Law Journal* 17 (1994), p. 58 (NYSE senior vice president and chief economist). But see R. Kosnik, "The Role of the SEC in Evaluating Foreign Issuers Coming to U.S. Markets," *Fordham International Law Journal* 17 (1994), p. S97.

83. See SEC Release No. 33-6896 (June 5, 1991). In this release, the SEC proposed a new exemptive rule and registration form under the Securities Act for foreign issuers' rights offerings of equity securities to existing US shareholders. The aggregate offering price would be capped at $5 million (US).

84. See SEC Release No. 33-6897 (June 5, 1991). Under this proposal, the SEC would create a new system of rules and forms whereby tender offers for a foreign issuer's securities could proceed in the United States on the basis of the applicable regulations of the target company's home jurisdiction where no more than 10 percent of the class of securities are held by US holders (other than US holders of more than 10 percent of that class). The proposed rules would apply to both third-party and issuer tender and exchange offers. Registration of securities issued in an exchange offer (or compliance with an exemption therefrom) would be accomplished under one of two available procedures: (1) an exempt offering where $5 million or less of the securities are offered in the United States or (2) a registered offering for larger qualifying exchange offers where 5 percent or less of the shares are held in the United States, using a streamlined registration form that "wraps around" home country documents. In addition, the SEC has proposed to formalize accommodations reached with the United Kingdom's Panel on Takeovers and Mergers to permit tender offers for the securities of a US-chartered company to be conducted under both US and UK law.

85. See note 5 and accompanying text.

HOW TO ATTRACT
US INVESTORS

Chapter 5

The Economic Clout of US Institutions

In recent years, US investors' appetite for foreign equities has become voracious. Moreover, it is largely the giant US *institutional* investors that have both dominated trading in foreign securities on US markets and reached outward into foreign equity markets. There are a relatively small number of these institutions engaged in foreign trading; knowing their identity and understanding what influences their investment and corporate governance decisions is of paramount importance to any company wanting to raise money through US equity markets or from US investors willing to invest abroad. Institutional investors' holdings in US companies have increased gradually enough that US companies have become somewhat accustomed to the institutions' increasingly obstreperous demands. To foreign companies, however, these demands may come as a shock—especially to those foreign companies that have little awareness of the rights US institutional investors take for granted.

INSTITUTIONAL SHARE OF US FINANCIAL ASSETS

US institutions occupy a commanding place not only in US markets but increasingly in worldwide capital markets. Assets of institutional investors grew to $9.5 trillion at the end of the third quarter of 1994 from $6.3 trillion in 1990—more than a 50 percent increase in four years. By 1994, institutional investors held as much as 22 percent of all US financial assets, and their percentage of equity market holdings had increased to 51.5 percent.

Figure 5–1 shows that institutional investors' assets as a percent of total US financial assets began a steep ascent after 1980. Throughout the

FIGURE 5–1

Institutional Investor Assets as a Percentage of US Financial Assets

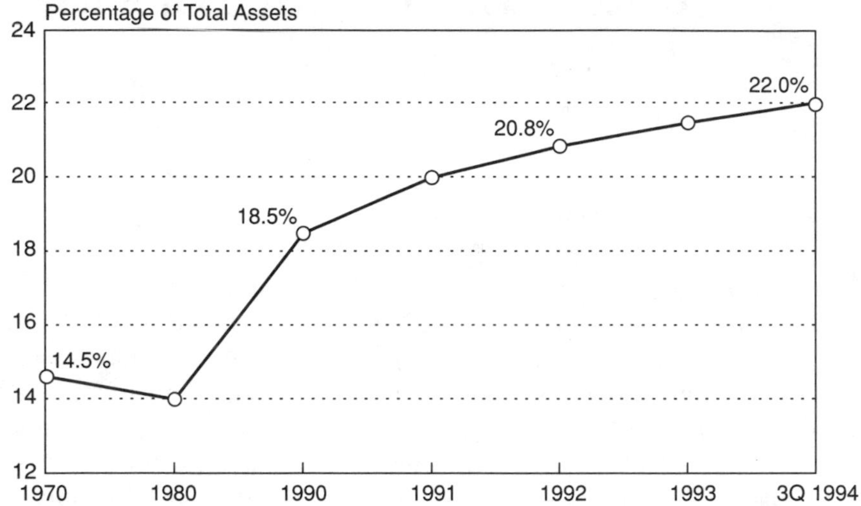

Source: *The Brancato Report on Institutional Investment* 2, ed. 1 (January 1995).

entire decade of the 1970s, institutions held just over 14 percent of US assets. In 1980 they had about the same proportion with which they entered the decade. During the next decade alone, however, they increased their share of US assets from approximately 14 percent to 18.5 percent. By the third quarter of 1994, as noted before, institutions held nearly 22 percent of US assets.

Beginning in 1970, all institutions' assets nearly tripled in one decade, from $672.6 billion in 1970 to $1.9 trillion in 1980. The next decade brought *more* than a tripling in assets, to $6.3 trillion in 1990. There was an additional staggering increase of more than 50 percent in the next four years, to $9.5 trillion at the end of the third quarter of 1994. Annual growth rates were fastest at 14.9 percent per year during the first half of the 1980s and then leveled off to a still respectable 10.8 percent per year during the latter half of the 1980s. Aided by the boom in the stock market, assets grew 13.3 percent from 1990 to 1993 but slowed to only a 3.4 percent increase during the first three quarters of 1994.

Table 5–1 breaks down these figures according to category of institutions, and Figures 5–2 and 5–3 similarly show growth in assets held by

TABLE 5–1
Institutional Investors Asset Growth by Category: 1980–1994

Type of Institution	Assets ($ billions)					Compounded Annual Growth Rate			% Growth:
	1980	1985	1990	1993	3rd Q. 1994	1980 1985	1985 1990	1990 1993	1993–3Q. 94
Pension funds	859.2	1,900.8	3,115.6	4,525.4	4,566.8	17.2%	10.4%	13.3%	0.9%
Private trusteed	504.4	1,156.0	1,743.0	2,570.8	2,510.3	18.0	8.6	13.8	–2.4
Private insured	158.2	346.7	636.1	833.0	872.8	17.0	12.9	9.4	4.8
State & local	196.6	398.1	736.5	1,121.6	1,183.7	15.2	13.1	15.1	5.5
Investment companies	118.0	435.8	967.3	1,662.9	1,802.5	29.9	17.3	19.8	8.4
Open-end mutual funds	113.0	426.3	914.6	1,552.0	1,686.4	30.4	16.5	19.3	8.7
Closed-end mutual funds	5.0	9.5	52.7	110.9	116.1	13.7	40.9	28.1	4.7
Insurance companies	518.7	790.6	1,328.4	1,675.7	1,751.1	8.8	10.9	8.0	4.5
Life insurance	321.0	479.2	772.1	1,004.2	1,051.9	8.3	10.0	9.2	4.8
Property & casualty	197.7	311.4	556.3	671.5	699.2	9.5	12.3	6.5	4.1
Bank & trust companies	342.2	550.7	759.1	1,132.6	1,179.1	10.0	6.6	14.3	4.1
Foundations	48.2	102.1	142.5	194.4	204.2	16.2	6.9	10.9	5.0
All Institutions	1,886.3	3,780.0	6,312.9	9,191.0	9,503.7	14.9	10.8	13.3	3.4

Source: *The Brancato Report on Institutional Investment.* 1, ed. 1 (December 1993), and 2, ed. 1 (January 1995).

FIGURE 5–2
Institutional Investor Growth: 1980–1994

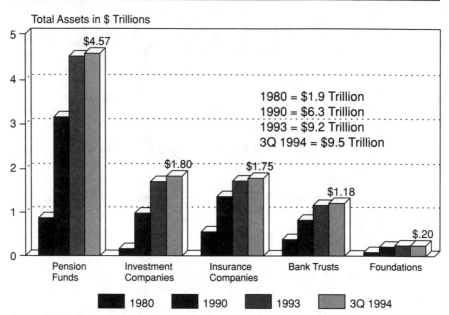

Source: *The Brancato Report on Institutional Investment* 2, ed. 1 (January 1995).

each type of institutional investor from 1980 through the third quarter of 1994. Pension funds accounted for the largest dollar increase of any type of institution between 1980 and 1994: Assets rose from $860 billion in 1980 to $4.6 trillion in 1994, over a five-fold increase. Since 1985, average private trusteed (corporate) pension fund growth has been outpaced by growth in the public pension fund sector, although proceeding from a smaller base. The most rapid growth of any institutional investor category took place in the open-end investment company category. (This is the statutory terminology for a mutual fund, indicating that it stands ready to redeem its shares on demand.) In virtually all years from 1980 on, mutual funds have significantly outstripped total institutional asset growth as well as growth for all other categories.

While foreign issuers may have a sense of the institutional investor market from examining their total assets and the shifts in asset growth among institutionas, a key factor in understanding US institutional investors is realizing that institutions may not manage all their assets—they

FIGURE 5–3
Institutional Investor Assets by Category: 1970, 1980, and 1994

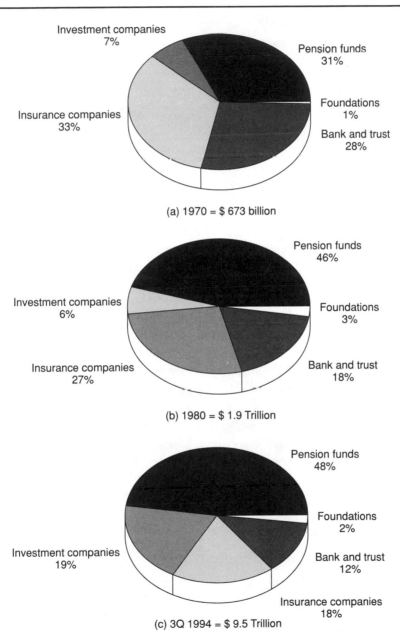

(a) 1970 = $ 673 billion

(b) 1980 = $ 1.9 Trillion

(c) 3Q 1994 = $ 9.5 Trillion

Source: *The Brancato Report on Institutional Investment* 2, ed. 1 (January 1995).

FIGURE 5–4
Holdings vs. Management of Assets: 1993

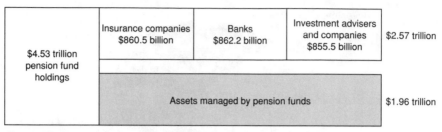

| $4.53 trillion pension fund holdings | Insurance companies $860.5 billion | Banks $862.2 billion | Investment advisers and companies $855.5 billion | $2.57 trillion |
| | Assets managed by pension funds | | | $1.96 trillion |

Source: *The Brancato Report on Institutional Investment* 2, ed. 1 (January 1995).

may allocate these assets to other institutions to manage on their behalf. Thus, there are substantial differences between money held by institutions as prime fiduciaries and money actually managed by the institutions. For example, Figure 5–4 shows that while pension funds held a total of $4.53 trillion in assets in 1993, they allocated significant portions of these assets for *management* to external investment advisors, investment companies, life insurance companies, and bank and trust companies. In 1993, therefore, pension funds actually managed only $1.96 trillion out of their $4.53 trillion in assets, while a total of $2.57 trillion was delegated to other institutions to manage. Thus, as Table 5–2 shows, pension funds *held* 49.2 percent of 1993 institutional investor assets but *actually managed* only 21.2 percent of institutional assets. Money allocated to banks

TABLE 5–2
Institutional Investor Holdings versus Management

Institution	% Assets Held	% Assets Managed
Pension funds	49.2%	21.2%
Private trusteed	28.0	16.0
State & local	12.2	5.3
External investment advisors	0.0	8.5
Investment companies	18.1	25.8
Insurance companies	18.2	26.0
Banks	12.3	18.1
Foundations	2.1	0.4
Total	100.0	100.0

Source: *The Brancato Report on Institutional Investment* 2, ed. 1 (January 1995).

to manage, primarily from pension funds, increases their influence in the markets: in 1993 they held 12.3 percent of assets as institutional investors themselves but managed 18.1 percent of total institutional investor assets. Insurance companies, similarly, held 18.2 percent of institutional assets in 1993 while their managed assets amounted to 29.8 percent. In terms of assets, therefore, the key groups to focus on when planning a strategy to attract US institutional investor capital are not only pension funds but investment companies, insurance companies (although they primarily invest in debt securities), and banks.

INSTITUTIONAL SHARE OF US EQUITY MARKETS

Figure 5–5 and Table 5–3 trace the share of US equity markets held by institutions since earlier decades. Overall, the market value of institutional equity holdings increased from $53 billion (12.6 percent of total US equity markets) in 1960 to $166 billion (19.4 percent of total US equity markets) in 1970. During the next decade, equity investments grew to

FIGURE 5–5
Institutional Ownership of US Equity: 1960–1994

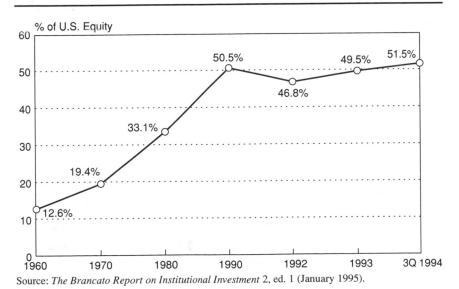

Source: *The Brancato Report on Institutional Investment* 2, ed. 1 (January 1995).

TABLE 5–3
Institutional Investors Holdings of Total Outstanding Equity: 1950–1994
($ billions)

Year	Market Value of Total Outstanding Equity	Market Value of Total Institutional Equity Holdings	Percent Institutional Equity
1950	142.7	8.7	6.1 %
1960	421.2	52.9	12.6
1970	859.4	166.4	19.4
1980	1,568.9	519.9	33.1
1988	3,105.5	1,519.9	48.9
1989	3,812.9	1,905.7	50.0
1990	3,543.7	1,790.0	50.5
1991	4,869.4	2,283.6	46.9
1992	5,540.9	2,590.6	46.8
1993	6,186.5	3062.5	49.5
3rd Q. 1994 p	6,135.1	3162.5	51.5

Notes: p = preliminary.

Values of total outstanding equity from The Board of Governors, Federal Reserve System.

Source: *The Brancato Report on Institutional Investment* 2, ed. 1. (January 1995).

$520 billion (33.1 percent of the total US equity market). The decade of the 1980s saw a staggering increase in the total percent of market equities held by institutions: from 33.1 percent of total outstanding equity in 1980 to 50.5 percent in 1990. By 1992, however, the proportion of total equity accounted for by institutional investors actually declined several percentage points to just under 47 percent. Of this decline, 2.3 percentage points alone was attributable to a decline in the share of total equity markets held by private pension funds. By 1993, however, institutional equity share had recovered to 49.5 percent and reached an all-time high of 51.5 percent by the end of the third quarter of 1994.

INSTITUTIONAL INVESTMENT IN THE LARGEST 1,000 US CORPORATIONS

Figure 5–6 shows that institutions have substantially and consistently increased their holdings of the largest 1,000 US corporations: from 46.6 percent of total stock in 1987 to 55.8 percent of total stock by year-end

FIGURE 5–6
Institutional Ownership in the Top 1,000 US Corporations: 1987–1994

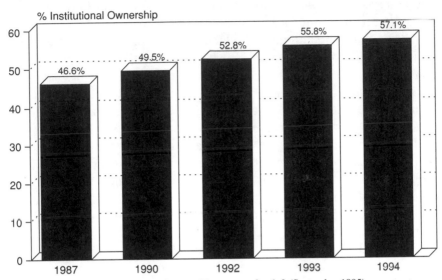

Source: *The Brancato Report on Institutional Investment* 2, ed. 3 (September 1995).

1993 and then to 57.1 percent by year-end 1994. At present, concentration is greatest for the largest 250 companies (with average institutional holdings of 58.0 percent) and then declines for the remaining 750 companies. It is worthwhile to note that institutional ownership in these smaller capitalization companies is increasing more rapidly, as institutions have begun to take a more aggressive investing stance and have looked beyond the largest "blue chip" companies to seek out new investment opportunities—although these large institutions are still generally constrained[1] to invest in companies with a minimum capitalization. Thus, for example, the highest increase in institutional ownership took place in the smallest capitalization group (top 750 to 1,000 companies) where ownership increased 12.7 percentage points from 37.7 percent in 1987 to 50.4 percent in 1993.

As already mentioned, institutional ownership in the largest 1,000 corporations steadily increased, reaching 55.8 percent in 1993. This would appear to be in contrast to findings discussed above which reported that the share of total outstanding equities held by institutions increased until 1990 and then declined from over 50 percent in 1990 to approximately 47 percent by 1992. Data in Table 5–4 explain how institutional ownership can increase in the largest companies while it declines as a percent of the equity markets as a whole; largely, this is because the top 1,000 corporations are accounting for a lower percentage of total market value. Repurchases and restructurings in the largest 1,000 companies have lowered their growth in total outstanding stock market value, to the extent that it has not kept pace with overall equity market growth, especially that of the burgeoning small capitalization sector. This, coupled with the tendency of large institutions to seek high capitalization stocks, is responsible for these seemingly anomalous trends.

There were significantly more companies with higher concentrations of institutional holdings in 1993 than in prior years. For example, in 1987, only 0.4 percent, or four companies out of the top 1,000, had institutional ownership in excess of 90 percent. By 1993, this percentage grew to 3.5 percent or 35 companies out of the 1,000 with institutional ownership in excess of 90 percent.

Finally, when broken down by industry grouping, there is substantial variation in the institutional holdings for different industries (see Table 5–5). Utility companies have the lowest institutional investment, while manufacturing and transportation companies have the highest. The electric equipment industry leads all individual industry groupings, with 66.9 percent institutional ownership in 1993.

MANAGEMENT BY TYPE OF INSTITUTION IN THE LARGEST US CORPORATIONS

This section examines a different series of data, which are provided by Georgeson & Company and are based on the Vickers database of the statements that investment managers must file with the Securities and Exchange Commission under Rule 13F. These 13F filings list holdings according to the managers who are actually responsible for investing the holdings. Thus, if a pension fund delegates investment authority to a bank, the holding will show up in the database under the bank category and not the pension fund category.

As might be expected, institutional management in the 13F filing series increases, as does ownership in the top 1,000 corporations, over the period 1985 through mid-1994 (see Table 5–6). Average institutional management in the top 25 companies increased from 36.1 percent of

TABLE 5–4
Relative Growth in Market Value, All Domestic Corporations versus Top 1000: 1990–1993

	1990 ($ billions)	Percentage Change	1991 ($ billions)	Percentage Change	1992 ($ billions)	Percentage Change	1993 ($ billions)
Market value of all domestic corporations	3,327.2	37.6%	4,578.3	14.1%	5,225.9	9.1%	5,700.1
Market value of top 1,000 corporations	2,950.0	14.4%	3,375.0	13.8%	3,841.7	8.0%	4,149.0
Market value of top 1,000 as a percentage of market value of all domestic corporations	88.6%		73.7%		73.5%		72.8%
Percentage of top 1,000 corporations held by institutional investors	49.5%		51.0%		53.0%		55.8%

Source: *The Brancato Report on Institutional Investment* 1, ed. 3 (September 1994). Calculated from Federal Reserve Flow of Funds data and from the *Business Week* Top 1,000 database.

TABLE 5–5

Institutional Investor Concentration of Ownership in the Top 1,000 US Corporations by Industry Grouping: 1987–1993

Industry	Average Institutional Investor Holdings		
	1990	*1992*	*1993*
Aerospace	55.6%	62.0%	39.7%
Automotive	52.2	51.9	52.4
Banks	43.6	48.0	49.2
Chemicals	54.7	61.2	62.1
Conglomerate	53.5	55.5	63.0
Consumer	51.1	53.3	58.0
Container	40.6	52.4	54.5
Electrical equipment	58.8	56.0	66.9
Food	41.5	44.6	46.8
Fuel	51.6	55.6	61.0
Health care	54.5	54.7	55.5
Housing	45.9	50.7	48.6
Leisure	52.0	53.5	58.2
Manufacturing	57.7	59.5	64.2
Metals	50.1	57.1	53.6
Nonbank finance	54.2	55.9	60.1
Office equipment	55.3	64.6	66.4
Paper	62.2	57.9	59.0
Publishing/TV	40.2	42.8	46.5
Retailing	53.5	50.6	58.6
Services	47.1	57.9	57.1
Telecommunications	37.5	49.4	46.5
Transportation	61.1	63.5	65.3
Utilities	39.2	37.7	38.4

Source: *The Brancato Report on Institutional Investment* 1, ed. 3 (September 1994). Calculated from the *Business Week* Top 1,000 database.

holdings in 1985 to 45.3 percent of holdings in 1990 and then to 48.9 percent of holdings in mid-1994. Where the data for institutionally held telephone companies is omitted from the sample, average institutionally managed holdings increased from 38.2 percent in 1985 to 48.7 percent in 1990 and then to 51.3 percent in mid-1994.

Table 5–6 also breaks down the institutional holdings by type of institution. In mid-1994, banks had the largest investment discretion, managing 18.8 percent of the outstanding stock of the largest 25 companies, or more than a third of all institutional holdings.

In mid-1994, institutional holdings in the top corporations (ranked by

TABLE 5-6
Managed Holdings by Type of Institutional Investor in the Largest 25 US Corporations: 1985, 1990, and mid-1994

	1985 Average	Percentage Point Change 1985–1990	1990 Average	Percentage Point Change 1990–1994	1994 Average
Average Institutional holdings in the largest 25 companies	36.1%	9.2	45.3%	3.6	48.9%
22 Non-telephone companies	38.2	10.6	48.7	2.6	51.3
3 telephone companies	21.3	4.0	25.3	5.4	30.7
By Institutional Investor Category:					
Banks	15.2%	1.9	17.1%	1.7	18.8%
Money managers	10.9	5.7	16.5	-1.8	14.7
Insurance companies	3.1	-0.8	2.3	1.1	3.4
Investment companies	2.0	0.1	2.1	3.6	5.7
Corporate pensions	1.8	-0.2	1.6	1.0	2.6
Public, academic, & foundation	0.9	4.4	5.3	-1.7	3.6

Note: Data for 1985 and 1990 are as of December 31st; data for 1994 are latest 13F filings in the Georgeson database as of August 1, 1994. This database is continually updated with quarterly filings; the bulk of the filings cover either the first or second quarter of 1994.

Source: For 1985 and 1990 data: Brancato, Columbia Institutional Investor Project, based on CDA Spectrum database of 13F Filings. For 1994 data: Georgeson & Company based on Vickers database of 13F Filers as cited in *The Brancato Report on Institutional Investment* 1, ed. 3 (September 1994).

market value) ranged from highs of 74.1 percent for Intel and 73.7 percent for Motorola to lows in the 30 percent range for the telephone companies in the top 25 sample. Like institutional *ownership* in the top 1,000 sample, institutional *management* in the largest capitalization companies is more concentrated.

Table 5–7 summarizes the trends in managed holdings by the largest 5, 10, 20, and 25 institutional investors. In 1985, the largest 5 institutions held 8.5 percent of the stock in the top 25 companies. By mid-1994, the largest 5 institutions held 11.2 percent of the stock in the top 25 companies—these 5 institutions thus held 23 percent of the 25 companies' stock in the hands of all the 13F-filing institutions.

US INSTITUTIONAL INVESTOR TRADING PATTERNS

Commentators attempting to describe the trading habits of institutional investors in simple terms have made some widely varied and often directly contradictory observations. Some people hold the perception, for example, that institutional investors trade only for short-term gain, while others argue that they cannot actively trade because they *are the market* and would disrupt it too much if they were active traders. Similarly, there is a common perception that institutions are responsible for excessive turnover in US stock markets; on the other hand, some say that excessive turnover cannot possibly appeal to institutional investors because they make their investments to fulfill long-term beneficiary payout requirements. Careful analysis shows that most of the conflicting observations are true at some time because trading behavior varies from one kind of investor to another and among the same investors under different circumstances.

Analysis of equity turnover for the year ended September 30, 1994, shows an aggregate annual turnover of 43.6 percent for all institutional investors. (see Table 5–8). The analysis was conducted using the Georgeson & Company, Inc., database and is based on 13F filings with the Securities and Exchange Commission. Money managers had the highest turnover rate, at 55.7 percent, while corporate pensions managing their own funds had the lowest turnover, at 19.9 percent. The turnover data cover money managed directly by the institution.

Even more revealing than aggregate turnover numbers, however, are

TABLE 5-7
Concentration of Institutional Investor Holdings by the Largest 25 Institutions in the Largest 25 US Corporations: 1985, 1990 and mid-1994

	1985		1990		1994	
	Average Percent Held	*Distribution of Institutional Shares Held*	*Average Percent Held*	*Distribution of Institutional Shares Held*	*Average Percent Held*	*Distribution of Institutional Shares Held*
All institutions	36.1%	100%	45.3%	100%	48.9%	100%
Top 5 institutional investors	8.5	23	10.6	23	11.2	23
Top 10 institutional investors	12.6	35	15.1	33	16.1	33
Top 20 institutional investors	17.9	49	20.8	46	22.5	46
Top 25 institutional investors	19.8	55	22.9	51	24.8	51

Source: *The Brancato Report on Institutional Investment* 1, ed. 3 (September 1994). Calculated from the Georgeson & Company database.

TABLE 5–8
Turnover by Investment Strategy and Type of Institution: 1994

	Aggressive Growth	Growth	Balanced*	Indexed Only	Overall Portfolio Average
Corporate pensions	3.1%	29.2%	17.6%	15.2%	19.9%
Public pension funds	neg.**	40.9	25.2	9.6	20.9
Mutual fund managers	74.1	67.3	55.2	neg.**	50.5
Money managers	67.7	67.7	47.0	34.3	55.7
Insurance companies	32.8	54.6	32.5	neg.**	44.7
Banks	52.7	60.0	27.3	20.3	29.5
Overall average	63.9%	63.4%	39.2%	18.0%	43.6%

Notes: Data calculated for year ended September 30, 1994.

All data weighted by value of portfolio devoted to each investment strategy. Strategies shown are the four most prevalent.

* Balanced; encompasses a variety of investment strategies and may include some indexed investments.

** neg. = negligible

Source: *The Brancato Report on Institutional Investment* 1, ed. 2 (April 1994). Calculated using the Georgeson & Company database.

turnover data obtained by analyzing the portfolios of money managed by each type of institutional investor and classified according to a variety of investment strategies such as those listed in Table 5–8: "aggressive growth," "growth," "balanced portfolio," and "indexed only." When institutional practices are broken down in this way, we find that, for the year ended September 30, 1994, turnover is most vigorous under the aggressive growth strategy, especially as pursued by mutual fund managers (74.1 percent) and money managers (67.7 percent). At the low end of the turnover range, public pensions managing their own indexed funds have only 9.6 percent turnover. The lowest turnover among all portfolio subsegments can be found within the aggressive growth investment strategy of the portfolios of corporate pension funds that manage their own money (3.1 percent). Turnover thus varies by a factor of more than 20 from the lowest to the highest portions of the various portfolios. Moreover, it is the "activist" public pension funds which, when they manage their own money, tend to hold their assets longest in indexed portfolios—a fact that should be of great interest to companies seeking equity capital.

For all institutions, only a small proportion (3.3 percent) of equity under management was turned over rapidly in portfolios with an aggressive growth strategy. Growth investments accounted for 24.1 percent of equity value, and balanced investments accounted for 26.3 percent. By contrast, 14.2 percent of institutional equity was devoted to an indexed only strategy. More specifically, indexation is pursued most by public pension funds, with 52.2 percent of their portfolios under management allocated. This compares with 37.2 percent of corporate pension fund equities that are indexed.

INSTITUTIONAL INVESTMENT IN FOREIGN EQUITIES

The *London Times* has described the difficulty of gathering international financial data as "rather like taking a blurred snapshot of a fast moving target." While recognizing the potential for failing to capture all international equity flows, *The Brancato Report on Institutional Investment* nevertheless estimates that total US equity holdings of foreign corporations dramatically increased from $91.5 billion in 1988 to $245.9 billion in 1993. (See Chapter 1 for a breakdown of the aggregate investment flows derived from purchases of foreign stock by US investors.) This chapter demonstrates how significant a presence US institutions are in the purchase of foreign securities.

Institutional presence in foreign equity markets has been dramatically increasing. Table 5–9 illustrates that the principal institutional investors making foreign equity investments (pension funds and mutual funds) increased their equity holdings from $97.7 billion in 1990 to $236 billion in 1993. This represents an aggregate increase in pension fund assets devoted to foreign equities from 3.1 percent in 1990 to 5.0 percent in 1993 and an increase in mutual funds assets from 1.7 percent to 2.6 percent.

Institutions account for the bulk of foreign equity investments made by US investors. Furthermore, it is the largest pension funds that account for the largest concentration of such foreign equity investments. The largest funds surveyed by Greenwich Associates (those with assets over $1 billion) are the major holders of international equities, controlling 88.8 percent of all institutional holdings of foreign stocks in 1993.

Table 5–10 shows that the 25 largest pension fund holders of international equity (ranked by year-end holdings) held $85.3 billion in interna-

TABLE 5-9

Assets Held in International Equities by Type of Institution: 1990–1993
($ Billions)

	1990		1991		1992		1993	
	Foreign Equities	Percentage of Total Assets	Foreign Equities	Percentage of Total Assets	Foreign Equities	Percentage of Total Assets	Foreign Equities	Percentage of Total Assets
All US pension funds * & endowments **	82.2	3.1%	102	3.1%	135	3.8%	195	5.0%
Mutual funds	15.5	1.7	27.7	2.6	32.7	2.6	41.0	2.6
Total	97.7	2.8	129.7	3.0	167.7	3.5	236.0	4.3

Notes: * Includes all US private trusteed and state & local pension funds.

** Assets invested in international equity mutual funds by pension funds and endowments are included in this category and were subtracted from the mutual fund category to prevent double counting.

Source: *The Brancato Report on Institutional Investment* 1, ed. 3 (September 1994). Estimated using data from Baring Securities and the Investment Company Institute.

TABLE 5–10
International Equities Held by the 25 Pension Funds with the Largest Foreign Portfolios: 1989–1994 ($ Millions)

Ranked by 1993 Holdings of International Equities	1989		1991		1993		1994	
	International Equities	% of Total Assets	International Equities	% of Total Assets	International Equities	% of Total Assets	International Equities	% of Total Assets
1. TIAA-CREF	4,000	4.9%	5,470	5.5%	10,197	8.2%	13,195	9.9%
2. California Public Employees (CalPERS)	2,700	5.0	6,371	9.9	9,292	12.0	11,190	14.3
3. IBM	NA	NA	NA	NA	5,781	17.1	5,838	16.5
4. California State Teachers	0	0.0	0	0.0	2,223	4.6	4,938	10.1
5. AT&T	2,085	4.9	2,554	5.7	3,864	7.2	4,693	8.9
6. New York State & Local	83	0.2	683	1.4	2,651	4.6	4,164	6.9
7. General Electric	1,653	5.7	1,597	5.1	2,833	7.5	3,890	11.1
8. New York City Retirement	0	0.0	1,827	3.7	2,986	8.2	3,609	10.2
9. Wisconsin Investment Board	380	1.9	934	4.1	2,089	7.1	3,369	11.2
10. New York State Teachers	0	0.0	311	0.0	317	0.7	3,039	7.4
11. Oregon Public Employees	1,115	10.0	1,209	9.6	2,400	14.1	2,700	15.6
12. Pennsylvania Public School	0	0.0	328	1.6	750	2.9	2,600	10.3
13. Texas Teachers	0	0.0	650	2.2	1,636	4.5	2,329	6.4
14. Los Angeles County	0	0.0	892	8.0	1069	6.8	2,139	13.7
15. Maryland State	0	0.0	180	1.4	519	3.0	2,109	12.7
16. NYNEX	853	5.3	1,368	8.2	2,150	11.7	2,068	11.6
17. Colorado Public Employees	1,152	12.5	1,299	11.9	1,315	9.5	2,016	14.0
18. Minnesota State Board	0	0.0	0	0.0	1130	5.9	2,014	10.6
19. GTE	1,459	11.7	1,715	11.5	2,140	12.7	1,975	13.9
20. Connecticut Trust	680	8.5	1,229	13.1	1,935	17.6	1,971	17.7
21. U.S. West	1,150	11.7	1,174	12.5	1,542	13.6	1,902	16.9
22. Du Pont	380	2.0	862	4.2	2,194	9.6	1,826	8.0
23. Florida State Board	0	0.0	0	0.0	898	2.5	1,754	4.6
24. Illinois Teachers	493	5.8	838	8.5	1,349	11.5	1,547	12.8
25. Virginia Retirement	9	0.0	595	4.4	1074	6.5	1,521	9.2
Total Top 25	17,690	3.8%	30,653	5.2%	61,911	7.7%	85,328	10.5%

Notes: * As of September 30th of each year.
Source: *Pensions and Investments.*

tional stocks in 1994. These funds, therefore, accounted for 29.6 percent of the $288.5 billion of foreign equity held by US investors. (See Table 1–3 above.) Their investments in international equities rose nearly five-fold, from $17.7 billion at year-end 1989 to $85.3 billion at the end of 1994. Foreign issuers will want to capture the attention of these largest funds, which are the fastest-growing foreign investment segment of the market as well as a highly organized and closely assembled potential audience.

NOTES

1. As fiduciaries, institutional investors may be subject to numerous constraints under federal law, through the Employee Retirement Income Security Act of 1974 and its amendments and companion state statutes, relating to the quality of the securities in which they invest, the risk (which may be related to the amount of capitalization and a stock's liquidity), and the diversity of their portfolios. As a practical matter, large institutions may not invest in stocks of companies under a certain size merely because they have so much money to invest on a daily basis that they need to place investments in large blocks to manage the transaction flow.

Chapter 6

Corporate Governance Concerns

Corporations attempting to understand the institutional investors' perspective on corporate governance should remember that the seeds of current discontent were sown during the early 1980s when takeovers became unusually common in the United States. Until that time, most institutional investors would never have considered voting against management. Reactions by target managements taken in response to raiders, however, led to a breach of investor confidence. Institutional investors began to perceive that managements were entrenching themselves to protect their offices and benefits, while not necessarily acting in the best interest of shareholders. The wounds opened then continue to fester today in an atmosphere of acrimony between managements and shareholders in the United States. The key to rebuilding the confidence that was lost depends largely on whether each side—corporations and institutional investors—can understand the other's corporate governance concerns and whether both parties can devise strategies to bridge the confidence gap.

The term *corporate governance,* well known by now in the United States, may still be unfamiliar to corporations in other countries; it is used throughout this book to refer to the governing structure of corporations and how the balance of power to direct the affairs of the corporation is divided between managements, boards of directors, and shareholders. In comparing the differences in governance in various countries, it is critical to remember that different ownership structures affect the corporation's governance structure and the role of each of the participants in the governance process. For example, family-owned businesses tend to have managers who are owners. Also, a strong CEO may have developed a company through personal leadership. In both cases, the thought of shareholders as *owners* is anathema to management. Owners/managers often believe the role of shareholders is to provide capital at an attractive rate of return and, if they are not satisfied, shareholders are free to sell their stock in the company. Yet certain institutional investors quite vocally remind managers that *they* are the corporation's *owners,* even if they hold only a small percentage of the company's stock. The clash between shareholders and managers arising from a fundamental and diametrically opposed view of the role of shareholders leads to considerable acrimony. Further complicating the corporate governance debate is the dramatically changing role of the board of directors in US corporations, as shareholders press for more active boards to monitor the CEO and the direction of the corporation. Additional board oversight may be even less welcomed than investor oversight by many strong CEOs who have traditionally shaped and even controlled their boards.

This chapter explores the development of the changing roles of shareholders, managers, and boards in the United States. It first lays out the context in which institutional investors developed their present concerns about corporate governance issues, then describes a prime factor driving institutional investor activism—the fiduciary standards to which these institutions themselves are held accountable. Then, it discusses the four most pressing corporate governance issues for activist institutions: affording shareholder representation; structuring corporate boards; setting executive compensation; and evaluating corporate performance. The last chapter of this book suggests the key factors that managements, board, and shareholders should keep in mind to minimize conflicts in the corporate governance area, as companies position themselves to enter US securities markets and attract US institutional investor capital.

THE RISE OF US INSTITUTIONAL INVESTOR ACTIVISM

While institutions are very different and act on the basis of different investment objectives and governance perspectives (as was discussed in the Introduction and Chapter 5), they have evolved in their activism through several distinct stages of activity. Institutions have directed investments away from corporations they consider socially undesirable; opposed certain management initiatives to discourage takeovers and the market for corporate control; pressed for structural and operational changes in company boards of directors; and more actively monitored performance in at least a segment of their portfolio companies (see Box 6–1). The most ac-

Box 6–1

Stages of Institutional Investor Activism

Social Investing

For decades, a number of individual investors have pressured corporations to adopt social policies concerning consumer protection, the environment, and withholding investments in countries perceived to be undemocratic, such as the former South Africa. A few noted individuals in the United States pursued this strategy by making public statements at annual company meetings to attract media attention. These individuals were joined by some of the large institutional investors, especially by pension fund managers for church groups. These individuals and institutions learned that becoming schooled in proxy voting tactics could be at least as effective as their media strategy, and might, in fact, provide more leverage over the company if enough votes could be amassed among the shareholders. A number of social issues continue to be raised today, especially by church groups and, until recently, many state legislatures banned public pension funds from investing in companies doing business in South Africa. On the whole, however, the largest institutional investors have tended to be more concerned with financially based issues.

Fighting Anti-Takeover Initiatives

During the mid-1980s, institutions were faced with an array of what they perceived to be management entrenchment devices to reduce shareholder value and eliminate the market for corporate control. Devices, for example, included payment of "greenmail" by management (takeover devices are explained in the text of this chapter) or awarding "golden parachutes" to provide executives with exorbitant compensation if they lost their jobs following a merger. Shareholders were also faced with a series of initiatives by management to prevent them from receiving a premium offered by a bidder (via "poison pills" and other strategies). Institutions expanded their proxy voting activist skills to oppose management initiatives to block takeovers and to protect their right to decide whether to "tender" or surrender their shares to a bidding company for the premium generally offered.

Pressing for Structural Governance Changes within the Corporation

In the late 1980s and early 1990s, shareholders became increasingly concerned with the formal structure of the corporation and the role of its board of directors. Institutions focused on *structural* issues such as whether there

Box 6–1 (continued)

should be a separate CEO and chairman; the number of "outside" directors who were independent of management; the composition of key board committees such as the audit, nominating, and compensation committees; proxy voting mechanics; and other issues institutions could affect through proxy voting mechanisms. Institutional shareholders learned that voting their stock represented an economic value, not only in takeovers, but to influence the direction of the corporation. Federal and state regulatory oversight of certain institutional investors reinforced this belief by requiring fiduciaries to vote their stock as a matter of fiduciary responsibility. Institutions focused on the board as the means to improve the corporation and its accountability to them, and they chose certain corporate governance structures as the pivotal point of pressure most easily accessible to them through the now familiar proxy voting mechanism.

Monitoring Performance
While important, many institutions now consider the structural governance initiatives mentioned above to be merely surrogate measures for performance. Thus, by the mid-1990s, institutions had shifted their focus to performance-related issues including measuring and evaluating the performance of the board, the CEO, and the company. Executive compensation and the link, if any, between executive pay and corporate performance also concerns institutions as they scrutinize corporate performance more closely.

tivist of these institutions—led by the public pension funds and, to a growing degree, the private pension funds, investment managers, and banks—have emerged from these stages of activism with a sharp focus on four key governance issues, which will be discussed in the remainder of this chapter:

- Affording shareholders representation and the ability to vote their proxies.
- Structuring the corporation so that its board of directors performs appropriate oversight to protect the interests of shareholders.
- Setting appropriate levels of executive compensation to provide incentives to management while protecting shareholders.
- Evaluating and monitoring corporate performance.

The Takeover Period

The 1980s takeover period began with overnight "raids," or rapid and secret attempts to take control over corporations. Legendary takeover financiers, such as T. Boone Pickens, Carl Icahn, Sir James Goldsmith, and Saul Steinberg, bought small stakes in some of America's largest corporations then initiated bids for a controlling share of stock at a premium over the current stock price. The premium would generally apply to only 51 percent of the outstanding shares, and if the raider were successful in gaining this percent, which he needed to control the company, he could offer significantly less for the remaining 49 percent of "minority" shares. In some cases, raiders got control, then used the company's own assets to pay off the debt they incurred when they borrowed funds to buy the 51 percent control block in the first place. Institutional investors became concerned that they might be in breach of their own fiduciary duties if they did not tender their shares to the raider at the premium (or at least sell their stock to "arbitrageurs," who were traders who offered less than the premium price but more than the current market price, in the hope of making a profit on the difference—"arbitraging"—if and when the merger was completed).

Companies first targeted by raiders, or put "into play," tended to be oil companies, for which the book value—the value that might be received if the assets were sold—was considerably higher than the current market share value. This made it more attractive to a raider to buy oil company assets than to start a company to drill for new reserves.

Meanwhile, the whole trading atmosphere on Wall Street was shifting to encourage swift turnover of stock, increasing the rapidity with which these merger raids took place. There were three principal reasons this shift occurred. First, changes were gradually occurring in the long-standing post-1945 tax structure. Until the mid 1970s, an individual investor might have a marginal income tax rate of 75 percent and capital gains tax rate on assets held for at least one year of only 25 percent. This meant that an investor buying stock would want to hold that stock for a year and a day in order to pay the 25 percent capital gains tax on the profit, instead of the 75 percent marginal tax rate applicable to general income including assets held less than one year. But the lowering of marginal tax rates in the 1970s and the effective elimination of capital gains tax rates reduced the incentive to hold stock and produced a climate in which there were virtually no negative tax effects on individuals from trading.

Second, following the enactment of the Employment Retirement Income Security Act (ERISA) in 1974, investment money began to shift from large individual accounts in brokerage houses to institutional ownership, especially through pension funds—a trend described in detail in Chapter 5. Vast quantities of assets were being amassed in the accounts of institutional investors, which were tax-exempt and therefore immune from the tax consequences of trading stock.

Third, Wall Street itself underwent a major change with the removal of fixed commissions paid to stock brokers for executing orders for traded stock. The floating commissions enacted in 1968 were intended to encourage competition among brokers. This precipitated a restructuring of the brokerage industry that led to a number of mergers among brokerage houses and a diminution in their research department capabilities, which relied upon "fundamental" research-oriented analysts who performed in-depth analysis on companies and tended to look for longer-term prospects when recommending stock or placing client investments. Meanwhile, the advent of computers in the 1970s permitted a gradual shift from "fundamental" research-oriented investment strategies to a greater degree of computerized program trading, which has contributed to the increase in daily volatility in the stock market. These events conspired to create a "casino" atmosphere surrounding the stock market and a decidedly unsettling and suspicious feeling between managements (who thought shareholders were selling the company out) and shareholders (who were driven by the need to earn returns on their investments in a climate of rapid trading and sometimes frantic merger bidding wars).

Greenmail: The Initial Abuse

Greenmail occurs when a company is compelled to repurchase from a shareholder a block of stock at a premium over the current market price, as its only practical recourse for preventing a takeover attempt. During the 1983–1984 period, noted financiers started buying chunks of stock, threatened to initiate a takeover, and then waited to be "bought out" at a premium over market value. The value of company repurchases of large blocks of stock, presumably made to pay greenmail, amounted to $1.47 million in 1983 and more than tripled in one year to $4.6 million in 1984.[1] As huge premiums over the market price, frequently in excess of 35 percent, were paid to Saul Steinberg, Rupert Murdoch, Sir James Goldsmith, and others, institutions questioned managements' motives for transferring this wealth to the raiders at their expense.

Managements defended their discriminatory payments of greenmail on the grounds they needed to keep their companies from falling into the hands of unscrupulous financiers who would strip them of assets and reduce overall, long-term shareholder value. Some of the raiders, on the other hand, justified their actions in populist terms, arguing that companies were worth more if they were broken up and that they were not raiders but legitimate financiers intent on increasing value for *all* shareholders. Institutions were clearly caught in a swirl of offers and counteroffers.

After a widely publicized case involving the Walt Disney Company became the center of public attention highlighting the practice of greenmail, institutional investors, especially those heading public pension funds, began to sue corporations to block greenmail payments. In 1984, under the leadership of California State Treasurer Jesse Unruh, a group of public pension funds formed the Council of Institutional Investors (CII) to serve as a forum for raising corporate governance issues. The council had its first working meeting in February 1985, when public pension fund members met to question greenmail payments such as those made in the Phillips Petroleum and Walt Disney cases. Having tested their proxy voting skills in the area of social activism (see Box 6–1), some of these institutional investors began to use the proxy process to press for antigreenmail amendments to corporate charters. These were designed to eliminate greenmail by providing that, unless permitted by a vote of a majority of the shares owned by the nonparticipating shareholders, a corporation cannot purchase any of its shares at a premium over the market price from a shareholder who has held a certain percentage or more of stock for less than a certain number of years. Antigreenmail charter proposals could be approved either by shareholder vote or by the vote of the board of directors. According to the Investor Responsibility Research Center (IRRC), in 1984, two companies adopted antigreenmail charter amendments; by mid-1985, shareholders in approximately 60 companies had voted in favor of such amendments, while boards of directors for another three companies had approved them.[2] Then, in the mid-1980s, two forces acted to curb greenmail abuses: the first was a court ruling in the now famous Walt Disney case in which Saul Steinberg attempted to greenmail Disney;[3] the second was a change in the tax laws in 1985 excluding payments to shareholders in excess of current market value—excess greenmail payments—from the normal business expense deductibility provisions of the Internal Revenue Service (IRS) code. By that time, however, public pension funds had already become energized against

managements who appeared to put their own interests before those of
their shareholders.

Poison Pills

Like greenmail, poison pills became a "lightning rod" for shareholder activism. Poison pills derive their name from their onerous provisions, and
they generally take the form of rights or warrants issued to shareholders
that are worthless unless they are triggered by a hostile acquisition attempt. For example, if a raider crosses a 20 percent stock purchase
threshold without obtaining the approval of the company's board, other
shareholders get a two-for-one split, but the raider does not; therefore, he
suffers an immediate dilution. Although poison pills have undergone significant metamorphoses in response to various court challenges by shareholders over the years, the general practice of instituting poison pills was
another major takeover tactic that served to unite shareholders against
managements.[4] Box 6–2 provides a brief description of the major provisions corporations in the United States have instituted during the past 10
years to defend themselves against either unwanted bidders or against institutional investors seeking greater governance power over the corporation. (Box 6–3, which appears later in this chapter, provides an account of
the major proposals shareholders have brought to the ballot either to combat the corporate defenses listed in Box 6–2 or to further other corporate
governance aims.)

INSTITUTIONAL INVESTORS AS FIDUCIARIES

Private corporate pension funds (and the so-called "Taft Hartley" labor
union pension funds) operate under federal regulations established by the
Employment Retirement Income Security Act (ERISA) of 1974. Robert
Monks, former administrator of the Department of Labor's Pension and
Welfare Benefits Administration, says no one anticipated that the impact
of establishing ERISA on the course of investments in the United States
would be so dramatic. According to Monks: "I once asked the chief sponsor of ERISA, the late Senator Jacob Javits, whether he had any idea that
the money gathered under this statute would reach such proportions, and
he said, 'I have never been accused of modesty, but I will tell you in all
sincerity that it never occurred to me.'"[5] Monks and his coauthor, attor-

Box 6–2

Corporate Defensive Provisions of Concern to Institutional Investors

Takeover-Related Provisions

Anti-greenmail provisions: Greenmail refers to the practice of accumulating a block of stock in a company, then selling the stock back to the company in a private transaction at an above-market price. In exchange for the greenmail payment, the greenmail recipient often signs a standstill agreement, which limits his ability to seek control of the company for a certain period of time. In an effort to discourage greenmail, some companies have adopted charter and bylaw amendments that prohibit such above-market purchases unless the same offer is made to all shareholders or unless shareholders approve the transaction by a majority or supermajority vote. Technically, antigreenmail provisions are not takeover defenses; taken in tandem with other measures, however, some observers say the provisions deter the accumulation of large blocks of stock that often precede a takeover attempt.

Consider nonfinancial effects of mergers: Some companies have adopted provisions that require or allow their boards of directors to evaluate the impact a proposed change in control could have on employees, host communities, suppliers, and other constituencies. Some state laws allow corporations' directors to consider such factors, whether or not the company has specifically adopted a charter or bylaw provision permitting it to do so.

Fair price provisions: Fair price provisions require a bidder to pay all shareholders a "fair price"—usually defined as the highest price the bidder paid for any of the shares it acquired in a target company during a specified period of time before the commencement of a tender offer. Most fair price provisions do not apply if a merger is approved by the target's board or if the bidder obtains a specified supermajority level of approval for the merger from the target's shareholders.

Poison pills: Shareholder rights plans are among the more complicated antitakeover devices. Although their terms and conditions vary considerably, the purpose of a poison pill is to force all potential bidders to negotiate with a target company's board of directors. If the board approves the deal, it is often able to redeem the pill. If the board does not approve the bid and the potential acquirer proceeds anyway, the pill is "triggered," causing actions that would make the target financially unattractive or dilute the voting power of the potential acquirer.

Under a typical plan, shareholders are issued rights to purchase stock in

Box 6–2 (continued)

their own company or in the acquiring company at a discount price (usually half) if a hostile bidder acquires a certain percentage (usually 10, 15, or 20 percent) of the outstanding shares. Unlike anti–takeover charter and bylaw amendments, poison pills do not generally have to be submitted to shareholders for ratification. Requests to authorize large amounts of additional common or preferred stock, which do require shareholder approval, frequently are seen as standby measures for companies that have adopted, or may adopt, poison pills.

Supermajority vote to approve merger: Supermajority provisions establish shareholder vote requirements that are higher than the minimum levels set by state law to approve a merger or other business combination. They typically require the approval of the holders of two-thirds, 75 or 80 percent or more of the shares for actions that otherwise would require simple majority approval. Supermajority vote requirements are often combined with fair price provisions.

Provisions Related to Company Boards of Directors
Classified board: A classified board is one in which directors are divided into separate classes, with the directors in each class elected to overlapping three-year terms. Staggering directors' terms makes it more difficult for dissidents to seize control of a target company immediately, even if they control the majority of a company's stock, since only one-third of the directors stand for election in any one year.

Cumulative voting: Cumulative voting permits shareholders to apportion the total number of votes they are entitled to cast in the election of directors in any fashion they desire. The total number is equal to the number of directors to be elected at the meeting multiplied by the number of shares voted. With cumulative voting, each shareholder may cast the total number of votes he or she is entitled to cast for one director or apportion them among the candidates desired.

The use of cumulative voting enables the holders of a minority of a company's stock to elect one or more directors even if they are unable to muster sufficient support on a straight voting basis; for example, the owners of 11 percent of the voting shares in a corporation that is electing 10 directors can be assured of electing one director if they vote all the shares cumulatively for one nominee. The greater the number of directors to be elected, the lower the level of support needed to elect directors cumulatively. Many companies oppose cumulative voting.

Box 6–2 (continued)

Shareholder Voting Issues

Confidential voting: Firms that use secret ballots designate either an independent third party or company employee sworn to secrecy to tabulate and review all proxy votes. In most instances, management agrees not to look at individual proxy cards. Most companies reserve the right to examine individual proxy cards in the event of a contested election. The intended purpose of secret ballots is to eliminate pressures and potential conflicts of interest faced by fiduciaries who vote shares on behalf of others.

Dual class stock: Some companies have two or more classes of common stock. The voting rights attached to each class of stock may (but do not always) vary from the one vote per share standard.

Under some voting schemes, one class of stock will be granted super voting rights—typically 5, 10, or more votes per share. In other instances, a class of shares may carry no voting rights. Some companies also provide one or more classes of stock with special rights, such as the ability to name a certain percentage of the directors. In other instances, such as at General Motors, stock is split into separate classes that reflect the company's various business operations.

Dual class capitalization plans are not anti-takeover measures per se; they only help management (or another insider group) deter takeovers when they control the class of stock with higher or special voting rights.

Limited shareholder ability to act by written consent or to call a special meeting: Some companies have adopted charter or bylaw amendments that restrict or prohibit shareholders from taking action by written consent or calling a special meeting. Typically, the written consent limits will (1) set a supermajority approval standard; (2) require unanimous consent; or (3) ban the practice outright.

Unequal voting rights: Unequal voting rights provisions limit the voting rights of certain types of holders or grant special rights to a particular class of shareholder. One variety, time-phased voting, gives shareholders who have owned their stock for a specified period of time, typically four years, a higher number of votes per share than more recent purchasers. Another unequal voting device, known as a substantial shareholder provision, reduces or caps the voting power of the holder once a certain ownership threshold, typically 10 or 20 percent, has been reached.

Source: Investor Responsibility Research Center, *Corporate Takeover Defenses,* 1993.

ney Nell Minow, describe the idea behind ERISA as simple: Congress wanted to make it worthwhile for private companies to create pension plans for their employees, and then it wanted to protect the money after the plans had been created. The statute was designed to resolve conflicts of interest and liability that had left the private pension system uncertain and, in some cases, chaotic. One massive federal law was to preempt all state law in this area. ERISA pension funds are modeled on trust law, whereby a fiduciary must act for the "exclusive benefit" of pension plan participants. This system is designed to prevent pension plan sponsors from investing undue amounts in risky, illiquid, or self-dealing transactions. Initially, ERISA applied only to private corporate pension plans, but, through a series of state laws, most public pension funds have by reference and regulation become covered by the same ERISA principles.

Former SEC Commissioner Bevis Longstreth quotes from the language of the statute when he describes what constitutes a *prudent person's behavior* with respect to investing ERISA funds:

> The duties of an ERISA fiduciary relating strictly to prudence are twofold. First, he must act in all manners regarding the pension plan, not simply its investments, "with the care, skill, prudence, and diligence under the circumstances then prevailing that any prudent man acting in any like capacity and familiar with such matters would use in the conduct of an enterprise of a like character and with like aims." Diversification, which trust law treats as one facet of the general duty of prudent investment, appears in ERISA as a separate statutory duty. The fiduciary must "diversif[y] the investments of the plan so as to minimize the risk of large losses, unless under the circumstances it is clearly prudent not to do so."[6]

The duties of a fiduciary are also defined by the statute to apply to a pension fund's investment managers as well as its trustees. According to Longstreth, ERISA also posits a formidable scheme of sanctions for breach of fiduciary duty. A fiduciary who makes an imprudent investment or violates the duty to diversify the plan's assets is personally liable for any losses and is subject to suit brought in federal court by the Secretary of Labor, a plan participant or beneficiary, or another fiduciary. The regulations interpreting ERISA's prudent-person standard grant a "safe harbor," whereby the statutory duty is considered to be satisfied with respect to a particular investment if the fiduciary has thoroughly considered the following: the investment's place in the whole portfolio; the risk of loss and the opportunity for gain; and the diversification, liquidity, cash flow, and overall return requirements of the pension plan. With takeovers and their potential for realizing significant short-term profits through exercising the tender-offer stipulations, "prudent" institutional investors were faced with a dilemma: Should they sell and take the premium, or should they hold for the long term and back management as they had traditionally done?

By the mid- to late-1980s, many of the largest public pension funds had become active in submitting anti–takeover shareholder proposals, but private corporate pension fund managers were, understandably, reluctant to pressure other corporations to remove their protective devices. Money managers and bank custodians, even if assured anonymity in the few cases where confidential proxy voting existed, were also reluctant to exercise their voting power in contests for corporate control to vote against their current or potential clients. Thus, proxy voting, never vigorous to begin with, became something that private pension funds, money managers, and banks generally wanted to avoid.

The Avon Letter Requires Proxy Voting

In 1988, however, the Department of Labor (DOL) pension administrator Robert Monks began to force fiduciaries, such as the reluctant private corporate pension fund managers, to vote their proxies. Monks wrote a letter of instruction (such letters issued by the DOL are similar to opinions set forth by a judge in a court of law) addressed to Helmuth Fandel, the chairman of the retirement board of Avon Products Inc. and dated February 23, 1988 (the "Avon letter"). The letter clearly set forth Monks' opinion that ownership powers, including proxy voting, have an economic value; are an asset of a pension plan; and are therefore subject to the same fiduciary standards as other plan assets. In the Avon letter, the Department of Labor asserted that the fiduciary act of managing plan assets that are shares of corporate stock includes voting proxies pertaining to those shares of stock. The responsibility for voting proxies therefore lies exclusively with the plan trustee unless the trustee delegates this authority to a named fiduciary, which might be, for example, an investment manager. This investment manager would not be relieved of the fiduciary responsibility to vote proxies merely because he or she was following directions of some other person regarding the voting of these proxies, or, in turn, had delegated this responsibility to yet another person. Compliance with this provision requires proper documentation of the activities that are subject to monitoring, including maintaining accurate records of proxy voting.

The Avon letter was followed by a series of increasingly focused statements and rulings by the Department of Labor that—along with the rising activism of public pension funds—provided considerable momentum to the corporate governance movement. The Department of Labor was taking a position it clearly vowed to monitor: that the right to vote must be exercised with the same fiduciary standards as money is invested, with care, skill, prudence, and diligence. According to Monks and Minow, the 1989 Department of Labor's "Proxy Project Report" underscored the department's commitment to this issue:

> A fiduciary who fails to vote, or casts a vote without considering the impact of the question, or votes blindly with management would appear to violate his duty to manage planned assets solely in the interests of the participants and beneficiaries of the plan. We will be vigilant in assuring that pension fund fiduciaries handle proxy voting as they handle any other corporate asset— namely not for the benefit of themselves or third parties, but for the benefit of participants and beneficiaries.[7]

Even after the departure of Monks from the DOL, the department has persistently, and under various Republican and Democratic administrations alike, put pressure on fiduciaries to become more active in corporate governance. In a letter from Monks' successor at the DOL, dated January 23, 1990, and, ironically, addressed to Robert Monks himself, who had left the Department of Labor to found Institutional Shareholder Services, Inc. (ISS), the Department of Labor further extended the pension funds' voting responsibility. In this letter, the DOL established the directive that a fiduciary has the obligation to monitor the voting activities of the investment managers it hires, and that the named fiduciary, which might be, for example, an investment manager, must act solely in the interest of the *participants and the beneficiaries* and without regard to his or her relationship to the *plan sponsor.* This ruling was intended to keep the pressure up to vote proxies by ensuring that not only prime fiduciaries but also investment managers to whom these prime fiduciaries have delegated voting authority will, in turn, vote their shares with regard to the shareholder interest.

The Department of Labor Recommends Monitoring Governance and Performance

DOL Interpretive Bulletin 94-2, issued on July 28, 1994, codifies all the Department of Labor's statements, letters, and prior rulings with regard to the duty of employee benefit plan fiduciaries to vote proxies. The DOL Bulletin reiterates the department's earlier position that voting proxies is a fiduciary act of plan asset management. Recognizing that pension plan investments wield considerable influence, Secretary of Labor Robert B. Reich issued the 1994 bulletin to urge pension plan officials to actively monitor the management of companies in which they invest. Reich is quoted in the press release accompanying the Interpretive Bulletin: "Responsible shareholder activism by pension plan managers can improve the long-term company performance, increasing the return to plan participants and strengthening the competitive advantage of American business." The Interpretive Bulletin states that pension plan managers may actively monitor and communicate with corporate management, independently or together with other shareholders, as a means to improve corporate performance and investment return. The DOL reaffirms its long-standing position that plan officials are responsible for voting proxies, unless that responsibility has been delegated to an investment manager. In that case, plan officials should monitor the manager's activities, a principle that was established with the letter to ISS discussed above. The Bulletin clarifies that these principles also apply to proxies on foreign investments. Plan officials, however, can properly decline to vote foreign investment proxies where they judge the cost would outweigh any benefits. The DOL's Interpretive Bulletin puts fiduciaries under considerable pressure, unless they can justify their lack of action on the basis of excessive cost, to become actively involved in a broad range of corporate governance issues if there is reason to believe that such monitoring or communication is likely to enhance the value of the fiduciary's investment. The DOL cites areas for activism, including voting for board of director candidates who are independent, evaluating executive compensation, evaluating a corporation's investment in its workforce, and monitoring financial and nonfinancial[8] measures of corporate performance:

> An investment policy that contemplates activities intended to monitor or influence the management of corporations in which the plan owns stock is consistent with a fiduciary's obligations under ERISA, where the re-

sponsible fiduciary concludes that there is a reasonable expectation that such monitoring or communication with management, by the plan alone or together with other shareholders, is likely to enhance the value of the plan's investment in a corporation, after taking into account the costs involved. Such a reasonable expectation may exist in various circumstances, for example, where plan investments in corporate stock are held as long-term investments or where a plan may not be able to easily dispose [of] such an investment.

Active monitoring and communication activities are generally concerned with such issues as the independence and expertise of candidates for the corporation's board of directors and assuring that the board has sufficient information to carry out its responsibility to monitor management. Other issues may include such matters as consideration of the appropriateness of executive compensation, the corporation's policy regarding mergers and acquisitions, the extent of debt financing and capitalization, the nature of long-term business plans, the corporation's investment in training to develop its work force, other workplace practices, and financial and non-financial measures of corporate performance. Active monitoring and communication may be carried out through a variety of methods including by means of correspondence and meeting with corporate management as well as by exercising the legal rights of a shareholder.[9]

Shareholders Cast Proxy Votes on the Issues

In October 1992, the Securities and Exchange Commission extensively revised its disclosure regulations on shareholder communication and executive compensation. (Revisions in compensation disclosure will be discussed later in this chapter.) The new regulations permit more direct communication between shareholders, managements, and the public. Prior to the release of the new rules, communications on how shareholders intended to vote had to be cleared by the SEC before release to the public. Investors feared talking to each other because they might inadvertently form a "group" under SEC regulations and would therefore be required to make various filings with the commission. The October 1992 regulations removed these restrictions and permitted investors to freely make known their voting intentions and to discuss them with other shareholders and the press. This considerably opened up dialogue surrounding the proxy voting process.

The Investor Responsibility Research Center (IRRC), a Washington, D.C., based research firm, tracks shareholder proposals and compiles voting results. IRRC reports that the number of corporate governance proposals offered by sharcholders in 1995 at companies in IRRC's 1,500-firm universe surpassed the total number offered in 1994. As of June 1, 1995, IRRC had tracked more than 520 proposals that were offered for 1995 meetings, compared with 466 in all of 1994. However, given the broad new communications latitude of the October 1992 proxy reform regulations, an increasing number of communications between institutional investors and companies take place behind the scenes in meetings that frequently result in negotiated settlements to replace the introduction of formal shareholder proposals. More than 40 proposals were dropped during the 1994 proxy season prior to meetings as a result of negotiated settlements, and an undisclosed number were never made public since they were disposed of through private negotiations between managements and shareholders. IRRC's data tracking shareholder proposals therefore significantly *understates* the amount of proxy voting activity by the activist institutions.

Box 6–3 summarizes shareholder initiatives introduced during two recent proxy voting "seasons" in the United States. (Proxy voting seasons are generally during the first five months of the calendar year when the bulk of US corporations hold their annual meetings.) Foreign issuers should view these data as indicative of strong interest in proxy voting, even though many US institutional investors actually consider the annual meeting to be irrelevant and a waste of corporate resources. The focus is now on increasingly high levels of negotiations which occur prior to the public forum of the company's annual meeting.

Shareholders Meet with Managements and Boards

Structuring effective communications, including personal meetings with institutional investors, may become critical to company management wishing to attract US institutional investor capital. Institutional investors generally have two types of people involved in communications with companies: personnel concerned with evaluating investments and personnel concerned with evaluating corporate governance. On the investment decision-making side, many institutional investors who are actively managing their own portfolios function like Wall Street security analysts ("sell side" analysts—so named because they are associated with firms that sell stock). These institutional investment personnel want to meet with the company's chief financial officer (as analysts do) and want to be involved in conference calls when senior management announces earn-

Box 6–3

Summary of 1993 and 1994 Shareholder Initiatives

Poison Pills
In 1994, 11 shareholder proposals—down from the 18 in 1993—to redeem poison pill shareholder rights plans actually came to a vote. Despite the decrease in the number of these proposals voted on, poison pills still received the highest support of any corporate governance proposal—a staggering 54.8 percent, more than 10 percent higher than the 1993 average. Seven of the 11 poison pill proposals received majority votes, and 5 actually passed. All of the majority votes came on resolutions sponsored by proponents with ties to labor union pension funds.

Confidential Voting
Secret ballot proposals received the second greatest level of support from voters—receiving 40.6 percent in 1994—down from 41.7 percent in 1993. The number of proposals that came to a vote also was down—from 20 in 1993 to 12 in 1994. Three proposals got majority votes, with two actually passing. Five others topped 40 percent. In 1993, five proposals won majority votes.

Classified Boards
1994 was a banner year for proposals aimed at repealing staggered boards—with the first two such proposals ever to pass—at Mead and US Shoe. As of August 1st 1994, average support on the 37 such proposals to elect all directors annually was 35.7 percent, up 3.8 percent from 1993's average vote of 31.9 percent.

Golden Parachutes
Proposals to subject future golden parachutes to shareholder votes scored well in 1994, but not as well as in 1993. The average vote on the three proposals that came to vote was 36 percent—down from 1993's all-time high of 41.4 percent.

Cumulative Voting
As of August 1, 1994, there were 33 proposals to institute cumulative voting, which makes it easier for significant minority shareholders or dissidents to obtain board representation. Average support for the 33 proposals was 25.9 percent, up nearly 3 percent from the average support level of 23

Box 6–3 (continued)

percent in 1993. Nearly achieving a majority vote was a proposal at Genesco. The 48.5 percent support received by the proposal was the highest vote ever recorded on this issue by IRRC.

Separate CEO & Chairman
Average support for the five shareholder proposals to split the jobs of CEO and board chairman was 23 percent in 1994—a slight increase from 22.4 in 1993. NYCERS' (the New York City Employee Retirement System's) proposal to Baxter International received the season's highest vote of 30 percent of the votes cast.

Independent Nominating Committee
Like 1993, proposals calling for all-independent nominating committees fared poorly. Support for the six proposals recorded in 1994 by IRRC averaged 16 percent of voting. In 1993, there were only two such proposals, which averaged 26.7 percent.

Independent Directors
New board-related proposals aimed at expanding the role of independent directors have not fared as well as the other traditional corporate governance proposals. As of August 1, 1994, IRRC had recorded that only three of these proposals came to a vote. The three proposals averaged only 13.2 percent of the vote, as compared to the 20.2 percent averaged by the three proposals in 1993.

Restrict Executive Compensation
There were a high number of proposals addressing executive compensation in both 1993 and 1994. Despite this fact, shareholder support for these proposals was low in comparison with other corporate governance proposals. In 1994, average support for 33 proposals aimed at capping pay or linking it to some measure of performance was 14 percent. This represented a drop from 1993 support on 44 proposals of 18.4 percent.

Increase Disclosure of Executive Compensation
Average support for the 15 proposals in 1994 to increase disclosure of executive compensation was also very low at 9.8 percent. Similar proposals in 1993 averaged 9.2 percent.

Box 6–3 (continued)

Shareholder Advisory Committees
Shareholders at Sun gave minimal support (7.8 percent) to the 1994
season's only proposal, requesting the creation of a shareholder advisory committee.

Source: Investor Responsibility Research Center, *IRRC Corporate Governance Bulletin*, May/June, 1994.

---

ings results or significant events. Foreign ADR issuers have found it useful to establish offices in the United States to facilitate conference call
communications.

Corporate governance personnel, frequently senior staff from the office
of the pension fund's general counsel, are the primary people concerned
with corporate governance issues. While they receive input from the investment personnel, they are the ones from the pension fund likely to
write letters to and possibly request face-to-face meetings not only with
senior management but also with the CEO and perhaps outside or independent members of the board of directors as well. Setting up these face-
to-face meetings raises a number of questions for both companies and
shareholders. Speaking at the Kellogg Corporate Governance Conference on October 5, 1994, Michael A. Miles, former CEO of Philip Morris Companies, discussed the need for companies to develop specific policies to organize these special high-level governance-related meetings
with institutions. According to Miles, companies must address questions
such as which shareholders the company should meet with and how it can
avoid the charge of discrimination against small shareholders if it chooses
to meet only with its largest institutional investors. Both corporations and
institutions want to be careful to avoid transmitting "inside information"—the company because it needs to avoid improper disclosure and
the institution because it does not want to be precluded from trading the
company's stock.

Another important issue is at whose instigation the meeting should
take place. For example, in 1993, Ceridian, formed after a restructuring
of Control Data, initiated what was reported to be a productive meeting

with shareholders because it believed that institutional investors were not fully aware of some of the changes that were taking place following the restructuring. The meeting was organized, the agenda structured, and the parties met around a table in a collegial atmosphere. In 1994, on the other hand, Philip Morris shareholders requested a meeting first with management and then with the company's outside directors that did not go well. Indeed, the case serves as an important illustration of communications between corporations and institutional shareholders gone wildly awry. Jon Lukomnik, deputy comptroller for pensions, New York City Comptroller's Office, says: "The Philip Morris case was a comedy of errors turned into a tragedy." According to Lukomnik, after the company announced it was splitting off its tobacco units, senior governance officials at six pension funds asked for a meeting with management, but their request was denied. Then the company announced there would be no split. The same six funds asked for another meeting—this time not only with management but with directors, including the independent directors. The long-awaited meeting took place on September 21, 1994, in Manhattan. Lukomnik related his side:

> "We were told we would have independent directors but we had only one. It may have been a classic example of failed communication. There was a teacher/student setup in the room. Forty-five minutes was delegated for lecture, then cocktails. There were analyst packages on the chairs, and, when questioned about these, the company said 'Well, we do 30 of these meetings a year.' But the institutional investors became upset by this because we aren't analysts."

About half of the pension fund representatives including Lukomnik walked out of the meeting in protest, as did Sarah Teslik, Executive Director of the Council of Institutional Investors and the principal organizer of the meeting.

While the institutions thought they had been manipulated by the company, apparently the company thought it had been manipulated by the institutions. Word about the meeting spread, and the debacle was reported in the *New York Times* the following day. Many in the corporate community became less willing to meet with shareholders and when CalPERS requested a meeting with Philip Morris in April of 1995 the company flatly refused.

Many corporate executives experience a great deal of frustration in dealing with institutions. They have been used to meetings with securities analysts, which have, for decades, been the best vehicle for communicating with the investment community. According to a report by the Conference Board, a research organization that analyzes global business trends, some companies are, however, adapting to a new communications environment and are beginning to understand the nuances of dealing with the various parts of the institutional investor community; they are very careful not to treat as analysts the senior corporate governance staff who think of themselves as owners of the companies in which they invest. In the report, a UK head of corporate development explains the difference in approach between dealing with institutional investors and dealing with the brokerage "sell-side" analysts:

> In short order we found that instead of dealing with a few industry analysts we had a much larger audience of current and potential shareholders with different informational requirements. The people from the brokerage houses were interested in share price volatility. The institutional analysts wanted to know about the prospective earning power of the industry, the assets of the business, the quality of management and they would ask 'relative to the industry and the market is your share price underrated or overrated?' You cannot rely on intermediaries in responding to these kinds of inquiries because the relevant information includes discussions about the company's strategy and business plans."[10]

In considering the attendance list for company meetings with institutional shareholders, Miles recommends that corporate top management be in attendance at the meeting, regardless of whether the shareholders have requested that the meeting involve the outside directors. This is primarily because top management may be able to answer questions that independent directors alone may not be able to. Shareholders, on the other hand, may not want top management to be present throughout the meeting since they may believe that the problem with the company stems from management and they may wish to talk freely with the company's board of directors which, under state corporate law in the United States, appoints management. Most observers from the corporate and institutional investor communities agree, however, that the meetings should have a goal to achieve a reasonable outcome. Both sides know, as well, that if such a reasonable outcome is not possible, shareholders have the right to file proxy resolutions and to plead their case to the media.

AFFORDING SHAREHOLDER REPRESENTATION

The right to vote on a representational basis is deeply embedded in the culture of the United States. Similarly, the issue of "one share/one vote," to provide protection against any disenfranchisement of shareholders, is at the heart of institutional investors' perception of shareholder democracy. Indeed, the Council of Institutional Investors (CII) in its Shareholder Bill of Rights (see Appendix A) lists one share/one vote as its first issue. The CII believes that American corporations must be governed by principles of accountability and fairness; the Shareholder Bill of Rights was designed to ensure participation by shareholders not only in electing directors, the legal responsibility of shareholders under state corporate law, but also in the key financial decisions of the company. The one share/one vote principle that institutional investors adamantly endorse provides that each share of common stock, regardless of its class, shall be entitled to vote in proportion to its relative share in the total common stock equity of the corporation. Furthermore, institutional investors consider the right to vote "inviolate" and may not be abridged "by any circumstance or by any action of any person."

Most US institutional investors, and especially the public pension funds, believe that the right to vote is an extremely valuable asset they obtain when they purchase stock because, more and more frequently, the issues presented in proxies have potential economic impact on the value of their shares. As discussed above, shareholders reacted negatively during the 1980s, as a number of financial instruments were created to give managements an incentive to protect themselves against raiders (such as the payment of greenmail and the development of poison pills). By comparison, voting restrictions are seen by shareholders as an even more draconian device for management to unilaterally seize control of the destiny of the corporation and disenfranchise shareholders. Unequal voting rights should be of particular concern to non-US companies that wish to attract US institutional investor capital since, with rare exceptions, public pension funds will either not invest in companies with unequal voting rights, or if they do buy ADRs or shares in them they are likely to immediately press for equal voting rights. Money managers and bank investment managers, although considerably less vocal on the issue of unequal voting rights, have also begun to urge foreign companies to provide a one share/one vote governance structure, either on their own volition (because they believe it is good investment strategy) or at the behest of the public pension funds that delegate funds to them to manage. Private corporate pension funds, under financial pressure themselves to meet employee pension payout obligations, may press for equal voting rights in cases where they perceive such voting rights will affect the value of their investments.

According to Institutional Shareholder Services (ISS), the most common of the mechanisms used to establish a system of unequal voting rights within the corporation is to institute *dual class voting,* which refers to companies designating two classes of voting stock, one of which carries more votes per share than the other. For example, class A common stock may have 1 vote per share and class B 10 votes per share. Another type of unequal voting rights would be *time-phased voting,* which refers to voting rights that increase with the length of time the stock is held by one investor. For example, an investor may have 1 vote per share held up to five years, after which the investor has 10 votes per share.

Two controversies surrounding the one share/one vote issue illustrate how deeply the principle is embedded in US institutional investors' perception of minimum standards of corporate governance. The first involved proposals by the NYSE and the other organized stock exchanges in the United States to permit listed companies to establish classes of stock with unequal voting rights, while the second involved a vigorous international debate over Rupert Murdoch's attempt to impose dual listing for the Australian company News Corp.

The New York Stock Exchange and One Share/One Vote

In 1985, after more than 50 years of imposing, with very rare exceptions, a uniform standard on the companies listed on the exchange, the New York Stock Exchange (NYSE) proposed to rescind its one share/one vote rule.[11] The NYSE had permitted a dual-class system, where different classes of stock have different voting rights, which was limited primarily to companies that were controlled by families. During the takeover wave of the 1980s, dual class listing began to appeal to a number of corporations as a painless way to fend off a takeover. At the same time, while the NYSE had been the preeminent place for listing stock, the American Stock Exchange (AMEX) and the National Association of Securities Dealers Quotation System (NASDAQ) were actively competing for listings. A number of companies announced their intention to abandon the

NYSE for the other exchanges that permitted dual-class systems, and to sustain its competitive position the NYSE submitted a proposal to rescind its one share/one vote rule to the Securities and Exchange Commission. (While the NYSE is a self-regulatory body, the SEC must approve its procedural rules.)

The SEC, however, moved to prohibit the NYSE from rescinding the rule, by taking the unprecedented step of imposing a listing standard on all of the exchanges; this not only kept the one share/one vote standard at the NYSE but imposed it on the other exchanges as well. The SEC justified its action upholding one share/one vote as being at the heart of its regulatory ability to ensure confidence in the markets. The SEC rule, however, was narrowly drawn since it permitted companies that had already issued dual classes of stock to keep them. In addition, it also allowed companies that issued stock for the first time to issue stock with unequal voting rights, on the theory that investors are aware of the implications of such unequal voting rights when they purchase first-time issues. The SEC rule, however, did prohibit companies from issuing dual-class stock in exchange offers, which, according to ISS, were the avenue by which many companies had created unequal voting arrangements. Obviously, these arrangements could frequently be initiated during a takeover situation where stock is used as part of the transaction. The SEC found that such exchange offers were coercive because the monetary premium offered would likely encourage the individual investors to exchange their voting shares for nonvoting shares despite the fact that public shareholders, as a class, were better off when they had higher voting rights.

The Business Roundtable, which favored the dual class listing as a means of reducing the power of institutional shareholders, challenged the SEC ruling on the grounds that the SEC lacked jurisdiction—that the exchanges were not obligated to set listing policies based on a directive from the SEC. The courts upheld the Business Roundtable and rescinded the SEC's ruling. For several years, the issue remained unresolved although the SEC began to put pressure on the exchanges to come up with their own compromise. Then, in the summer of 1994, in response to urging by the new SEC chairman, Arthur Levitt Jr., the exchanges forged an agreement for a proposed rule change whereby they would amend their own self-regulatory procedures. On July 8, 1994, the NYSE proposed a rule change pursuant to Rule 19b-4 under the Securities Exchange Act of 1934, which would adopt the listing standards in large part originally suggested in the SEC ruling that had been overturned. Under the compromise proposed rule change, corporations may not revise voting to *eliminate* the one share/one vote privilege for outstanding shares; however, companies are permitted to list dual class in *initial* listings, where shareholders would understand the implications of the dual listings.[12]

Rupert Murdoch and One Share/One Vote

In November 1993, Rupert Murdoch proposed to issue dual class shares for the Australian-based News Corp. Since the proposal would clearly have disenfranchised them, this change in governance did not appeal to US institutional investors, and they vigorously opposed Murdoch's attempt to circumvent the one share/one vote principle and limit their voting rights. Ironically, the News Corp. incident occurred at the same time that the major US stock exchanges were struggling to unify their position on voting rights. The uproar in the United States and Australia over News Corp. is credited with having prompted them to finalize the terms of their agreement over voting rights.

The controversy began when the largely family-owned News Corp. (controlled by Rupert Murdoch) announced its intention to issue dual-class, or supervoting, shares—this represented an attempt to lock in the Murdoch family's control despite its shrinking ownership. The Australian Stock Exchange (ASX) initially appeared receptive to the Murdoch supervoting plan as revealed in its "differential voting rights discussion paper" of November 1993. When the proposed action by the ASX to allow differential voting rights became public in Australia, it became front page news. The Australian Investment Managers' Group (AIMG), later renamed Australian Investment Managers' Association (AIMA), became publicly involved. This is the organization of the major money managers with investment control over a large share of Australian investments. (In Australia, the more activist institutions appear to be the investment managers who work through the AIMA; whereas, in the United States, the activists tend to be the public pension funds who work through the Council of Institutional Investors.) AIMA's chairman, Peter Griffin, debated the ASX chairman, Laurie Cox, in the major financial papers in Australia. A number of large US pension funds such as CalPERS and Wells Fargo publicly objected to Murdoch's attempt to disenfranchise them. (Coincidentally, Richard Koppes, general counsel of CalPERS, was in Australia when the issue was first made public; Koppes made a number of public statements in opposition to the Murdoch proposal, although CalPERS did not, in fact, own any News Corp. stock at the time.)

As opposition mounted, Murdoch threatened that if the ASX did not amend its listing rule (3K(2)(a)) to accommodate him, he might take his listing business to the New York Stock Exchange, which had, as previously noted, permitted differential voting. Thus, the conflict became an international one in which the Australian Stock Exchange was pressured to change its own rules or lose one of its major listed companies to a US exchange, where it thought it would receive more favorable treatment. The ASX indicated it would review the matter. The ASX was criticized for sacrificing an important governance principle on self-serving grounds since it derives revenues from trading, and if Murdoch moved the listing of stock to the US exchanges that would permit the dual listing the ASX and other exchange firms would lose business. CalPERS' public opposition to the News Corp. voting proposal was representative of the view of US institutions generally: They would not tolerate an abrogation of their voting rights. Koppes also pointed out his concerns that institutional investors would lose confidence in the Australian securities markets as a whole if the ASX were to make what was generally regarded as a self-serving decision to allow News Corp. the differential voting rights.

After numerous discussions between US and Australian exchanges, and under obvious pressure from a highly organized transpacific institutional investor base, in February 1994, the board of the Australian Stock Exchange decided not to amend its listing rule. The ASX's announcement on differential voting rights said that the exchange had been in correspondence with the New York and London stock exchanges and that it would not change the listing rules to provide for differential voting rights. However, Australian observers note that the ASX retains the power to administer the rule flexibly, primarily for the purpose of allowing companies that newly issue stock to do so with differential voting rights on grounds that this is a matter of mutual consent, in that investors would be forewarned of the "weak" voting position of any such new issuances. To this extent, the ASX's procedures are similar to those adopted by the US exchanges. At stake, clearly, was not only the corporate governance principles pertaining to News Corp. but, more importantly, the confidence that major institutional investors would have in the integrity and transparency of the entire Australian securities market.

The ASX's decision, coupled with the July 1994 agreement by the NYSE, the AMEX, and the NASD, seems to have put this issue to rest in the United States and Australia. Foreign issuers in other countries, however, should be particularly concerned with their own attempts to restructure their voting in light of this international incident, lest they fall into the sort of controversy that Rupert Murdoch did. Finally, the News Corp. case, like the Hanson plc case discussed earlier in this book, signal the important evolution of the *international* activist institutional shareholder, as groups from Australia, the United Kingdom, and even on the European continent communicate and press, increasingly in transcontinental unison, for basic shareholder rights.

STRUCTURING BOARDS OF DIRECTORS

The most common legal corporate structure in the United States is for shareholders to elect the board of directors and for the board to appoint and monitor the performance of top management. Based on this distribution of power, institutional investors see boards of directors as pivotal in the governance process, and they have pressed for changes to transform the composition of boards from what some regard as hand-picked colleagues of the chairman to independent directors who will act on behalf of the shareholders to monitor management and improve corporate performance.

Indeed, a recent Conference Board report affirms that boards of US corporations are steadily becoming more independent.[13] Boards have increasingly eliminated directors whose connection with the company can conflict with their ability to exercise independent judgment on corporate matters before them. The Conference Board survey covered composition of boards; presence of outside directors on nominating, audit, and compensation committees; existence of a separate CEO and Chairman; and other governance issues. The Conference Board's survey, which is unique in that it compares changes in board composition over more than 10 years, was released in August of 1993 and is based on responses from 546 domestic and foreign corporations. Its major findings with respect to US corporations are as follows:

- Seventy-six percent of board chairmen are also the company chief executive, as was the case reported in the earlier 1972 Conference Board survey.
- Almost every company surveyed has an audit committee as part of its board. In 1972, only 45 percent reported such a committee.

This important independent committee faces major new challenges, including complex financial controls over far-flung operations, the increase in lawsuits alleging improper disclosure, and increasingly high-tech auditing procedures that are replacing paper documents in some industries.

- Ninety-one percent of the surveyed firms' boards have a compensation committee, compared with 69 percent in 1972. Members of these committees are being subjected to complaints about high executive pay packages and are being charged with complying with recent disclosure regulations requiring compensation committees to inform shareholders of the rationale behind executive pay decisions.

- Sixty-four percent of respondents have a nominating committee for directors, up from only 8 percent in a 1972 Conference Board survey. Some respondents say that this committee is necessary because the personal network of the CEO and the board is no longer sufficient for recruiting high-quality candidates who can commit the time it takes to be an effective director today.

- Sixty percent of corporations responding to the survey now have boards that are "independent" in that they have no directors who represent a major customer, or a major supplier or who are related to, or have a significant business connection with, a member of the company's management.

- Outsiders currently comprise a majority of the board membership in 94 percent of the manufacturing and financial firms surveyed and in 93 percent of the nonfinancial service companies surveyed.

- More than 60 percent of all companies have no more than two members of management on their board.

- Chief executives have often initiated reductions in the number of inside board members in their firms. The director-selection process has been changing in ways that decrease the CEO's influence and increase the proportion of independent candidates for director positions.

- Survey participants say that strategy formulation is the corporate activity that the board most influences. Boards also influence human resources and financial management and, to a lesser extent, operations control, risk management, and external relations.

- The independent board action mentioned most often—by a third of respondents—is modifying management's recommendations for the CEO's pay.

- Nine percent of companies say the board has asked the CEO to re-sign or retire early.

- Fifty-nine percent of the surveyed companies say their boards have "considerable" influence in getting the information they desire. Thirty-nine percent say that directors "regularly" make independent inquiries about corporate affairs, and 86 percent say it is company policy that a director may make a direct request for relevant information.

- At board meetings, directors spend two-thirds of their time on three main concerns: strategy matters (a median of 25 percent of meeting time), financial management (21 percent), and operations control (20 percent).

One issue of board structure and governance that can be expected to be in the spotlight during the next few years is how to make boards more diverse in ethnic and gender composition. This is a specific shareholder goal of funds such as TIAA-CREF—the Teachers' Insurance and Annuity Association-College Retirement Equities Fund—which is the largest of the US pension funds and represents college teachers throughout the country. Another proposal is to separate the roles of the chairman of the board and the CEO, positions which tend to be held by the same individual in approximately three-quarters of the companies in the United States. In other countries, such as the United Kingdom and Australia, the general practice is to separate the two functions. The argument in favor of separating the roles stems from the belief that a separate and independent chairman who is not an employee of the company will be in a better position to impartially evaluate the chief executive and communicate with the board. In companies where the roles remain combined in one individual, a number of boards have elected a "lead director." A lead director serves as a surrogate or alternate chairman of the board, to ensure that channels of communication are open between management and the board and not lodged—and sometimes bottled up—in one person fulfilling the dual role of chairman and CEO.

The General Motors Guidelines on Corporate Boards

In 1993, General Motors' board of directors made a landmark decision to split the functions of chairman and chief executive. Then, in April of 1994, General Motors' new chairman, John Smale, unveiled[14] the board's approved guidelines for corporate governance (see Appendix B for the complete guidelines). These guidelines have rapidly become the leading standard in the United States against which institutional investors measure desirable corporate governance practices pertaining to boards of directors. The guidelines call for the election of a lead director in the event that the chairman is not an independent member of the board. According to the guideline entitled Lead Director Concept:

> The Board adopted a policy that it have a director selected by the outside directors who will assume the responsibility of chairing the regularly scheduled meetings of outside directors or other responsibilities which the outside directors as a whole might designate from time to time.
>
> Currently, this role is filled by the non-executive Chairman of the Board. Should the Company be organized in such a way that the Chairman is an employee of the Company, another director would be selected for this responsibility.

There are certain similarities between the GM guidelines and those recommended in the United Kingdom in December 1992 by the Committee on the Financial Aspects of Corporate Governance. (The report is referred to as the Cadbury Report after the Chairman of the Committee, Sir Adrian Cadbury.) On the lead director concept, the Cadbury Report recommends:

> Given the importance and particular nature of the chairman's role, it should in principle be separate from that of the chief executive. If the two roles are combined in one person, it represents a considerable concentration of power. We recommend, therefore, that there should be a clearly accepted division of responsibilities at the head of a company, which will ensure a balance of power and authority, such that no one individual has unfettered powers of decision. When the chairman is also the chief executive, it is essential that there should be a strong and independent element on the board.[15]

The GM Board Guidelines also include a very important and somewhat radical commitment to evaluate the performance of directors, if even on an aggregate basis.[16]

> The Committee on Director Affairs is responsible to report annually to the Board an assessment of the Board's performance. This will be discussed with the full Board. This should be done following the end of each fiscal year and at the same time as the report on Board membership criteria.
>
> This assessment should be of the Board's contribution as a whole and

specifically review areas in which the Board and/or the Management believes a better contribution could be made. Its purpose is to increase the effectiveness of the Board, not to target individual Board members.

The California Public Employees' Retirement System (CalPERS) quickly embraced the GM guidelines as evidence of exemplary board self-evaluation and of generally good corporate governance practice. On May 12, 1994, CalPERS wrote to the corporations representing the largest 200 domestic equity holdings within its portfolio. In its letter, CalPERS challenged these 200 companies to follow GM's lead and undergo the same type of self-analysis. CalPERS acknowledged that specific governance models must differ according to industry and company but urged boards to seek the benefits to be derived through the *process* of defining the structure by which the board will operate and the disciplines it will follow in fulfilling its duties. It was this *process,* as revealed by companies' responses to CalPERS' challenge, that formed the basis of CalPERS' "report card" evaluation (see Appendix C). CalPERS sent a second letter on August 25, 1994, to nonresponding companies. Follow-up letters and correspondence continued into the winter of 1994, and CalPERS announced that it would issue updates of its report card on how companies are adhering to the GM guidelines as companies respond and alter their guidelines accordingly.

With regard to monitoring changes in boards of directors, there is, in fact, considerable similarity between the approaches embodied in the General Motors Guidelines, the Cadbury Report initiatives, and CalPERS' report card evaluations. All depend on disclosure to exert pressure for voluntary corporate compliance, rather than regulatory or legal change in board structure and evaluation requirements. Also, all appear to have had some impact in encouraging change and conformance with the voluntary guidelines. While many companies may not necessarily agree with the general principles set forth by GM or Cadbury, they may move towards conformance anyway so as to avoid a demerit on report cards kept not only by CalPERS but by many US institutional investors. Finally, support for board evaluation has come not only from shareholders; many board members who served on the National Association of Corporate Directors' Blue Ribbon Commission to evaluate directors welcomed having an established set of procedures they can use to argue for change without being considered "traitors" to their own companies.

SETTING EXECUTIVE COMPENSATION

In the shareholder community, discontent over high levels of executive compensation has been brewing for some years. The Securities and Exchange Commission acted in October 1992 to vastly broaden the disclosure requirements for executive compensation. This section provides a potential issuer in US securities markets with some insight into the controversy surrounding executive compensation: what kinds of compensation packages are acceptable to shareholders and what kinds trigger action by institutional investor activists.

Of course, foreign issuers are subject to the full panoply of the executive pay disclosure rules only if they file the periodic reports or registration statements with the SEC that are required for US companies. Foreign issuers registering securities or filing annual reports on Form 20-F (as discussed in Chapters 3 and 4) are required merely to disclose executive and director compensation on an aggregate basis, without naming individual officials. If the issuer provides home-country pay disclosure for specific officers or directors, however, the same disclosure must be reported to US shareholders in Form 20-F. Those companies qualifying for the Rule 12g3-2(b) exemption, whose securities trade primarily in the US over-the-counter market, have no such disclosure obligation unless imposed by their country of domicile.

Despite the regulatory latitude afforded foreign issuers in this area, management considering the feasibility of either entering the US securities markets or expanding an existing US presence should remain mindful that the SEC's rigorous new executive compensation disclosure standards were partially the result of mounting shareholder demands for concise, yet understandable information on precisely how and how much senior managers and directors of public companies are paid. Even more importantly, the new standards compel board compensation committees to explain the extent to which executive pay awards are linked to corporate performance. Armed with this information, shareholders have penalized directors for abusive compensation practices at the corporate ballot box. In sum, strong shareholder demand for quantified, individualized compensation data—typically expressed in the form of inquiries as to how executive and/or director compensation leads to improved corporate performance—ultimately may compel foreign companies to furnish far more disclosure than otherwise prescribed by law or SEC rule.

Jon Lukomnik, Deputy Comptroller for Pensions, New York City Comptroller's Office, sees no one governance issue as more directly representing a transfer of wealth from shareholders to management than executive compensation. According to Lukomnik, focusing on the compensation issue is also an easy way to understand whether the board of directors is putting the shareholders' interests first and an easy way of asking the fundamental question: Are corporate directors executing their proper authority? And while executive compensation is currently the focus of most of the contention, directors' own compensation is increasingly of shareholder concern as well.

Executive Pay Packages

The typical objectives in structuring the total executive compensation package are to attract exceptionally qualified executives, retain them, motivate them in the short and the long term, provide recognition, and provide security. According to the National Association of Corporate Directors' Blue Ribbon Commission Report on Executive Compensation, total compensation for an executive can be defined as the sum of annualized pretax base salary, annual bonus, estimated grant value of medium- or long-term incentive compensation, and value of qualified and supplemental benefits, including deferred compensation and perquisites.[17]

A typical senior executive today might receive some or all of the following (see Box 6–4 for an explanation of key terms):

- Base salary.
- Annual bonus or short-term incentive.
- Medium- or long-term incentives that may include:
  - Stock options.
  - Stock appreciation rights (SARs).
  - Restricted stock.
  - Phantom stock.
  - Performance units paid in the form of stock or cash.

- Tax-qualified or broad-based benefit plans that may include:
  - Pension plans.
  - Medical and dental plans.
  - Savings plans.
  - Life insurance plans.
  - Disability plans.

Box 6–4

Elements in Typical US Executive Pay Plans

1. **Base salary** reflects the impact of experience and sustained performance. Salary is usually set on the basis of "market rate" (what similar companies pay for similar jobs).

2. **Annual bonus** rewards achievement of an annual target. Most typically a percent of profits goes into a pool, which is allocated to the participants, usually on the basis of each one's contribution to annual profitability as measured by growth in earnings per share or rate of return on equity.

3. **Long-term incentives** are designed to reward future performance for periods greater than one year. They are subdivided into the following:

   a. **Performance unit or share plans:** Awards of cash or stock related to financial measures, most often cumulative increases in earnings per share over a three- to five-year period.

   b. **Stock options:** Nontransferable rights to purchase shares of employer stock at a fixed price over a stated period (usually 10 years). Increases in share price over time increase the potential value of stock or the actual value of stock acquired and held. Incentive stock options (ISOs) meet Internal Revenue Code requirements. SARs are stock appreciation rights which give a recipient, in lieu of exercising one stock option in whole or in part, the right to receive an amount in cash or stock equal to appreciation in the stock price since the date of the grant.

   c. **Restricted stock:** Grants of shares of stock or stock equivalents restricted from sale or transfer for a period of continued employment (anywhere from 3 to 10 years).

   d. **Phantom stock:** Analogous to company stock most often used by private companies or divisions of public corporations. Conceptually similar to an SAR.

Source: The Conference Board

- Supplemental benefit plans that may include:
  - Deferred compensation plans.
  - Supplemental executive retirement plans (SERPs).
  - Excess retirement plans.
  - Supplemental medical and disability plans.
  - Supplemental life insurance plans.

- Perquisites that may include:
  - Club memberships.
  - Financial planning or counseling.
  - Use of company automobiles and company planes.
  - Airline club memberships.
  - Chauffeurs.

From 1993 to 1994, chief executive officer salaries and bonuses in a sample of 350 of the largest US corporations grew 11.4 percent compared with the 8.1 percent increase registered during the period 1992 to 1993. At the same time, corporate profits grew 28.5 percent, according to William M. Mercer Inc., the firm performing the annual survey for *The Wall Street Journal*. The median CEO salary and bonus in Mercer's 1994 survey reached $1,294,316, up from $1,174,398 in 1993 (see Table 6–1 for a detailed accounting of CEO compensation).

SEC Compensation Disclosure Regulations

During the early 1990s, the Securities and Exchange Commission undertook a major review of its shareholder voting and proxy regulations, which also included a review of executive compensation disclosure regulations. At the same time, there was a public uproar in Congress over the issue of excessive executive compensation, fueled by the perception that executives were being paid unfairly high amounts as the country struggled during a recession, company profits fell, and unemployment escalated. Numerous pieces of legislation to limit executive compensation were introduced in the Congress, and one significant bill passed that limited the deductibility of executive compensation in excess of one million dollars, unless shareholders approved the compensation and unless the compensation could be shown to be linked to corporate performance.[18] In comparison to the Congressional approach, the SEC consistently took the position that *disclosure* rather than *regulation* to impose dollar compensation limits was desirable. The SEC's position was based on the belief that the disciplinary effect of the markets, aided by full and fair disclosure mandated by SEC rules, should ultimately operate to curb any perceived abuses in the area of executive pay.

In February 1992, the SEC began to reinforce shareholder monitoring of executive compensation by changing its interpretation of the "ordinary business" exclusion of Rule 14a-8(c)(7) to permit shareholders to express their views on executive and director compensation through the vehicle of shareholder proposals carried in registrant proxy statements. Then, on October 15, 1992, the SEC adopted new executive compensation disclosure requirements for proxy statements and other reports filed by domestic reporting companies.[19] The new regulations require that the following be included in the registrant company's proxy statement:

1. A summary table containing detailed information on the total compensation for the last three years for the CEO and each of the four other most highly paid executives (Figure 6–1).

2. A performance graph comparing the companies' five-year cumulative total shareholder returns with those of other companies in peer group and/or compared to the Standard and Poor's 500 average or other broad equity market index (Figure 6–2).

3. A compensation committee report describing the factors affecting the committee's decisions regarding CEO and other executive compensation and discussing the relationship between such compensation and the company's performance in the past fiscal year.

4. Option/stock appreciation rights tables disclosing various information regarding stock options and SARs, including potential appreciation rates and unrealized gains on outstanding options.

5. Expanded disclosure for incentive stock option repricings, potential lack of independence of compensation committee members, and details of new compensation plans subject to shareholder approval.

Figure 6–1 provides an example of the key summary compensation table and Figure 6–2 provides an example of the comparison of the five-year cumulative total shareholder return graphs required by the SEC.

Institutional Shareholder Concerns

Many large institutional investors candidly state they are not in a position to analyze the nuances of individual company pay packages. Kurt N. Schacht, general counsel of the State of Wisconsin Investment Board, says that institutional investors are focused on four key compensation issues:

1. The extent to which management has a significant stock ownership stake in the company.

2. The fairness of issuing stock options and other grants to executives.

TABLE 6–1
The Wall Street Journal/William M. Mercer 1994 CEO Compensation Survey (in $ Thousands)

| Industry | Executive | 1994 Salary | 1994 Bonus | 1994 Salary + Bonus | % change from 1993 | Long-term Compensation | | Total Direct Compensation | Present Value of Options Grants |
						Options	Other		
Basic Materials									
Alcoa	Paul H. O'Neill	700.2	750.0	1,450.2	39.0%	1,436.5	0.0	2,886.7	5,574.9
Bethlehem Steel	Curtis H. Barnette	550.0	121.0	671.0	34.2%	101.9	611.3	1,384.2	656.3
Dow Chemical	Frank P. Popoff	935.0	700.0	1,635.0	10.2%	1,374.5	175.8	3,185.3	2,463.4
DuPont	Edger S. Woolard Jr.	840.0	1,185.0	2,025.0	63.0%	1,693.3	0.0	3,718.3	1,231.6
Scott Paper	Albert J. Dunlap	705.8	2,500.0	3,205.8	NA	0.0	3,181.3	6,387.0	12,396.4
Industrial									
Deere	Hans W. Becherer	764.1	874.5	1,638.6	78.7%	1,305.1	413.9	3,357.7	459.1
Federal Express	Frederick W. Smith	650.1	470.0	1,120.1	103.5%	0.0	0.0	1,120.1	3,131.5
Tenneco	Dana G. Mead	878.2	900.0	1,778.2	NA	0.0	647.3	2,425.4	1,534.0
Union Pacific	Drew Lewis	880.0	1,500.0	2,380.0	3.5%	0.0	0.0	2,380.0	8,061.7
Westinghouse	Michael H. Jordan	1,000.0	700.0	1,700.0	NA	0.0	185.0	1,885.0	NA
Technology									
AT&T	Robert E. Allen	1,109.0	2,253.6	3,362.6	40.8%	0.0	1,885.6	5,248.2	1,046.5
Boeing	Frank Shrontz	844.8	749.2	1,594.0	NA	877.3	218.4	2,689.7	479.3
General Electric	John F. Welch Jr.	1,850.0	2,500.0	4,350.0	10.1%	3,259.4	0.0	7,609.4	4,899.6
IBM	Louis V. Gerstner Jr.	2,000.0	2,600.0	4,600.0	NA	0.0	0.0	4,600.0	6,225.9
Rockwell International	Donald R. Beall	815.0	1,300.0	2,115.0	23.3%	0.0	0.0	2,115.0	1,976.3
Cyclical									
Delta Airlines	Ronald W. Allen	475.0	0.0	475.0	−2.6%	0.0	0.0	475.0	2,278.5

Disney	Michael D. Eisner	750.0	9,907.2	10,657.2	1321.0%	0.0	0.0	10,657.2	NA
Gannett	John J. Curley	800.0	750.0	1,550.0	19.2%	0.0	0.0	1,550.0	1,824.5
Goodyear	Stanley C. Gault	995.0	1,162.5	2,157.5	10.4%	0.0	1,014.4	3,171.9	2,400.4
Nike	Philip H. Knight	750.0	150.0	900.0	-4.3%	0.0	0.0	900.0	NA
Noncyclical									
Anheuser-Busch	August A. Busch III	940.0	1,232.0	2,172.0	18.3%	0.0	0.0	2,172.0	1,485.0
Coca-Cola Co.	Roberto C. Goizueta	1,548.2	2,823.0	4,371.2	19.6%	6,218.8	1,463.6	12,053.5	NA
General Mills	H. Brewster Atwater Jr.	608.1	241.6	849.7	-38.7%	0.0	60.4%	910.1	5,550.3
Johnson & Johnson	Ralph S. Larsen	920.0	586.7	1,506.7	12.6%	0.0	535.8	2,042.5	783.0
Kellogg	Arnold G. Langbo	800.0	688.5	1,488.5	N/A	0.0	0.0	1,488.5	1,439.1
Financial									
American Express	Harvey Golub	800.0	2,040.0	2,840.0	N/A	0.0	1,799.9	4,639.9	1,942.0
Citicorp	John S. Reed	1,275.0	3,000.0	4,275.0	3.0%	825.0	0.0	5,100.0	4,675.7
Mellon	Frank V. Cahouet	826.7	430.0	1,256.7	-9.3%	0.0	28.6	1,285.2	2,047.6
NationsBank	Hugh L. McColl Jr.	900.0	2,100.0	3,000.0	15.4%	0.0	10,725.0	13,725.0	NA
Salomon	Robert E. Denham	1,000.0	0.0	1,000.0	-51.1%	0.0	0.0	1,000.0	NA
Utilities									
Bell Atlantic	Raymond W. Smith	831.2	778.7	1,609.9	-4.7%	0.0	400.9	2,010.8	11,173.2
Bell South	John L Clendenin	588.5	765.0	1,353.5	-6.5%	223.6	215.6	1,792.7	849.6
GTE	Charles R. Lee	784.6	1,219.5	2,004.1	14.3%	0.0	698.1	2,702.2	899.2
US West	Richard D. McCormick	700.0	560.0	1,260.0	0.0%	0.0	0.0	1,260.0	746.7
Union Electric	Charles W. Mueller	400.0	120.0	520.0	N/A	0.0	0.0	520.0	NA
Energy									
Atlantic Richfield	Mike R. Bowlin	715.7	600.0	1,315.7	NA	0.0	0.0	1,315.7	4,703.7
Chevron	Kenneth T. Derr	1,000.0	700.0	1,700.0	-6.3%	0.0	1,403.0	3,103.0	1,287.1
Exxon	Lee R. Raymond	1,300.0	550.0	1,850.0	NA	671.9	941.8	3,463.6	2,595.2
Mobil	Lucio A. Noto	770.8	525.0	1,295.8	NA	850.1	609.7	2,755.6	1,034.0
Texaco	Alfred C. DeCrane Jr.	927.5	595.1	1,522.6	NA	509.9	769.1	2,801.6	1,513.2

Source: The Wall Street Journal/William M. Mercer 1994 CEO Compensation Survey, *The Wall Street Journal*, April 12, 1995, pp. R1–R16.

FIGURE 6–1
Summary Compensation Table

(a) Name and Principal Position[2]	Annual Compensation[1]				Long-term Compensation			(i) All Other Compensation ($)[7]
	(b) Year	(c) Salary ($)	(d) Bonus ($)	(e) Other Annual Compensation ($)[3]	Awards		Payouts	
					(f) Restricted Stock Award(s) ($)[4]	(g) Options/SARs (#)[5]	(h) LTIP Payouts ($)[6]	
CEO	---							
A	---							

B	---							

C	---							

D	---							
	---							

[1] Compensation deferred at election of executive includable in category and year earned. If salary or bonus deferred under LTIP, must disclose in footnotes the amount deferred.

[2] Includes CEO and four most highly compensated executive(s) whose salary and bonus exceed $100,000.

[3] Includes (a) perquisites if aggregate value exceeds $50,000 or 10 percent of salary plus bonus (nature and value of perquisites representing 25 percent of total must be disclosed in footnotes), (b) above-market interest of preferential dividends paid or payable on deferred compensation, (c) earnings with respect to long-term incentive plans paid or payable prior to settlement or maturation, (c) tax reimbursements or "gross ups," and (e) preferential discounts on stock. Three year phase-in.

[4] Footnote disclosure of shares with less than three-year vesting, aggregate number and value of restricted shares held at year-end, and treatment of dividends. Need not include stock with performance-related vesting conditions, which may be treated at LTIP award.

[5] Total number of options or stand-alone SARs (even if payable only in cash) reported. Repriced options treated as new grants.

[6] Covers amounts paid or payable (not awards) under long-term plans. Does not include stock-based plans conditioned only on continued employment or passage of time.

[7] Residual category-components identified in footnotes. Includes but not limited to (a) termination and change of control payments, (b) accrued or contingent above-market or preferential earnings on deferred compensation, (c) accrued or contingent earnings on long-term incentive compensation, (d) registrant contributions to defined contributions plans, and (e) specified premiums on executive split-dollar insurance arrangements. Three year phase-in.

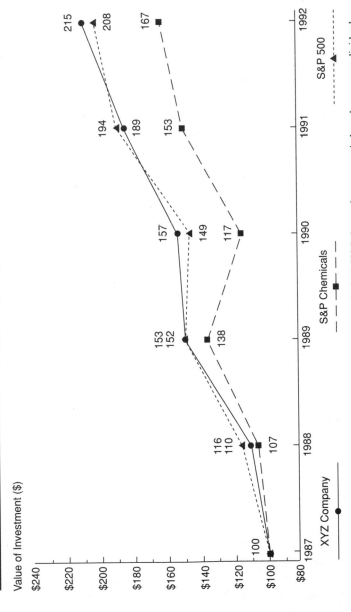

FIGURE 6–2

Comparison of Five-year Cumulative Total Return Versus S&P 500 and S&P Chemicals Index

Value of Investment ($)

XYZ Company ●————●

S&P Chemicals ■——————■

S&P 500 ▲ ‑ ‑ ‑ ‑ ‑ ▲

Assumes $100 invested on 1/1/88 in XYZ Company common stock, S&P 500 Index, and peer group index; also assumes dividend reinvestment.

3. Designing pay-for-performance packages that provide a meaningful correlation between corporate results and compensation.

4. The role of the compensation committee and its proper determination and processes.[20]

In support of these principles, the State of Wisconsin Investment Board has actively opposed compensation packages that result in what it considers to be unfair dilution and it has been especially adamant about opposing repricing stock options that enable executives to take advantage of stock options even if the company's stock has fallen to lower prices than when the options were originally offered. Richard M. Schlefer, assistant vice president of the College Retirement Equities Fund, agrees that evaluating executive compensation is generally so complex that the investor can only recommend the following general policies, standards, and processes for setting executive compensation:

- Compensation should include salary and performance components.
- Salary should have a defined relationship to salaries in industry peer groups.
- Total compensation should be adequate to attract, motivate, and retain quality talent.
- Performance measures should relate to key characteristics accepted within the particular industry to measure success. Performance should be measured over time periods adequate to assess and link actual performance with responsibilities.
- Compensation should be determined by the compensation committee of a board and care should be taken to avoid interlocking compensation committee memberships with other boards.
- Stock options and restricted stock awards should be integrated with other elements of compensation to formulate a competitive package.
- The board should set forth annually in the proxy statement the criteria used to evaluate performance of the chief executive officer and other senior management. TIAA-CREF supports the spirit of the SEC rules on enhanced executive compensation disclosure and compensation committee reports to shareholders.
- TIAA-CREF opposes any ban on "golden parachute" severance agreements. It abstains on resolutions calling for prior shareholder ratification of golden parachute severance agreements, but TIAA-CREF supports resolutions that call for shareholder approval of golden parachutes that exceed Internal Revenue Service guidelines.

- Stock option, stock purchase, stock appreciation rights, savings, pensions, bonus, and management incentive award proposals are scrutinized closely by TIAA-CREF. Consideration should be given to the need of the company to attract, motivate, and reward people. This must be balanced against the concerns of shareholders. (TIAA-CREF guidelines for voting proxies on these issues are listed in Appendix D.)

Notwithstanding these general principles, TIAA-CREF notes that certain types of executive compensation practices raise warnings, or "red flags," to institutional investors. These are spelled out in the Teachers' Insurance and Annuity Association-College Retirement Equities Fund (TIAA-CREF) Policy Statement (see Appendix D). While Schlefer notes considerable difficulty in obtaining valid company-specific data, a company's *policies*, which now must be disclosed in its proxy statement, can raise red flags, which call for further research. Red flags may be a sign of procedural faults in the development of a compensation plan or may reveal a history of abusive practices. TIAA-CREF will also vote against a plan that does not raise a red flag if the company's current practice or history of awards causes serious concerns about the way the plan would be administered. For example, a red flag would be raised if the total potential dilution from existing and proposed compensation plans exceeds 15 percent over the duration of the plan or 1.5 percent per year. TIAA-CREF may permit an exception to this policy in the case of plans proposed by companies in high-technology industries, which routinely pay executives more in stock and for which coverage extends through at least middle management levels. Also, TIAA-CREF says it may increase the threshold of dilution to 20 percent for firms whose market equity capitalization is under $100 million. Appendix D also shows that TIAA-CREF, like the State of Wisconsin Investment Board and other US institutional investors, is similarly interested in opposing abusive compensation practices that dilute shareholder value and that reward executives even if stock price has not appreciated (such as proposals to reprice stock options).

EVALUATING CORPORATE PERFORMANCE

There can be no doubt that institutional shareholders are most satisfied when the companies in their portfolios produce favorable results, in the form of either share price increases or dividend payout or a combination of both. When asked what institutional investors want from corporations,

Jon Lukomnik, Deputy Comptroller for Pensions, New York City Comptroller's Office, responded, "What do I want? Returns, returns, returns."

But, as noted earlier, if institutions are not pleased with performance, rather than observing the "Wall Street Walk" (i.e., selling their shares in companies), many institutional investors, especially the public pension funds, are targeting underperforming companies in their portfolio for special attention. Several years ago, the California Public Employees' Retirement System (CalPERS) was the first of the large public institutions to issue a "hit list," a list of underperforming companies. In 1994, the Council of Institutional Investors whose members number in excess of 90 public and private corporate pension funds began to issue its own list of underperformers. Both these lists are based on broad gauges of how companies' returns compare to others in their industry and to the overall market averages (such as the Standard & Poor's 500 company average.) Another method for targeting underperforming companies is that used by Robert Monks and Nell Minow, who left Institutional Shareholder Services Inc. (ISS) to found LENS, Inc.—a "corporate governance fund" that does extensive research and invests in a small number of underperforming companies with the intention of actively participating in corporate policy to turn them around and obtain improved returns. When a company surfaces on a CalPERS or CII list or in the LENS portfolio, this is widely reported in the press, and the company comes under intense scrutiny by other institutional investors as well. This section first describes how companies achieve the dubious distinction of ending up on one of the various institutional investor "hit lists"; then it discusses how institutions look at performance.

Institutional Investors Target Underperforming Companies

Table 6-2 lists CalPERS' corporate governance "targets" and the issues related to each from the inception of CalPERS' formal corporate governance activities in November 1987 through September 1992. The table, from a Wilshire Associates study performed under contract to CalPERS, shows a movement from *takeover* issues, such as poison pills, to *structural* issues, such as confidential voting, shareholder committees, and independent directors, and then to *performance* issues, such as corporate performance and executive compensation. How does CalPERS make its judgments about companies? Stephen Nesbitt, head of Wilshire Associates, explains:

In most instances, the targeted companies are selected by CalPERS' staff during the summer based on issues viewed as important. Subject to CalPERS' Board approval in the fall, letters are sent, generally to the targeted company's CEO, sometime between late October and early December. The letters identify what CalPERS takes issue with and request a response or meeting to give management the opportunity to explain why CalPERS should support management's position. The letters have been accompanied by a shareholder proposal. Depending upon filing dates, a shareholder proposal may either precede or follow these meetings.

Outcomes vary. Agreements with companies are sometimes reached early on. In other cases, the shareholder proposal is published in the proxy for vote. Settlement has also been reached after a proxy is published.[21]

Prior to 1990, CalPERS selected its targets on the basis of specific governance issues such as poison pills; subsequently, however, CalPERS' approach has involved a more fundamental effort to improve corporate operating and stock performance by exerting more aggressive pressure on the companies' managements and boards of directors. This shift in focus was also accompanied by a shift in analytical basis for choosing target companies. CalPERS began to hire outside consultants to analyze shareholder returns relative to industry peer groupings on a number of quantitative bases (shareholder returns, return on equity, return on invested capital, etc.) by company relative to industry peer groupings. For 1994, CalPERS identified a "Failing 50" list of companies, from which it selected a "Focus 10" list of the worst performers slated for direct action: Boise Cascade, CPI Corp., Eastman Kodak, First Mississippi, IBM, Navistar International, US Shoe, USX/ Marathon, Westinghouse, and Zenith. ISS reports that three of the 1994 worst performing companies—Boise Cascade, Westinghouse, and IBM—were carryovers from CalPERS' 1993 list. CalPERS communicated with the remaining 40 companies on the 1994 "Focus 50" list to notify them that they could find themselves on next year's shorter "Focus 10" list if they did not improve their performance.

CalPERS' shift in emphasis towards evaluating performance is also reflected by a change in tactics: While the pension fund would normally file a shareholder proposal to be put on the proxy ballot for its poison pill and board structural initiatives, in targeting corporate performance, CalPERS has stepped up the pressure for direct communications with managers and boards. Following the issuance of its "Focus 10" list, CalPERS communicated directly with the chairman of each company's board beginning in September 1993, requesting meetings with the outside directors to discuss

TABLE 6-2
CalPERS' Corporate Governance Target: 1987–1992

Company	Date	Issue(s)	Excess Returns	
			-5 Years	*+5 Years**
Alcoa	11/24/87	Poison pill	-10%	-38%
Consolidated Freightways	11/12/87	Poison pill	-26	-138
Gillette	11/06/87	Poison pill	98	264
Great Northern Nekoosa	12/04/87	Poison pill	160	22
Ryder	11/10/87	Confidential voting	-29	-92
Texaco	12/02/87	Poison pill	-48	75
US Air	12/11/87	Poison pill	-110	-172
Avon	11/21/88	Poison pill	10	112
Bell & Howell	01/02/88	Poison pill	40	1
Continental Corporation	12/15/88	Confidential voting	-39	-69
First Interstate	11/19/88	Confidential voting	-50	-43
Halliburton	11/10/88	Poison pill	-113	-51
Lockheed	11/28/88	Delaware "opt out"	-89	17
Whirlpool	11/10/88	Confidential voting	-64	82
EG&G	11/09/89	Confidential voting	-131	-42
Kmart	12/01/89	Abstentions	-72	-10
Occidental Petroleum	12/20/89	Shareholder committee	-82	-79
TRW	11/14/89	Shareholder committee	-94	16
Armstrong World	11/05/90	Pennsylvania antitakeover	-68	123
Boise Cascade	10/26/90	Performance	-92	-42
General Motors	01/05/90	Performance, independent directors	-93	-1
Hercules	10/19/90	Performance	-104	322
Inland Steel	11/09/90	Confidential voting	-62	-26
ITT	11/05/90	Performance, exec compensation	-40	58
Northrup	11/30/90	Performance, Delaware "opt out"	-137	90

Company	Date	Issue		
Scott Paper	11/05/90	Pennsylvania antitakeover	-24	-35
Sears	9/11/90	Performance, shareholder committee	-104	129
WR Grace	12/06/90	Performance, exec compensation	-57	39
American Express	11/07/91	Performance, exec compensation	-113	55
Chrysler	11/07/91	Performance, shareholder committee	-126	323
Control Data	11/07/91	Performance, shareholder committee	-153	120
Dial Corporation	11/07/91	Executive compensation	-20	-4
IBM	11/07/91	Performance	-91	-63
Polaroid	11/07/91	Performance	-100	-1
Salomon Brothers	11/07/91	Performance, independent directors	-114	46
Time Warner	11/26/91	Performance	-52	89
Advanced Micro Devices	10/22/92	Performance	-82	9
Champion International	04/04/92	Performance	-89	7
MacFrugals	10/22/92	Performance	-99	38
Pennzoil	10/14/92	Performance	-68	-11
Sizzler International	10/22/92	Performance	-67	-18
Westinghouse	09/15/92	Performance	-101	-25

* For those companies on CalPERS' list less than five years, excess returns are calculated through January 4, 1994.

Source: Stephen L. Nesbitt, "Long-Term Rewards From Corporate Governance," Wilshire Associates Incorporated, January 4, 1994, p.2.

company performance. By February 1994, CalPERS had met with outside directors representing 8 of the 10 companies.

James Heard, President of ISS, describes the results of CalPERS' communications with its 1994 "Focus 10" companies:

> One of the eight, Navistar, has agreed to designate a "lead director" from
> among outside directors. This falls short of formally separating the offices of
> chairman and CEO, which some critics of board performance strongly advo-
> cate, but it is intended to enhance board autonomy and accountability to
> shareholders.
>
>   CalPERS submitted shareholder proposals to Boise Cascade and US Shoe,
> requesting both companies to eliminate classified boards and elect all direc-
> tors annually. Again, the intent is to make the board more accountable to
> shareholders by making it easier to replace directors. CalPERS is continuing
> to monitor developments at Eastman Kodak, IBM and Westinghouse, and it is
> still in discussions with CPI Corp. and First Mississippi.[22]

In 1995, CalPERS chose a "Focus 9" group of companies: Boise Cascade, First Mississippi, Jostens, Kmart, Melville, Navistar International,
Oryx Energy; US Shoe Corp, and Zurn Industries. During the 1995 proxy
season, according to ISS:

> Successful meetings with Navistar, Kmart, and US Shoe led CalPERS to drop
> its shareholder proposals with those companies. However, the fund will con-
> tinue to monitor the companies' performance as well as initiatives submitted
> by other shareholders.[23]

While the New York City pension funds have been active for some
years in corporate governance, focusing primarily on board accountability and oversight, they too have begun to evaluate companies not only on
their governance structure but also on their performance. The methods
used include measuring one-, three-, and five-year total shareholder
returns compared to industry-specific returns for the same period. In addition, these funds are using seven other screens to evaluate potential targets, including corporate governance profiles, public databases, institutional ownership, and any shareholder proposal's potential impact on the
funds' portfolio. The New York City Employees Retirement System
(NYCERS) selected 15 target companies in 1995, seven of which were
chosen under their new process because they returned an aggregate of *minus* 46.3 percent over five years, compared to 61.5 percent return of the
Standard and Poor's 500 index.[24] NYCERS also pursues meetings with
company management and boards and has reportedly been successful in

prompting Oryx Energy to adopt a confidential voting policy as well as to convince other companies to increase their number of independent directors and to press for establishing a nominating committee comprised solely of independent directors.

Maryellen Anderson, former assistant treasurer for the state of Connecticut, says that the Council of Institutional Investors produced its own September 1994 "target list" of 20 companies through a similar type of analysis comparing shareholder returns by company and by industry. "This kind of accepted security analysis should produce no surprises on the Council's list of poor performers," according to Anderson.

Another approach to evaluating performance is taken by the LENS Fund. The LENS 1994 annual report (fiscal year ending July 31, 1994) presents the highlights of the fund's first two full years of operation as an active "money manager" in what may be regarded as the first "corporate governance fund." The LENS investment strategy of active management is grounded in what Monks and Minow believe to be well-established principles of "value" investing:

> We invest in companies that have unrealized value, and then we use the wide variety of initiatives available to shareholders to encourage a company's managers and directors to make the necessary changes to realize that value. We invest in companies that have strong assets undervalued by the market. . . .
>
> Andrew Carnegie once said that the best investment strategy is to put all your eggs in one basket and then watch the basket. Our strategy is to watch not just the basket but the eggs; and we make sure that the eggs understand that they are being watched. We have found that boards of directors, like subatomic particles, behave differently when they know they are being observed. Our initiatives are designed to create this difference. Our experience has shown that shareholder involvement can add value.[25]

Unlike CalPERS and the other major public pension funds, LENS invests in only a small number of companies and becomes much more involved with its portfolio companies; that is, LENS is engaged in "relational investing" whereby an investor seeks to develop an in-depth relationship with that investor's portfolio companies. By the end of 1994, LENS had invested in seven companies: Sears Roebuck, Eastman Kodak, American Express, Westinghouse, Scott Paper, Borden, and Stone & Webster. It also evaluates companies for future investment potential and has formed its own group of "focus companies," which include candidates outside the United States. Nell Minow has often pointed out that the CEOs in virtually all the companies in the LENS portfolio resigned sometime following LENS' taking a position in the company and frequently amid considerable media attention; she is quick to add that LENS was surely not responsible for the CEOs' departures. However, intense scrutiny from the institutional investor community can rapidly spread to involve boards of directors who may make changes in top management if faced with a chairman/CEO who remains deaf to investors' concerns over performance.

LENS' primary focus in companies it is involved in continues to be the board, and its initiatives have been directed toward ensuring that each company's board of directors devotes the time, the energy, and the independent analysis necessary to create long-term shareholder value. In comparison to the active relational investment strategy of LENS, which is directed at a small number of companies, most of the large public pension funds such as the New York State Common Retirement Fund, the state funds of Connecticut and Pennsylvania, and CalPERS, are substantially indexed, which means they invest in a "basket of stocks" such as the Standard and Poor's 500. Since they do not generally sell stocks in their indexed funds, and they maintain that they are invested for the long-term, these institutions get involved in companies mainly through the "value added" of their proxy voting and, more recently, through their personal attention to a small list of underperforming companies culled from their portfolios, which might contain in excess of 2,000 stocks. The State of Wisconsin Investment Board is a notable exception since it pursues both an active investing and voting strategy. An important development in the institutional investor movement may be signaled by Richard Koppes of CalPERS when he said that, although the fund is largely indexed at this time, it might consider taking a more relational investing approach whereby it might invest in a small number of stocks with the intention of becoming more actively involved—thus shifting a portion of its assets to pursue an approach like LENS' approach.

The Relationship Between Corporate Governance and Performance

There is considerable debate about whether shareholder activism leads to increased performance. The two right columns in Table 6–2 summarize the Wilshire Study calculations for the increase in value to shareholders resulting from CalPERS' corporate governance program, as measured by "excess returns," or the difference between the targeted company's total return and the S&P 500 index total return. For each targeted company, excess return is measured over two periods: the five years prior to CalPERS' initial involvement with the company and the five years after (if a five-year history is available; if not, through the date of the study, which is January 4, 1994).

The Wilshire study finds:

- For the five years prior to CalPERS' first established contact, the average targeted company's total return was 7.1 percent per year, while the S&P 500 total return was 15.0 percent per year. This 7.9 percent annual shortfall (15.0 minus 7.1) or 66.4 percent cumulative shortfall over five years was spread across most of the targeted companies. Only 4 of the 42 companies outperformed the S&P 500 index in the prior five years.

- After CalPERS first establishes contact with the targeted companies, underperformance is arrested and excess return turns positive and continues over the five years after a CalPERS initiative. The cumulative excess return over the five years averages 41.3 percent for each company or 7.2 percent per year.[26]

Thus far, neither NYCERS nor the CII has been identifying hit list candidates long enough to meaningfully track changes in performance. LENS, however, claims that for the year ending July 31, 1994, its portfolio companies have had an average total return of 14.5 percent compared with 5.17 percent for the S&P 500. For the full two years of operations, LENS has a two-year annualized return of 23.6 percent from its investment activities compared with a 6.97 percent return for the S&P 500.

Company reaction to claims by institutional investors that their activism creates shareholder value is not readily quotable, since few companies have wished to publicly disagree with entities with such economic clout. Privately voiced criticisms of the CalPERS' study performed by Wilshire point out that, while the correlation might exist, the cause-and-effect relationships implied in the studies have not been proved. Whether returns improved because of shareholder activism remains a strongly contested subject. Moreover, most corporate managements find it difficult to believe that pension fund fiduciaries, especially the senior corporate governance staff who are clearly not following the company on an in-depth analytical basis, could know enough about their business to productively provide "oversight." Corporations quite frankly resent the intrusion and further resent the increasingly broad areas of performance issues institutions delve into. Institutions say they do not want to micromanage the companies, yet they do press for considerable details in certain operational zones of activity. Institutions say they are dealing with the company's direction and strategy, but corporations believe they go too far in their demands to discuss matters they believe should be left to the discretion of management.

The whole matter is hotly debated in the United States, as the Securities and Exchange Commission has declined to draw distinctions as to what constitutes a proper avenue for shareholder oversight, pending the resolution of a major case by the courts that would provide the SEC with that direction. Moreover, as institutions press for additional disclosure of future corporate plans, companies react negatively on the grounds that they will expose themselves to shareholder litigation if discussions about future direction later prove incorrect. As frustrating as the issues are, those corporate managers who react with outright hostility to the institutions, however, risk another type of fallout. Should board members begin to question why management is so intractable in the face of shareholder questions about performance, the whole corporate managerial structure could unravel rather quickly and unpredictably, frequently ending up with the unseating of a CEO. The best way to manage the situation is to anticipate it well in advance, communicate effectively with shareholders, and, above all else, build an impressive and defensible record of company performance.

NOTES

1. For further discussion and data see Carolyn Kay Brancato, "Greenmail and the Market for Corporate Control: Impact on Shareholders, Issues of Fairness and Recent Developments," Congressional Research Service, Report No. 85-181E, August 27, 1985.

2. "1985 Proxy Season Laden With Shark Repellents," *IRRC Corporate Governance Bulletin,* II, no. 3 (June 1985), p. 52.

3. Until the landmark ruling in the Walt Disney case, courts generally gave target companies' directors almost complete discretion. In the Disney case, Saul Steinberg's Reliance Group Holdings Inc. purchased 4.2 million shares, or 12 percent, of Walt Disney Productions. Reliance launched a tender offer for control of Disney, but it withdrew its offer when Walt Disney bought it out at a profit to Reliance of $60 million. Immediately after the repurchase agreement was announced, the stock plummeted and, shortly thereafter, numerous shareholder suits were filed. The courts found that management's action to repurchase Reliance's holdings were difficult to

understand except as defense strategies against a hostile takeover in which the company was trying to make itself appear less attractive. The opinion also referred to the greenmailers' profits as "ill-gotten gain," especially in light of the fact that Disney was borrowing the $325 million repurchase price and additionally burdening the company with an increased debt load that could adversely affect Disney's credit rating. Brancato, Greenmail, pp. 6–10.

4. In fact, not all poison pills enacted by companies automatically trigger institutional investor opposition. If institutional investors perceive a company to be unfairly under attack by a raider who is not likely to return to shareholders the value they believe will be generated by current management, they will support action by current management to institute a poison pill.

5. Robert A.G. Monks and Nell Minow, *Power and Accountability* (New York: Harper-Collins, 1991), p.187.

6. Bevis Longstreth, *Modern Investment Management and the Prudent Man Rule* (New York: Oxford University Press, 1986), pp. 32–33.

7. US Department of Labor, "1989 Proxy Project Report," as cited in Monks and Minow, p. 194.

8. Nonfinancial measures of corporate performance are those that track "intangible" assets, such as customer satisfaction, employee satisfaction and retention, intellectual capital, quality control, and so on. See, for example, Carolyn Kay Brancato, "New Corporate Performance Measures," The Conference Board, Report No. 1118, 1995.

9. US Department of Labor, Interpretive Bulletin 94-2, Pension and Welfare Benefits Administration, Part 2509, Interpretive Bulletins Relating to the Employment Retirement Income Security Act of 1974, pp. 26–28.

10. Ronald E. Berenbeim, "Company Relations with Institutional Investors," The Conference Board, Report No. 1070-94-RR, 1994, p. 25.

11. For a more complete discussion see *The ISS Corporate Ownership Manual* (Bethesda, Maryland: Institutional Shareholder Services, January 1990), Chapter 4, pp. 4–56.

12. New York Stock Exchange, Inc., Filing number SR-NYSE-94-20, amendment number 1 for proposed rule change by the New York Stock Exchange, pursuant to Rule 19b-4 under the Securities Exchange Act of 1934, July 8, 1994.

13. Jeremy Bacon, "Corporate Boards and Corporate Governance," The Conference Board, Report No. 1036, 1993.

14. "GM Board Guidelines on Significant Corporate Governance Issues" (white paper), which accompanied presentation, "Industry Leadership and the Responsibility of the Board of Directors," Remarks by John G. Smale, chairman, General Motors Corporation, at the Council of Institutional Investors, Washington, D.C., April 15, 1994.

15. Report of the Committee on the Financial Aspects of Corporate Governance (Cadbury Report), United Kingdom, December 1, 1992, section 4.9.

16. For procedures to evaluate directors as a whole and individually see Ronald E. Berenbeim, "Board Evaluation and Performance," The Conference Board, Report No. 1081-94-RR, 1994; and National Association of Corporate Directors, "Report of the NACD Blue Ribbon Commission on Performance Evaluation of Chief Executive Officers, Boards, and Directors," Washington, D.C., July 1994.

17. Guidelines for Corporate Directors: Report of the NACD Blue Ribbon Commission on Executive Compensation National Association of Corporate Directors, Washington, D.C., 1993, p. 7.

18. In 1993, the US Congress passed and the president signed the Omnibus Budget Reconciliation Act of 1993, adding Section 162(m) to the Internal Revenue Code. This provision denies a publicly held company a deduction for compensation paid to certain top executives to the extent that the compensation exceeds $1 million per executive in a taxable year. The compensation applies to most forms of compensation, including cash, stock, and stock options. The IRS issued proposed regulations on December 15, 1993, to provide guidance on some of the broader issues raised by Section 162(m). Until the final rules are adopted, companies should comply with the proposed regulations and subsequent IRS staff pronouncements. A company is publicly held and therefore subject to provision of Section 162(m) if its common equity securities are registered on the last day of the company's taxable year. In order to qualify for the exclusion for performance-based compensation, compensation must satisfy the following requirements: (1) it is payable solely on account of the attainment of one or more performance goals; (2) the performance goals are established by a compensation committee, consisting of at least two directors, all of whom must be "outside" directors; (3) the material terms of the compensation and performance goals are disclosed to and approved by the corporation's shareholders in a separate vote before the compensation is paid; and (4) the compensation is paid after the compensation committee certifies that the goals have been achieved.

19. SEC release numbers 33-6962, 34-31327, and IC-19032, pertaining to Regulation S-K. These new requirements became effective immediately upon publication in the October 21, 1992, *Federal Register* (Vol. 57, No. 204, pp. 48126-48159).

20. Kurt N. Schacht, General Counsel, State of Wisconsin Investment Board. Comments before the Investor Responsibility Research Center's 1994 Forum for Shareholders and Corporations: Voting on Executive Pay, New York City, October 13, 1994.

21. Stephen L. Nesbitt, "Long-Term Rewards from Corporate Governance," Wilshire Associates Inc., January 5, 1994, p. 3.

22. James E. Heard, "CalPERS Names '94 Targets, Study Links Governance to Returns," *ISS Issue Alert,* Institutional Shareholders Services, Inc., Bethesda, Maryland, IX, no. 2 (February, 1994), pp. 1 and 11.

23. Peter R. Gleason, "Proxy Season 1995: Negotiations and New Players," *Issue Alert,* Institutional Shareholders Services, Inc., Bethesda, Maryland, X, no. 2 (February 1995), p.1.

24. *Ibid.* p. 4.

25. LENS, Inc., Annual Report, period ending July 31, 1994, p. 4.

26. Nesbit, p. 5.

Conclusions

The dramatic growth of foreign company entrance into US securities markets affords unprecedented opportunity for corporations around the world to expand. Having access to the largest and most trusted securities markets in the world can benefit companies in the numerous ways discussed in this book. The channels for entry are described, as companies can choose to enter the private capital markets, the unlisted over-the-counter equity markets or the listed markets for trading equities either over-the-counter or on one of the stock exchanges. While the technical route companies choose to enter US markets is important, this book is intended to show companies not only the procedures they must follow to enter US markets but where the pools of capital are and how to position themselves to attract them. Knowledge of the US institutional investor base is imperative to success. Moreover, the spread of the US style of institutional activism as described in this book will affect companies throughout the world, whether or not they actually make the decision to enter US markets.

The *Financial Times* of September 13, 1993 reported:

> In the annals of business history, 1993 may go down as the year that shareholder activism went global. At annual meetings around the globe, boards of directors have found themselves facing shareholders who take an active interest in the performance and management of the business—and are willing to cast votes against executive resolutions with which they disagree.

International shareholder activism has indeed become a force with which companies throughout the world must reckon, especially as communications between shareholder groups improve. Not only are US institutional investors increasingly active in pressing for their agenda in US companies and in foreign companies they hold in their portfolios, their brand of activism is spreading rapidly to shareholder groups in other countries.

A worldwide network of institutions was formed during a watershed conference call in mid-1994 with representatives from the major shareholder groups in the United States, Australia, Switzerland, and the United Kingdom on the line. Sarah Teslik, Executive Director of the Council of Institutional Investors, is reported to have joined the conference call with the following words of salutation: "Hello World." Then, on March 29, 1995, the International Corporate Governance Forum was launched from the Watergate Hotel in Washington, D.C. The group, chaired by CalPERS' chairman, Bill Crist, included shareholder representatives from Australia, Canada, France, Ireland, Italy, Sweden, Switzerland, the United Kingdom, and the United States. Its purpose is to encourage the international exchange of corporate governance ideas and information. It is intended that the group be lodged in the offices of the Council of Institutional Investors in Washington, D.C.

Corporations should be aware that, although institutions may approach corporate governance from different positions, they will be sharing information on proxy voting and strategies they intend to use to exert pressure on corporations throughout the world. As representatives of the principal providers of scarce capital, these institutional investors wield sufficient clout that they can be ignored only at the peril of managements and boards. According to Bruce Babcock, a senior official from ISS who analyzes global proxy voting trends:

> The providers of this scarce capital are setting the standards. . . . Pension assets in the United States and the United Kingdom are becoming the critical source for liquid investment capital throughout the world. . . .
>
> In this context, the international corporate governance activities of US institutional shareholders are beginning to have a great impact. The corporate governance standards that US institutions use in making investment decisions are the basis for many of the changes being made overseas. . . . Overseas stock exchanges and corporations are taking a keen interest in the new US Department of Labor guidelines on overseas proxy voting, which establish the ability to vote as one of the criteria that ERISA funds must review when making an overseas investment decision. . . . US standards will likely set the baseline for future improvement in international corporate governance. While ten years ago some critics complained that US proxy rules were too stringent, they are today the standard against which markets worldwide measure themselves.[1]

The corporate response to the growing worldwide shareholder activist movement is not favorable. One general counsel of a major US corporation views it as "downright scary." Foreign issuers and US domestic companies can, however, anticipate the concerns of institutional investors and can minimize the risks of dealing with them. Models of interaction developed in the United States—sometimes through difficult confrontations—can be used to agree on the proper roles of shareholder, management, and boards elsewhere in the world, despite historical and cultural differences. One such model is articulated by Ira M. Millstein, chairman of the Columbia Institutional Investor Project. Speaking at Columbia's conference on relational investing in May of 1993, Millstein sets forth some basic principles concerning the evolving relationships between shareholders and companies:

- The institutions' task as shareholders is to see to it that the corporation has the best board members available and that they are functioning to monitor management.
- Importantly, boards should act in a timely manner to remove failing managers while shareholders should act to remove failing boards.
- A search continues for how to avoid waiting for a crisis to remove failing managers and boards. Today's Relationship Investing Conference attempts to move the process of monitoring up a notch— perhaps relationship investing is a search for a process by which financial institutions can become involved in their corporate investments' major problems and policy issues, at an early stage.[2]

As institutional investors vary in their investment characteristics, so too will the contours of their relationships with their portfolio companies vary. However, in general, US and international institutions will likely press for changes according to the principles of activism developed in the United States and discussed at length in this book.

First, investors will press for assurances that managements are not acting in their own interests at the expense of shareholders. Devices that managements might use to entrench themselves could include poison pills and instituting unequal voting rights. Companies should make sure that their plans to list shares or restructure do not disenfranchise current shareholders. In this context, companies should review the principles set forth in the Council of Institutional Investors' Bill of Shareholder Rights (see Appendix A). Companies wishing to attract US institutional investments should be certain that their procedures afford adequate opportunity for these institutions to vote their proxies; otherwise, institutions may be less interested in investing in these companies if they risk running afoul of their own fiduciary obligations as set forth by the Department of Labor and other relevant state authorities.

US and international institutional investors are likely to continue to pressure boards of directors to structure themselves to provide sufficient independence and oversight over management. Companies should carefully review the General Motors Guidelines (see Appendix B) for recommended board structures and procedures. Shareholders are most concerned about having independent directors to monitor management and to serve on critical board committees such as the audit and compensation committees. Where chairmen and CEO functions reside in the same individual, institutions prefer to see a "lead director" emerge to assure them that communications from management to boards are not locked up in one individual. Letting shareholders know that companies have a process to evaluate boards of directors, both collectively and individually, gives a clear signal to investors that boards are willing to tackle the difficult performance issue for themselves, and should, therefore, be more enlightened when it comes to evaluating the performance of the corporation.

Companies should involve their boards of directors, especially their independent directors, in strategic planning processes so that, if they are approached either formally or informally by institutions, they will be knowledgeable about and supportive of the company. A company's board members can be an invaluable asset to management; however, they need to be kept informed. Moreover, as shareholders have put boards increasingly in the public eye, boards are understandably worried about their own liability. Therefore, managements should take special care to communicate effectively with company boards of directors.

Executive compensation raises an important substantive issue for institutional investors. While most institutions agree that compensation should be set to motivate superior performance, they would prefer for compensation to be balanced, and they become concerned if management is perceived to be rewarding itself at the expense of shareholders. Institutions have also urged managers to set pay levels according to performance. At the very least, US institutions are used to extensive disclosure about the methods and levels of compensation; foreign issuers may not be required to provide such extensive information, but they will be under increasing pressure to do so. Companies should carefully review their executive compensation practices to see if they can meet the SEC's October 1992 reporting requirements for disclosing the elements of pay packages and for comparing shareholder returns to those of the company's "peer group." Companies should also carefully review the principles for setting compensation set forth by TIAA-CREF (see Appendix D). Is the compensation committee independent of management? Does the committee tie pay to performance for company executives? For its directors?

Finally, continued pressures on corporations to perform can be expected. Some institutions are explicitly beginning to evaluate companies on a longer-term basis. Companies may not be able to avoid getting onto one of these institutional investor "hit lists," but an effective corporate program to establish ongoing shareholder communications in face-to-face meetings can minimize the acrimony and give both sides positive goals to work towards in resolving their differences. Companies should build a rapport with institutional shareholders in advance of problems, especially if performance is down or anticipated to be.

Companies should establish procedures for evaluating corporate performance on a financial and nonfinancial basis. Companies should involve senior management, operational management, and their boards in this process. They should understand their key drivers of success and be able to communicate to shareholders how company strategy will translate into improved returns to investors. With the exception of some "traders" who are unlikely to want to have extensive discussions with management anyway, some institutions want to understand where a company is headed so they can provide the corporation with the "patient capital" it will need to achieve its long-term goals. It is well to remember that the goals of companies should be fundamentally aligned with the goals of shareholders: to achieve long-term growth and return value to investors.

Not all shareholders behave the same, but they do converge on the critical issues discussed in this book. Moreover, some institutional investors can be quite reasonable if companies know how to deal with them. In the end, corporations should remember two things: Institutional investors and corporations are both, ultimately, on the same side, and institutions succeed if corporations succeed. Robert Monks, speaking at the May 1993 Columbia conference on relational investing, summed up the potential links between the long-term investment focus of many large institutional investors and the long-term value of corporations.

"Relationship investors" become informed and interested partners insisting on competitiveness—meaning long-term superior returns. The long-term perspective reflects the fact that their fate is inextricably linked with the enter-

prise in which they invest. Investors like pension funds are not just permanent investors, they are permanent consumers, employees, and neighbors, and
that makes them permanent partners. A pension fund with a significant stake
in the company has no interest in short-term cost cutting that increases pollu-
tion, reduces research and development to undermine future productivity or
eliminates jobs. They will feel the adverse effects of "savings" like these in
excess of any short-term benefits in dividends or share price appreciation.[3]

Forging relationships between corporations and institutional investors
is worth considerable effort. It requires the development of new and more
comprehensive measures of performance and a common language for
corporations and institutions to discuss sophisticated long-term performance criteria and strategic goals and results. In the end, the lure of institutional investor capital can stimulate executives and boards of directors to view corporate governance in a new light for the benefit of all.

NOTES

1. Bruce Babcock, "Competition for Global Investment Heats Up," *ISS Global Proxy
   Review,* 3d quarter 1994, p. 1.
2. Ira M. Millstein, "The Institutional Investor Project," remarks to the Relational Investing Conference, Columbia Institutional Investor Project, New York City, May 6,
   1993, p. 11.
3. Robert Monks, "Relational Investing," remarks to The Relational Investing Conference, Columbia Institutional Investor Project, New York City, May 6, 1993, p. 8.

Council of Institutional Investors: Shareholder Bill of Rights

Preamble

American corporations are the cornerstones of the free enterprise system, and as such must be governed by the principles of accountability and fairness inherent in our democratic system. The shareholders of American corporations are the owners of such corporations and the directors elected by the shareholders are accountable to the shareholders. Furthermore, the shareholders of American corporations are entitled to participate in the fundamental financial decisions which could affect corporate performance and growth and the long range viability and competitiveness of corporations. This Shareholder Bill of Rights insures such participation and provides protection against any disenfranchisement of American shareholders.

I. One Share/One Vote

Each share of common stock, regardless of its class, shall be entitled to vote in proportion to its relative share in the total common stock equity of the corporation. The right to vote is inviolate and may not be abridged by any circumstance or by any action of any person.

II. Equal and Fair Treatment for All Shareholders

Each share of common stock, regardless of its class, shall be treated equally in proportion to its relative share in the total common stock equity of the corporation, with respect to any dividend, distribution, redemption, tender or exchange offer. In matters reserved for shareholder action, procedural fairness and full disclosure is required.

III. Shareholder Approval of Certain Corporate Decisions

A vote of the holders of a majority of the outstanding shares of common stock, regardless of class, shall be required to approve any corporate decision related to the finances of a company which will have a material effect upon the financial position of the company and the position of the company's shareholders; specifically, decisions which would:

(a) result in the acquisition of 5% or more of the shares of common stock by the corporation at a price in excess of the prevailing market price of such stock, other than pursuant to a tender offer made to all shareholders;

(b) result in, or [be] contingent upon, an acquisition other than by the corporation of shares of stock of the corporation having, on a pro forma basis, 20% or more of the combined voting power of the outstanding common shares or a change in the ownership of 20% or more of the assets of the corporation;

(c) abridge or limit the rights of the holders of common shares to:
  • consider and vote on the election or removal of directors or the timing or length of their term of office, or
  • make nominations for directors or propose other action to be voted upon by shareholders, or
  • call special meetings of shareholders or take action by written consent, or affect the procedure for fixing the record date for such action;

(d) permit any executive officer or employee of the corporation to receive, upon termination of employment, any amount in excess of two times that person's average annual compensation for the previous three years, if such payment is contingent upon an acquisition of shares of stock of the corporation or a change in the ownership of the assets of the corporation;

(e) permit the sale or pledge of corporate assets which would have a material effect on shareholder values; and

(f) result in the issuance of debt to a degree which would leverage a company and imperil the long term viability of the corporation.

IV. Independent Approval of Executive Compensation and Auditors

The approval of at least a majority of independent directors (or if there are fewer than three such directors, the unanimous approval of all such outside directors) shall be required to approve, on an annual basis: (a) the compensation to be provided to each executive officer of the corporation, including the right to receive any bonus, severance or other extraordinary payment to be received by such executive officer; and (b) the selection of independent auditors.

Source: The Council of Institutional Investors, Washington, D.C.

General Motors Board Guidelines on Significant Corporate Governance Issues

1. *Selection of Chairman and CEO*

    The Board should be free to make this choice any way that seems best for the Company at a given point in time.

    Therefore, the Board does not have a policy, one way or the other, on whether or not the role of the Chief Executive and Chairman should be separate and, if it is to be separate, whether the Chairman should be selected from the non-employee Directors or be an employee.

2. *Lead Director Concept*

    The Board adopted a policy that it have a director selected by the outside directors who will assume the responsibility of chairing the regularly scheduled meetings of outside directors or other responsibilities which the outside directors as a whole might designate from time to time.

    Currently, this role is filled by the non-executive Chairman of the Board. Should the Company be organized in such a way that the Chairman is an employee of the Company, another director would be selected for this responsibility.

3. *Number of Committees*

    The current committee structure of the Company seems appropriate. There will, from time to time, be occasions in which the Board may want to form a new committee or disband a current committee depending upon the circumstances. The current six Committees are Audit, Capital Stock, Director Affairs, Finance, Incentive and Compensation, and Public Policy.

4. *Assignment and Rotation of Committee Members*

The Committee on Director Affairs is responsible, after consultation with the Chief Executive Officer and with consideration of the desires of individual Board members, for the assignment of Board members to various committees.

It is the sense of the Board that consideration should be given to rotating committee members periodically at about a five year interval, but the Board does not feel that such a rotation should be mandated as a policy since there may be reasons at a given point in time to maintain an individual director's committee membership for a longer period.

5. *Frequency and Length of Committee Meetings*

The Committee Chairman, in consultation with Committee members, will determine the frequency and length of the meetings of the Committee.

6. *Committee Agenda*

The Chairman of the Committee, in consultation with the appropriate members of Management and staff, will develop the Committee's agenda.

Each Committee will issue a schedule of agenda subjects to be discussed for the ensuing year at the beginning of each year (to the degree these can be foreseen). This forward agenda will also be shared with the Board.

7. *Selection of Agenda Items for Board Meetings*

The Chairman of the Board and the Chief Executive Officer (if the Chairman is not the Chief Executive Officer) will establish the agenda for each Board meeting.

Each Board member is free to suggest the inclusion of item(s) on the agenda.

8. *Board Materials Distributed in Advance*

It is the sense of the Board that information and data that is important to the Board's understanding of the business be distributed in writing to the Board before the Board meets. The Management will make every attempt to see that this material is as brief as possible while still providing the desired information.

9. *Presentations*

As a general rule, presentations on specific subjects should be sent to the Board members in advance so that Board meeting time may be conserved and discussion time focused on questions that the Board has about the material. On those occasions in which the subject matter is too sensitive to put on paper, the presentation will be discussed at the meeting.

10. *Regular Attendance of Non-Directors at Board Meetings*

The Board is comfortable with the regular attendance at each Board Meeting of non-Board members who are members of the President's Council.

Should the Chief Executive Officer want to add additional people as attendees on a regular basis, it is expected that this suggestion would be made to the Board for its concurrence.

11. *Executive Sessions of Outside Directors*

The outside directors of the Board will meet in Executive Session three times each year. The format of these meetings will include a discussion with the Chief Executive Officer on each occasion.

12. *Board Access to Senior Management*

Board members have complete access to GM's Management.

It is assumed that Board members will use judgment to be sure that this contact is not distracting to the business operation of the Company and that such contact, if in writing, be copied to the Chief Executive and the Chairman.

Furthermore, the Board encourages the Management to, from time to time, bring managers into Board Meetings who: (a) can provide additional insight into the items being discussed because of personal involvement in these areas; and/or (b) represent managers with future potential that the Senior Management believes should be given exposure to the Board.

13. *Board Compensation Review*

It is appropriate for the staff of the Company to report once a year to the Committee on Director Affairs the status of GM Board compensation in relation to other large U.S. companies.

Changes in Board compensation, if any, should come at the suggestion of the Committee on Director Affairs, but with full discussion and concurrence by the Board.

14. *Size of the Board*

The Board presently has 14 members. It is the sense of the Board that a size of 15 is about right. However, the Board would be willing to go to a somewhat larger size in order to accommodate the availability of an outstanding candidate(s).

15. *Mix of Inside and Outside Directors*

The Board believes that as a matter of policy there should be a majority of independent Directors on the GM Board (as stipulated in By-law 2.12). The Board is willing to have members of Management, in addition to the Chief Executive Officer, as Directors.

But the Board believes that Management should encourage Senior Managers to understand that Board membership is not necessary or a prerequisite to any higher Management position in the Company. Managers other than the Chief Executive Officer currently attend Board Meetings on a regular basis even though they are not members of the Board.

On matters of corporate governance, the Board assumes decisions will be made by the outside directors.

16. *Board Definition of What Constitutes Independence for Outside Directors*

GM's By-law defining independent directors was approved by the Board in January 1991. The Board believes there is no current relationship between any outside director and GM that would be construed in any way to compromise any Board member being designated independent. Compliance with the By-law is reviewed annually by the Committee on Director Affairs.

17. *Former Chief Executive Officer's Board Membership*

The Board believes this is a matter to be decided in each individual instance. It is assumed that when the Chief Executive Officer resigns from that position, he/she should offer his/her resignation from the Board at the same time. Whether the individual continues to serve on the Board is a matter for discussion at that time with the new Chief Executive Officer and the Board.

A former Chief Executive Officer serving on the Board will be considered an inside director for purposes of corporate governance.

18. *Board Membership Criteria*

The Committee on Director Affairs is responsible for reviewing with the Board on an annual basis the appropriate skills and characteristics required of Board members in the context of the current make-up of the Board. This assessment should include issues of diversity, age, skills such as understanding of manufacturing technologies, international background, etc.—all in the context of an assessment of the perceived needs of the Board at that point in time.

19. *Selection of New Director Candidates*

The Board itself should be responsible, in fact as well as procedure, for selecting its own members. The Board delegates the screening process involved to the Committee on Director Affairs with the direct input from the Chairman of the Board as well as the Chief Executive Officer.

20. *Extending the Invitation to a New Potential Director to Join the Board*

The invitation to join the Board should be extended by the Board itself, by the Chairman of the Committee on Director Affairs (if the Chairman and CEO hold the same position), the Chairman of the Board, and the Chief Executive Officer of the Company.

21. *Assessing the Board's Performance*

The Committee on Director Affairs is responsible to report annually to the Board an assessment of the Board's performance. This will be discussed with the full Board. This should be done following the end of each fiscal year and at the same time as the report on Board membership criteria.

This assessment should be of the Board's contribution as a whole and specifically review areas in which the Board and/or the Management believes a better contribution could be made. Its purpose is to increase the effectiveness of the Board, not to target individual Board members.

22. *Directors Who Change Their Present Job Responsibility*

It is the sense of the Board that individual directors who change the responsibility they held when they were elected to the Board should volunteer to resign from the Board.

It is not the sense of the Board that the directors who retire or change from the position they held when they came on the Board should necessarily leave the Board. There should, however, be an opportunity for the Board via the Committee on Director Affairs to review the continued appropriateness of Board membership under these circumstances.

23. *Term Limits*

The Board does not believe it should establish term limits. While term limits could help insure that there are fresh ideas and viewpoints available to the Board, they hold the disadvantage of losing the contribution of directors who have been able to develop, over a period of time, increasing insight into the Company and its operations and, therefore, provide an increasing contribution to the Board as a whole.

As an alternative to term limits, the Committee on Director Affairs, in consultation with the Chief Executive Officer and the Chairman of the Board, will review each director's continuation on the Board every five years. This will also allow each director the opportunity to conveniently confirm his/her desire to continue as a member of the Board.

24. *Retirement Age*

It is the sense of the Board that the current retirement age of 70 is appropriate.

25. *Formal Evaluation of the Chief Executive Officer*

The full Board (outside directors) should make this evaluation annually, and it should be communicated to the Chief Executive Officer by the (non-executive) Chairman of the Board or the Lead Director.

The evaluation should be based on objective criteria including performance of the business, accomplishment of long-term strategic objectives, development of Management, etc.

The evaluation will be used by the Incentive and Compensation Committee in the course of its deliberations when considering the compensation of the Chief Executive Officer.

26. *Succession Planning*

There should be an annual report by the Chief Executive Officer to the Board on succession planning.

There should also be available, on a continuing basis, the Chief Executive Officer's recommendation as to his/her successor should he/she be unexpectedly disabled.

27. *Management Development*

There should be an annual report to the Board by the Chief Executive Officer on the Company's program for Management development.

This report should be given to the Board at the same time as the Succession Planning report, noted above.

28. *Board Interaction With Institutional Investors, the Press, Customers, Etc.*

The Board believes that Management speaks for General Motors. Individual Board members may, from time to time, meet or otherwise communicate with various constituencies that are involved with General Motors. But, it is expected that Board members would do this with the knowledge of the Management and, in most instances, at the request of Management.

Source: "GM Board Guidelines on Significant Corporate Governance Issues," (white paper), which accompanied presentation, "Industry Leadership and the Responsibility of the Board of Directors," Remarks by John G. Smale, Chairman, General Motors Corporation, at the Council of Institutional Investors, Washington, D.C., April 15, 1994.

California Public Employees' Retirement System:

Company Responses to Request for Board Governance Self-Evaluation
Prepared September 30, 1994

SURVEY SUMMARY

Overview

In the Spring of 1994, the Board of Directors of General Motors completed a self-imposed process of reviewing various corporate governance models. As a result, the GM Board issued a 28-point guideline, identifying its position with respect to these issues. On May 12, 1994, the California Public Employees Retirement System (CalPERS) wrote to the largest 200 domestic equity holdings within its portfolio. In this letter, CalPERS challenged these other companies to follow GM's lead and undergo the same type of self-analysis. CalPERS acknowledged that specific governance models must differ according to industry and company but urged boards to seek the benefits to be attained by the simple **process** of defining the structure by which the board will operate and the disciplines it will follow in fulfilling those duties. It was this **process,** as revealed by company responses to CalPERS' challenge, that form the basis of CalPERS' evaluation, below. CalPERS sent a second letter on August 25, 1994, to nonresponding companies.

Responses

A+	Excellent response	14	7.0%
A	Good response	31	15.5%
B	Good response but . . . Need more information	28	14.0%
C	Need more information	44	22.0%
D	Missed the point	27	13.5%
F+	Brush-off	15	7.5%
F	No response	41	20.5%
Number of companies		*200*	*100.0%*

Criteria

A+ Submitted a comprehensive list of guidelines. Response was signed by the chairman of the board. The board of directors was involved in the process.

A Provided an excellent list of guidelines. Not always clear as to involvement by the board in the response/process.

B Responded with minimal list of guidelines, with future more comprehensive review by the board possible; or indicated board already in the process of active review.

C Acknowledged corporate governance as an issue for board involvement. Future review by the board was possible.

D Sent a minimal response. Satisfied with their "own" corporate governance guidelines. Saw no benefit in formalizing such practices. Usually no board involvement.

F+ At least sent a letter, but essentially a "brush off." Saw no need to formalize corporate governance guidelines. Usually no board involvement.

F Chose not to respond.

*Responses to GM Guidelines
Letter*

A+—Excellent Responses

1. Airtouch Communications
2. Chevron Corporation
3. Cisco Systems
4. Dayton Hudson Corporation
5. Exxon
6. First Interstate Bancorp
7. FPL Group
8. International Business Machines (IBM)
9. J.C. Penney
10. Kmart
11. Merck
12. Northern Telecom
13. Time Warner
14. Westinghouse Electric Corporation*
15. WMX Technologies

*Responses to GM Guidelines
Letter*

A—Good Responses

1. Aetna
2. ALCOA
3. American Express
4. AMGEN
5. Bristol-Myers Squibb
6. Campbell Soup Co.
7. Chrysler Corp.
8. Corning Inc.
9. CSX Corp.
10. Dow Chemical Co.
11. Duke Power Company
12. Eastman Kodak Co.
13. Eli Lilly and Co.
14. Enron Corp.
15. Federal National Mortgage
16. General Mills, Inc.
17. Honeywell Inc.
18. International Paper

Responses to GM Guidelines Letter

F+ — Brush Offs

1. American Home Products Corp.
2. AMR Corp.
3. ARCO
4. Blockbuster
5. Capital Cities/ABC, Inc.
6. Consolidated Edison Co. of New York
7. CPC
8. Du Pont
9. Gannett
10. Johnson & Johnson
11. Ralston Purina Co.
12. The Southern Co.
13. United Technologies
14. Walgreen Co.
15. Xerox Co.

No Response to GM Guidelines Letter

F

1. Allied Signal Inc.
2. American Barrick
3. American International Group Inc.
4. Ameritech Corp.
5. Archer-Daniels-Midland Co.
6. Automatic Data Processing Inc.
7. Bankers Trust New York Corp.
8. Barnett Banks Inc.
9. Burlington Resources Inc.
10. CBS Inc.
11. Dean Witter Discover & Co.
12. Entergy Corp.
13. Federal Home Loan Mortgage Co.
14. First Union Corp.
15. Fleet Financial Group
16. GAP Inc.
17. GTE Corp.
18. H & R Block
19. Houston Industries Inc.
20. LIMITED Inc.
21. MASCO Corp.
22. McCaw Cellular Communications
23. MCI Communications
24. NBD Bancorp Inc.**
25. Novell Inc.

No Response to GM Guidelines Letter (continued)

26. Nucor Corp.
27. Oracle Systems Corp.***
28. Pacificorp
29. Peco Energy Co.
30. R.R. Donnelley & Sons****
31. Raytheon Co.
32. Royal Dutch Petroleum Co.
33. SCECORP
34. Seagram Co. Ltd.
35. Sysco Corp.
36. Tele-Communications
37. Toys 'R' Us Inc.
38. Wal-Mart Stores
39. Walt Disney Co.
40. Warner-Lambert Co.
41. Wm. Wrigley Jr. Co.

Source: California Public Employees' Retirement System

Notes: * Westinghouse: Not within CalPERS' 200 largest capitalized holdings, but voluntarily sought to participate in the survey. Not included in the Response Summary.

** NBD Bancorp Inc.: Letter addressed to chairman, who retired. Company returned letter to sender, rather than forward to new chairman.

*** Oracle Systems Corp.: Telephoned on September 30 and left message that did not receive May 12 letter, but did receive August 25 letter; preparing response.

**** R.R. Donnelley & Sons: Wrote on 8/24/94 indicating they would respond if sent additional copies of the mailings.

Appendix D

TIAA-CREF Guidelines for Voting Proxies on Executive Compensation

INTRODUCTION

In view of the fact that the issues involved in executive compensation are technical and complex, these guidelines for voting proxies on executive compensation are designed with the following principles in mind:

1. Focus on good practice (e.g, a board compensation committee composed entirely of independent directors; and a clear and convincing statement by the compensation committee in the proxy statement of the principles followed in developing the company's compensation package);

2. Recognize that we are only called upon to vote on compensation *plans,* not on the way a particular plan will actually be *administered;*

3. Recognize the difficulty of obtaining valid company-specific data (e.g., the true economic value of a company's total compensation package and its relation to packages at comparable firms);

4. Seek to affirm mainstream practice while focusing on extreme cases (i.e., where compensation plans violate TIAA-CREF's proxy voting guidelines *and* where further investigation shows a current failure to follow good practice, or a history of actual abuse including a lack of a reasonable relation between a company's financial performance and the compensation of its executives).

The following guidelines identify what TIAA-CREF believes are key issues, and "red flags" which call for further research on a particular portfolio company. If that research indicates procedural faults in the development of a compensation plan (such as lack of independence by the compensation committee), or a history of abusive practices, TIAA-CREF will vote against the plan. We will also vote against a plan that does not raise a "red flag" if the company's current practices or history of awards are such as to cause serious concerns about the way the plan would be administered.

VOTING GUIDELINES

Issue: Dilution from Stock-Based Plans

Red Flag: Total potential dilution from existing and proposed compensation plans (apart from restricted stock which is treated separately) exceeds 15% over duration of plan(s) or 1.5% per year.

Override: Increase threshold to 25% for plans proposed by companies in high technology industries in which coverage extends through at least middle management levels. Increase threshold to 20% for firms whose market equity capitalizations are under $100 million.

Comment: The two override conditions are each designed to address a specific consideration. The first addresses the needs of human-capital-intensive industries where generous stock-based grants are necessary to retain personnel and where significant contributions are made by individuals outside the ranks of senior management. The second override addresses the need to provide packages with sufficient value at lower capitalization firms, since a given level of dilution has a lower economic value the lower the market capitalization of the firm.

Issue: Reload Options

Red Flag: Proposal provides for granting reload options.

Override: Plan (i) limits the frequency with which options can be reloaded; (ii) provides for a reload only if market price increases a specified percent; and (iii) prohibits resale of shares purchased for which options were reloaded.

Comment: Reload options are automatically "reloaded" after exercise at the then-current market price. This creates an option that can be exercised several times over its full term. For this reason, reload options convey higher value to their recipients because they are, in effect, families of options. In addition, they enable the individual receiving them to reap the maximum potential benefit from options awards, by allowing him or her to take advantage of all increases in stock price that occur over the duration of the option with no attendant risk. This advantage is at odds with the payout structure of common stock, and thus can create a divergence between the interests of outside shareholders and the option recipient.

Issue: Option pricing

Red Flag: Unspecified exercise price or exercise price below 85% of fair market value on the date of the grant.

Override: Equivalent value transfer percentage from the proposed plan plus all other stock-based plans (apart from restricted stock which is treated separately) does not exceed the recommended maximum percentage of 2.25% over a ten-year period. For small capitalization firms, maximum value transfer percentage is 3.00%, and for firms in high technology industries, the maximum percentage is 3.75%.

Comment: Options that are at-the-money or out-of-the-money afford the recipient with no downside risk, and thus may encourage a "bet the bank" psychology that is not in the best interests of common shareholders. Granting options at a discount can overcome this shortcoming to some degree. However, the discretion to make in-the-money option grants can also lead to redundancy with other cash-based compensation plans. The override provides additional flexibility while concurrently guarding against potential abuses. It is based on the concept that there is a maximum permissible value transfer over the life of the plan. Therefore the override offers companies with less dilutive plans more flexibility with respect to the pricing of options.

The maximum permissible value transfer percentage of 2.25% is arrived at by multiplying the 15% recommended dilution level by the 15% permissible discount (.15 x [.]15 = .0225) to fair market value. Note that for companies where TIAA-CREF's guidelines allow greater dilution tolerances, those tolerances are substituted for the 15% dilution in the aforementioned calculation.

To calculate the value transfer percentage from existing and proposed option plans, add the sum of dilution from existing and proposed option plans times their respective discount from fair market value.

Issue: Restricted Stock

Red Flag: The proposed plan plus existing restricted stock plans provide equivalent value transfer percentage that exceeds recommended maximum of 2.25%. Note the actual value transfer percentage is simply the dilution from existing plus proposed restricted stock plans.

Override: For small capitalization firms, increase the maximum value transfer percentage to 3.00%, and for firms in high technology industries, increase the maximum percentage to 3.75%, consistent with dilution recommendation described above.

Comment: At many companies restricted stock awards are viewed as a substitute for some portion of cash compensation. To the degree that the use of restricted stock in lieu of cash injects the compensation package with an incentive-based component, these awards are a more effective means of transferring cash value.

We have designed our recommendations on restricted stock awards so that they transfer no more in the way of cash value than would an option plan that passes the recommended tests.

Issue: Coverage

Red Flag: Plan **is limited to a small number of** senior employees.

Override: Permit awards to a small number of employees at small capitalization companies whose market equity capitalizations are under $100 million.

Issue: Omnibus Plans/Redundancy

Red Flag: Proposed plan provides overlapping benefits either within the plan itself or with existing plans or with other proposed plans.

Override: Plans that give rise to redundancy to expire within two years or have remaining share authorizations that are less than 3% of outstanding stock.

Comment: Rather than blanket rejection of omnibus plans, we recommend that they be approved if they do not create redundancy in the compensation structure. For example, a proposal that seeks authorization for a plan that provides for stock options with tandem SARs, restricted stock, and performance units would be accepted under our proposed criteria as long as the company did not have other active plans that also provided for similar awards. The basic notion is to vote FOR any proposal whose elements would be approved on a sequential basis. In such instances, the omnibus plan is no more than a consolidation of awards that otherwise are provided for under distinct plans.

Many omnibus plans, however, do create redundancies. They frequently provide for not only the usual stock-based awards, but also various phantom awards that accomplish the same thing. Under our guidelines, TIAA-CREF would reject plans structured in this manner. The redundancy issue also pertains to plans that are not omnibus plans. Proposals seeking approval for a single type of award that is already granted through existing plans for which ample authorizations remain should be rejected.

Issue: Excess Discretion

Red Flag: Terms of awards, such as coverage, option price, or type of award provided for by the proposed plan, are not specified in the proposal.

Override: None.

Issue: Bundling

Red Flag: Vote on executive compensation plan is coupled with vote on one or more unrelated proposals.

Override: None.

Issue: Stock-Based Plans for Non-Employee Directors

Red Flag: Alone or in conjunction with either existing or proposed plans triggers any of the red flags discussed above.

Override: None.

Source: TIAA-CREF, Policy Statement on Corporate Governance

Index